THE HARVARD CLASSICS

EDITED BY CHARLES W ELIOT LL D

č

JOHANN WOLFGANG von GOETHE

FAUST, *Part I* · EGMONT
HERMANN AND DOROTHEA

CHRISTOPHER MARLOWE

DOCTOR FAUSTUS

WITH INTRODUCTION AND NOTES

VOLUME 19

P F COLLIER & SON COMPANY
NEW YORK

CONTENTS

Heavens! only look! What have we here!
In all my days ne'er saw I such a sight!
Jewels! which any noble dame might wear

—*p. 114*

INTRODUCTORY NOTE

JOHANN WOLFGANG VON GOETHE. the greatest of German men of letters, was born at Frankfort-on-the-Main, August 28, 1749. His father was a man of means and position, and he personally supervised the early education of his son. The young Goethe studied at the universities of Leipsic and Strasburg, and in 1772 entered upon the practise of law at Wetzlar. At the invitation of Karl August, Duke of Saxe-Weimar, he went in 1775 to live in Weimar, where he held a succession of political offices, becoming the Duke's chief adviser. From 1786 to 1788 he traveled in Italy, and from 1791 to 1817 directed the ducal theater at Weimar. He took part in the wars against France, 1792-3, and in the following year began his friendship with Schiller, which lasted till the latter's death in 1805. In 1806 he married Christiane Vulpius. From about 1794 he devoted himself chiefly to literature, and after a life of extraordinary productiveness died at Weimar, March 22, 1832. The most important of Goethe's works produced before he went to Weimar were his tragedy "Götz von Berlichingen" (1773), which first brought him fame, and "The Sorrows of Young Werther," a novel which obtained enormous popularity during the so-called "Sturm und Drang" period. During the years at Weimar before he knew Schiller he began "Wilhelm Meister," wrote the dramas, "Iphigenie," "Egmont," and "Torquato Tasso," and his "Reinecke Fuchs." To the period of his friendship with Schiller belong the continuation of "Wilhelm Meister," the beautiful idyl of "Hermann and Dorothea," and the "Roman Elegies." In the last period, between Schiller's death in 1805 and his own, appeared "Faust," "Elective Affinities," his autobiographical "Dichtung und Wahrheit" ("Poetry and Truth"), his "Italian Journey," much scientific work, and a series of treatises on German Art.

Though the foregoing enumeration contains but a selection from the titles of Goethe's best known writings, it suffices to show the extraordinary fertility and versatility of his genius. Rarely has a man of letters had so full and varied a life, or been capable of so many-sided a development. His political and scientific activities, though dwarfed in the eyes of our generation

3

by his artistic production, yet showed the adaptability of his talent in the most diverse directions, and helped to give him that balance of temper and breadth of vision in which he has been surpassed by no genius of the ancient or modern world.

The greatest and most representative expression of Goethe's powers is without doubt to be found in his drama of "Faust"; but before dealing with Goethe's masterpiece, it is worth while to say something of the history of the story on which it is founded—the most famous instance of the old and widespread legend of the man who sold his soul to the devil. The historical Dr. Faust seems to have been a self-called philosopher who traveled about Germany in the first half of the sixteenth century, making money by the practise of magic, fortune-telling, and pretended cures. He died mysteriously about 1540, and a legend soon sprang up that the devil, by whose aid he wrought his wonders, had finally carried him off. In 1587 a life of him appeared, in which are attributed to him many marvelous exploits and in which he is held up as an awful warning against the excessive desire for secular learning and admiration for antique beauty which characterized the humanist movement of the time. In this aspect the Faust legend is an expression of early popular Protestantism, and of its antagonism to the scientific and classical tendencies of the Renaissance.

While a succession of Faust books were appearing in Germany, the original life was translated into English and dramatized by Marlowe. English players brought Marlowe's work back to Germany, where it was copied by German actors, degenerated into spectacular farce, and finally into a puppet show. Through this puppet show Goethe made acquaintance with the legend.

By the time that Goethe was twenty, the Faust legend had fascinated his imagination; for three years before he went to Weimar he had been working on scattered scenes and bits of dialogue; and though he suspended actual composition on it during three distinct periods, it was always to resume, and he closed his labors upon it only with his life. Thus the period of time between his first experiments and the final touches is more than sixty years. During this period the plans for the structure and the signification of the work inevitably underwent profound modifications, and these have naturally affected the unity of the result; but, on the other hand, this long com-

panionship and persistent recurrence to the task from youth to old age have made it in a unique way the record of Goethe's personality in all its richness and diversity.

The drama was given to the public first as a fragment in 1790; then the completed First Part appeared in 1808; and finally the Second Part was published in 1833, the year after the author's death. Writing in "Dichtung und Wahrheit" of the period about 1770, when he was in Strasburg with Herder, Goethe says, "The significant puppet-play legend ... echoed and buzzed in many tones within me. I too had drifted about in all knowledge, and early enough had been brought to feel the vanity of it. I too had made all sorts of experiments in life, and had always come back more unsatisfied and more tormented. I was now carrying these things, like many others, about with me and delighting myself with them in lonely hours, but without writing anything down." Without going into the details of the experience which underlies these words, we can see the beginning of that sympathy with the hero of the old story that was the basis of its fascination and that accounted for Goethe's departure from the traditional catastrophe of Faust's damnation.

Of the elements in the finished Faust that are derived from the legend a rough idea may be obtained from the "Doctor Faustus" of Marlowe, printed in the present volume. As early as 1674 a life of Faust had contained the incident of the philosopher's falling in love with a servant-girl; but the developed story of Gretchen is Goethe's own. The other elements added to the plot can be noted by a comparison with Marlowe.

It need hardly be said that Goethe's "Faust" does not derive its greatness from its conformity to the traditional standards of what a tragedy should be. He himself was accustomed to refer to it cynically as a monstrosity, and yet he put himself into it as intensely as Dante put himself into "The Divine Comedy." A partial explanation of this apparent contradiction in the author's attitude is to be found in what has been said of its manner of composition. Goethe began it in his romantic youth, and availed himself recklessly of the supernatural elements in the legend, with the disregard of reason and plausibility characteristic of the romantic mood. When he returned to it in the beginning of the new century his artistic standards had changed, and the supernaturalism could now be tolerated only by being made symbolic. Thus he makes the career of Faust as a whole emblematic of the triumph of the persistent striving for the ideal over the temptation to find complete satisfaction in the sense, and prepares the reader for this interpretation by prefixing the "Prologue in Heaven." The elaboration of this symbolic element is responsible for such scenes as the Walpurgis-Night and the Intermezzo, scenes full of power and infinitely suggestive, but destructive of the unity of the play as a tragedy of human life. Yet there remains in this First Part even in its final form much that is realistic in the best sense, the carousal in Auerbach's cellar, the portrait of Martha, the Easter-morning walk, the character and fate of Margaret. It is such elements as these that have appealed to the larger reading public and that have naturally been emphasized by performance on the stage, and by virtue of these alone "Faust" may rank as a great drama; but it is the result of Goethe's broodings on the mystery of human life, shadowed forth in the symbolic parts and elaborated with still greater complexity and still more far-reaching suggestiveness—and, it must be added, with deepening obscurity —in the Second Part, that have given the work its place with "Job," with the "Prometheus Bound," with "The Divine Comedy," and with "Hamlet."

DEDICATION

Ye wavering shapes, again ye do enfold me,
As erst upon my troubled sight ye stole;
Shall I this time attempt to clasp, to hold ye?
Still for the fond illusion yearns my soul?
Ye press around! Come then, your captive hold me,
As upward from the vapoury mist ye roll;
Within my breast youth's throbbing pulse is bounding,
Fann'd by the magic breath your march surrounding.

Shades fondly loved appear, your train attending,
And visions fair of many a blissful day;
First-love and friendship their fond accents blending,
Like to some ancient, half-expiring lay;
Sorrow revives, her wail of anguish sending
Back o'er life's devious labyrinthine way,
And names the dear ones, they whom Fate bereaving
Of life's fair hours, left me behind them grieving.

They hear me not my later cadence singing,
The souls to whom my earlier lays I sang;
Dispersed the throng, their severed flight now winging;
Mute are the voices that responsive rang.
For stranger crowds the Orphean lyre now stringing,
E'en their applause is to my heart a pang;
Of old who listened to my song, glad hearted,
If yet they live, now wander widely parted.

A yearning long unfelt, each impulse swaying,
To yon calm spirit-realm uplifts my soul;

7

In faltering cadence, as when Zephyr playing,
Fans the Æolian harp, my numbers roll;
Tear follows tear, my steadfast heart obeying
The tender impulse, loses its control;
What I possess as from afar I see;
Those I have lost become realities to me.

PROLOGUE FOR THE THEATRE

MANAGER. DRAMATIC POET. MERRYMAN.

MANAGER

YE twain, in trouble and distress
True friends whom I so oft have found,
Say, for our scheme on German ground,
What prospect have we of success?
Fain would I please the public, win their thanks;
They live and let live, hence it is but meet.
The posts are now erected, and the planks,
And all look forward to a festal treat.
Their places taken, they, with eyebrows rais'd,
Sit patiently, and fain would be amaz'd.
I know the art to hit the public taste,
Yet ne'er of failure felt so keen a dread;
True, they are not accustomed to the best,
But then appalling the amount they've read.
How make our entertainment striking, new,
And yet significant and pleasing too?
For to be plain, I love to see the throng,
As to our booth the living tide progresses;
As wave on wave successive rolls along,
And through heaven's narrow portal forceful presses;
Still in broad daylight, ere the clock strikes four,
With blows their way towards the box they take;
And, as for bread in famine, at the baker's door,
For tickets are content their necks to break.
Such various minds the bard alone can sway,
My friend, oh work this miracle to-day!

POET

Oh of the motley throng speak not before me,
At whose aspect the Spirit wings its flight!

9

Conceal the surging concourse, I implore thee,
Whose vortex draws us with resistless might.
No, to some peaceful heavenly nook restore me,
Where only for the bard blooms pure delight,
Where love and friendship yield their choicest blessing,
Our heart's true bliss, with god-like hand caressing.

What in the spirit's depths was there created,
What shyly there the lip shaped forth in sound;
A failure now, with words now fitly mated,
In the wild tumult of the hour is drown'd;
Full oft the poet's thought for years hath waited
Until at length with perfect form 'tis crowned;
What dazzles, for the moment born, must perish;
What genuine is posterity will cherish.

MERRYMAN

This cant about posterity I hate;
About posterity were I to prate,
Who then the living would amuse? For they
Will have diversion, ay, and 'tis their due.
A sprightly fellow's presence at your play,
Methinks should also count for something too;
Whose genial wit the audience still inspires,
Knows from their changeful mood no angry feeling;
A wider circle he desires,
To their heart's depths more surely thus appealing.
To work, then! Give a master-piece, my friend;
Bring Fancy with her choral trains before us,
Sense, reason, feeling, passion, but attend!
Let folly also swell the tragic chorus.

MANAGER

In chief, of incident enough prepare!
A show they want, they come to gape and stare.
Spin for their eyes abundant occupation,
So that the multitude may wondering gaze,
You by sheer bulk have won your reputation,
The man you are all love to praise.

By mass alone can you subdue the masses,
Each then selects in time what suits his bent.
Bring much, you something bring for various classes,
And from the house goes every one content.
You give a piece, abroad in pieces send it!
'Tis a ragout—success must needs attend it;
'Tis easy to serve up, as easy to invent.
A finish'd whole what boots it to present!
Full soon the public will in pieces rend it.

POET

How mean such handicraft as this you cannot feel!
How it revolts the genuine artist's mind!
The sorry trash in which these coxcombs deal,
Is here approved on principle, I find.

MANAGER

Such a reproof disturbs me not a whit!
Who on efficient work is bent,
Must choose the fittest instrument.
Consider! 'tis soft wood you have to split;
Think too for whom you write, I pray!
One comes to while an hour away;
One from the festive board, a sated guest;
Others, more dreaded than the rest,
From journal-reading hurry to the play.
As to a masquerade, with absent minds, they press,
Sheer curiosity their footsteps winging;
Ladies display their persons and their dress,
Actors unpaid their service bringing.
What dreams beguile you on your poet's height?
What puts a full house in a merry mood?
More closely view your patrons of the night!
The half are cold, the half are rude.
One, the play over, craves a game of cards;
Another a wild night in wanton joy would spend.
Poor fools the muses' fair regards.
Why court for such a paltry end?
I tell you, give them more, still more, 'tis all I ask,

Thus you will ne'er stray widely from the goal;
Your audience seek to mystify, cajole;—
To satisfy them—that's a harder task.
What ails thee? art enraptured or distressed?

POET

Depart! elsewhere another servant choose
What! shall the bard his godlike power abuse?
Man's loftiest right, kind nature's high bequest,
For your mean purpose basely sport away?
Whence comes his mastery o'er the human breast,
Whence o'er the elements his sway,
But from the harmony that, gushing from his soul,
Draws back into his heart the wondrous whole?
With careless hand when round her spindle, Nature
Winds the interminable thread of life;
When 'mid the clash of Being every creature
Mingles in harsh inextricable strife;
Who deals their course unvaried till it falleth,
In rhythmic flow to music's measur'd tone?
Each solitary note whose genius calleth,
To swell the mighty choir in unison?
Who in the raging storm sees passion low'ring?
Or flush of earnest thought in evening's glow?
Who every blossom in sweet spring-time flowering
Along the loved one's path would strow?
Who, Nature's green familiar leaves entwining,
Wreathe's glory's garland, won on every field?
Makes sure Olympus, heavenly powers combining?
Man's mighty spirit, in the bard reveal'd!

MERRYMAN

Come then, employ your lofty inspiration,
And carry on the poet's avocation,
Just as we carry on a love affair.
Two meet by chance, are pleased, they linger there,
Insensibly are link'd, they scarce know how;
Fortune seems now propitious, adverse now,
Then come alternate rapture and despair;

And 'tis a true romance ere one's aware.
Just such a drama let us now compose.
Plunge boldly into life—its depths disclose!
Each lives it, not to many is it known,
'Twill interest wheresoever seiz'd and shown;
Bright pictures, but obscure their meaning:
A ray of truth through error gleaming,
Thus you the best elixir brew,
To charm mankind, and edify them too.
Then youth's fair blossoms crowd to view your play,
And wait as on an oracle; while they,
The tender souls, who love the melting mood,
Suck from your work their melancholy food;
Now this one, and now that, you deeply stir,
Each sees the working of his heart laid bare.
Their tears, their laughter, you command with ease,
The lofty still they honour, the illusive love.
Your finish'd gentlemen you ne'er can please;
A growing mind alone will grateful prove.

POET

Then give me back youth's golden prime,
When my own spirit too was growing,
When from my heart th' unbidden rhyme
Gush'd forth, a fount for ever flowing;
Then shadowy mist the world conceal'd,
And every bud sweet promise made,
Of wonders yet to be reveal'd,
As through the vales, with blooms inlaid,
Culling a thousand flowers I stray'd.
Naught had I, yet a rich profusion!
The thirst for truth, joy in each fond illusion.
Give me unquell'd those impulses to prove;—
Rapture so deep, its ecstasy was pain,
The power of hate, the energy of love,
Give me, oh give me back my youth again!

MERRYMAN

Youth, my good friend, you certainly require
When foes in battle round are pressing,
When a fair maid, her heart on fire,
Hangs on your neck with fond caressing,
When from afar, the victor's crown,
To reach the hard-won goal inciteth;
When from the whirling dance, to drown
Your sense, the night's carouse inviteth.
But the familiar chords among
Boldly to sweep, with graceful cunning,
While to its goal, the verse along
Its winding path is sweetly running;
This task is yours, old gentlemen, to-day;
Nor are you therefore less in reverence held;
Age does not make us childish, as folk say,
It finds us genuine children e'en in eld.

MANAGER

A truce to words, mere empty sound,
Let deeds at length appear, my friends!
While idle compliments you round,
You might achieve some useful ends.
Why talk of the poetic vein?
Who hesitates will never know it;
If bards ye are, as ye maintain,
Now let your inspiration show it.
To you is known what we require,
Strong drink to sip is our desire;
Come, brew me such without delay!
To-morrow sees undone, what happens not to-day;
Still forward press, nor ever tire!
The possible, with steadfast trust,
Resolve should by the forelock grasp;
Then she will ne'er let go her clasp,
And labours on, because she must.

On German boards, you're well aware,
The taste of each may have full sway;

Therefore in bringing out your play,
Nor scenes nor mechanism spare!
Heaven's lamps employ, the greatest and the least,
Be lavish of the stellar lights,
Water, and fire, and rocky heights,
Spare not at all, nor birds, nor beast.
Thus let creation's ample sphere
Forthwith in this our narrow booth appear,
And with considerate speed, through fancy's spell,
Journey from heaven, thence through the world, to hell!

PROLOGUE IN HEAVEN

The Lord. The Heavenly Hosts. *Afterwards*
Mephistopheles.

The three Archangels come forward

RAPHAEL

The Sun, in ancient guise, competing
With brother spheres in rival song,
With thunder-march, his orb completing,
Moves his predestin'd course along;
His aspect to the powers supernal
Gives strength, though fathom him none **may;**
Transcending thought, the works eternal
Are fair as on the primal day.

GABRIEL

With speed, thought baffling, unabating,
Earth's splendour whirls in circling flight;
Its Eden-brightness alternating
With solemn, awe-inspiring night;
Ocean's broad waves in wild commotion,
Against the rocks' deep base are hurled;
And with the spheres, both rock and ocean
Eternally are swiftly whirled.

MICHAEL

And tempests roar in emulation
From sea to land, from land to sea,
And raging form, without cessation,
A chain of wondrous agency,
Full in the thunder's path careering,

Flaring the swift destructions play;
But, Lord, Thy servants are revering
The mild procession of thy day.

THE THREE

Thine aspect to the powers supernal
Gives strength, though fathom thee none may;
And all thy works, sublime, eternal,
Are fair as on the primal day.

MEPHISTOPHELES

Since thou, O Lord, approachest us once more,
And how it fares with us, to ask art fain,
Since thou hast kindly welcom'd me of yore,
Thou see'st me also now among thy train.
Excuse me, fine harangues I cannot make,
Though all the circle look on me with scorn;
My pathos soon thy laughter would awake,
Hadst thou the laughing mood not long forsworn.
Of suns and worlds I nothing have to say,
I see alone mankind's self-torturing pains.
The little world-god still the self-same stamp retains,
And is as wondrous now as on the primal day.
Better he might have fared, poor wight,
Hadst thou not given him a gleam of heavenly light;
Reason he names it, and doth so
Use it, than brutes more brutish still to grow.
With deference to your grace, he seems to me
Like any long-legged grasshopper to be,
Which ever flies, and flying springs,
And in the grass its ancient ditty sings.
Would he but always in the grass repose!
In every heap of dung he thrusts his nose.

THE LORD

Hast thou naught else to say? Is blame
In coming here, as ever, thy sole aim?
Does nothing on the earth to thee seem right?

MEPHISTOPHELES

No, Lord! I find things there, as ever, in sad plight.
Men, in their evil days, move my compassion;
Such sorry things to plague is nothing worth.

THE LORD

Know'st thou my servant, Faust?

MEPHISTOPHELES

The doctor?

THE LORD

Right.

MEPHISTOPHELES

He serves thee truly in a wondrous fashion.
Poor fool! His food and drink are not of earth.
An inward impulse hurries him afar,
Himself half conscious of his frenzied mood;
From heaven claimeth he the fairest star,
And from the earth craves every highest good,
And all that's near, and all that's far,
Fails to allay the tumult in his blood.

THE LORD

Though in perplexity he serves me now,
I soon will lead him where more light appears;
When buds the sapling, doth the gardener know
That flowers and fruit will deck the coming years.

MEPHISTOPHELES

What wilt thou wager? Him thou yet shall lose,
If leave to me thou wilt but give,
Gently to lead him as I choose!

THE LORD

So long as he on earth doth live,
So long 'tis not forbidden thee.
Man still must err, while he doth strive.

MEPHISTOPHELES

I thank you; for not willingly
I traffic with the dead, and still aver
That youth's plump blooming cheek I very much prefer.
I'm not at home to corpses; 'tis my way,
Like cats with captive mice to toy and play.

THE LORD

Enough! 'tis granted thee! Divert
This mortal spirit from his primal source;
Him, canst thou seize, thy power exert
And lead him on thy downward course,
Then stand abash'd, when thou perforce must own,
A good man in his darkest aberration,
Of the right path is conscious still.

MEPHISTOPHELES

'Tis done! Full soon thou'lt see my exultation;
As for my bet no fears I entertain.
And if my end I finally should gain,
Excuse my triumphing with all my soul.
Dust he shall eat, ay, and with relish take,
As did my cousin, the renownèd snake.

THE LORD

Here too thou'rt free to act without control;
I ne'er have cherished hate for such as thee.
Of all the spirits who deny,
The scoffer is least wearisome to me.
Ever too prone is man activity to shirk,
In unconditioned rest he fain would live;
Hence this companion purposely I give,
Who stirs, excites, and must, as devil, work.
But ye, the genuine sons of heaven, rejoice!
In the full living beauty still rejoice!
May that which works and lives, the ever-growing,
In bonds of love enfold you, mercy-fraught,

And Seeming's changeful forms, around you flowing,
Do ye arrest, in ever-during thought!
> (*Heaven closes, the Archangels disperse.*)

MEPHISTOPHELES (*alone*)

The ancient one I like sometimes to see,
And not to break with him am always civil;
'Tis courteous in so great a lord as he,
To speak so kindly even to the devil.

THE TRAGEDY OF FAUST

DRAMATIS PERSONÆ

Characters in the Prologue for the Theatre
THE MANAGER.   THE DRAMATIC POET.   MERRYMAN.

Characters in the Prologue in Heaven
THE LORD.
RAPHAEL,   GABRIEL,   MICHAEL,   (The Heavenly Host).
MEPHISTOPHELES.

Characters in the Tragedy
FAUST.   MEPHISTOPHELES.   WAGNER, a Student.
MARGARET.   MARTHA, Margaret's Neighbour.
VALENTINE, Margaret's Brother.   OLD PEASANT.   A STUDENT.
ELIZABETH, an Acquaintance of Margaret's.
FROSCH,   BRANDER,   SIEBEL,   ALTMAYER,
(Guests in Auerbach's Wine Cellar).
Witches; old and young; Wizards, Will-o'-the-Wisp, Witch Pedlar,
Protophantasmist, Servibilis, Monkeys, Spirits, Journeymen,
Country-folk, Citizens, Beggar, Old Fortune-teller,
Shepherd, Soldier, Students, &c.

In the Intermezzo
OBERON.   TITANIA.   ARIEL.   PUCK, &c. &c.

PART I

NIGHT

A high vaulted narrow Gothic chamber.
FAUST, restless, seated at his desk.

FAUST

I HAVE, alas! Philosophy,
Medicine, Jurisprudence too,
And to my cost Theology,
With ardent labour, studied through.

And here I stand, with all my lore,
Poor fool, no wiser than before.
Magister, doctor styled, indeed,
Already these ten years I lead,
Up, down, across, and to and fro,
My pupils by the nose,—and learn,
That we in truth can nothing know!
That in my heart like fire doth burn.
'Tis true I've more cunning than all your dull tribe,
Magister and doctor, priest, parson, and scribe;
Scruple or doubt comes not to enthrall me,
Neither can devil nor hell now appal me—
Hence also my heart must all pleasure forego!
I may not pretend, aught rightly to know,
I may not pretend, through teaching, to find
A means to improve or convert mankind.
Then I have neither goods nor treasure,
No worldly honour, rank, or pleasure;
No dog in such fashion would longer live!
Therefore myself to magic I give,
In hope, through spirit-voice and might,
Secrets now veiled to bring to light,
That I no more, with aching brow,
Need speak of what I nothing know;
That I the force may recognise
That binds creation's inmost energies;
Her vital powers, her embryo seeds survey,
And fling the trade in empty words away.
O full-orb'd moon, did but thy rays
Their last upon mine anguish gaze!
Beside this desk, at dead of night,
Oft have I watched to hail thy light:
Then, pensive friend! o'er book and scroll,
With soothing power, thy radiance stole!
In thy dear light, ah, might I climb,
Freely, some mountain height sublime,
Round mountain caves with spirits ride,
In thy mild haze o'er meadows glide,
And, purged from knowledge-fumes, renew
My spirit, in thy healing dew!

Woe's me! still prison'd in the gloom
Of this abhorr'd and musty room!
Where heaven's dear light itself doth pass,
But dimly through the painted glass!
Hemmed in by book-heaps, piled around,
Worm-eaten, hid 'neath dust and mould,
Which to the high vault's topmost bound,
A smoke-stained paper doth enfold;
With boxes round thee piled, and glass,
And many a useless instrument,
With old ancestral lumber blent—
This is thy world! a world! alas!
And dost thou ask why heaves thy heart,
With tighten'd pressure in thy breast?
Why the dull ache will not depart,
By which thy life-pulse is oppress'd?
Instead of nature's living sphere,
Created for mankind of old,
Brute skeletons surround thee here,
And dead men's bones in smoke and mould.

Up! Forth into the distant land!
Is not this book of mystery
By Nostradamus' proper hand,
An all-sufficient guide? Thou'lt see
The courses of the stars unroll'd;
When nature doth her thoughts unfold
To thee, thy soul shall rise, and seek
Communion high with her to hold,
As spirit doth with spirit speak!
Vain by dull poring to divine
The meaning of each hallow'd sign.
Spirits! I feel you hov'ring near;
Make answer, if my voice ye hear!

(*He opens the book and perceives the sign of the
Macrocosmos.*)

Ah! at this spectacle through every sense,
What sudden ecstasy of joy is flowing!
I feel new rapture, hallow'd and intense,

Through every nerve and vein with ardour glowing.
Was it a god who character'd this scroll,
The tumult in my spirit healing,
O'er my sad heart with rapture stealing,
And by a mystic impulse, to my soul,
The powers of nature all around revealing.
Am I a God? What light intense!
In these pure symbols do I see,
Nature exert her vital energy.
Now of the wise man's words I learn the sense;

  " Unlock'd the spirit-world is lying,
   Thy sense is shut, thy heart is dead!
   Up scholar, lave, with zeal undying,
   Thine earthly breast in the morning-red!"

       (*He contemplates the sign.*)

How all things live and work, and ever blending,
Weave one vast whole from Being's ample range!
How powers celestial, rising and descending,
Their golden buckets ceaseless interchange!
Their flight on rapture-breathing pinions winging,
From heaven to earth their genial influence bringing,
Through the wild sphere their chimes melodious ringing!

A wondrous show! but ah! a show alone!
Where shall I grasp thee, infinite nature, where?
Ye breasts, ye fountains of all life, whereon
Hang heaven and earth, from which the withered heart
For solace yearns, ye still impart
Your sweet and fostering tides—where are ye—where?
Ye gush, and must I languish in despair?

  (*He turns over the leaves of the book impatiently, and
     perceives the sign of the Earth-spirit.*)

How all unlike the influence of this sign!
Earth-spirit, thou to me art nigher,
E'en now my strength is rising higher,
E'en now I glow as with new wine;
Courage I feel, abroad the world to dare,

The woe of earth, the bliss of earth to bear,
With storms to wrestle, brave the lightning's glare,
And mid the crashing shipwreck not despair.

Clouds gather over me—
The moon conceals her light—
The lamp is quench'd—
Vapours are rising—Quiv'ring round my head
Flash the red beams—Down from the vaulted roof
A shuddering horror floats,
And seizes me!
I feel it, spirit, prayer-compell'd, 'tis thou
Art hovering near!
Unveil thyself!
Ha! How my heart is riven now!
Each sense, with eager palpitation,
Is strain'd to catch some new sensation!
I feel my heart surrender'd unto thee!
Thou must! Thou must! Though life should be the fee!
(*He seizes the book, and pronounces mysteriously the sign
of the spirit. A ruddy flame flashes up; the spirit
appears in the flame.*)

SPIRIT

Who calls me?

FAUST (*turning aside*)
Dreadful shape!

SPIRIT

With might,
Thou hast compelled me to appear,
Long hast been sucking at my sphere,
And now—

FAUST

Woe's me! I cannot bear thy sight!

SPIRIT

To see me thou dost breathe thine invocation,
My voice to hear, to gaze upon my brow;
Me doth thy strong entreaty bow—
Lo! I am here!—What cowering agitation

Grasps thee, the demigod! Where's now the soul's deep
  cry?
Where is the breast, which in its depths a world conceiv'd
And bore and cherished? which, with ecstasy,
To rank itself with us, the spirits, heaved?
Where art thou, Faust? whose voice I heard resound,
Who towards me press'd with energy profound?
Art thou he? Thou,—who by my breath art blighted,
Who, in his spirit's depths affrighted,
Trembles, a crush'd and writhing worm!

FAUST

Shall I yield, thing of flame, to thee?
Faust, and thine equal, I am he!

SPIRIT

In the currents of life, in action's storm,
        I float and I wave
        With billowy motion!
        Birth and the grave
        A limitless ocean,
        A constant weaving
        With change still rife,
        A restless heaving,
        A glowing life—
Thus time's whirring loom unceasing I ply,
And weave the life-garment of deity.

FAUST

Thou, restless spirit, dost from end to end
O'ersweep the world; how near I feel to thee!

SPIRIT

Thou'rt like the spirit, thou dost comprehend,
Not me!   (*Vanishes.*)
        FAUST (*deeply moved*)
    Not thee?
    Whom then?

I, God's own image!
And not rank with thee! *(A knock.)*
Oh death! I know it—'tis my famulus—
My fairest fortune now escapes!
That all these visionary shapes
A soulless groveller should banish thus!
    (WAGNER *in his dressing gown and night-cap, a lamp*
        in his hand. FAUST *turns round reluctantly.*)

WAGNER

Pardon! I heard you here declaim;
A Grecian tragedy you doubtless read?
Improvement in this art is now my aim,
For now-a-days it much avails. Indeed
An actor, oft I've heard it said, as teacher,
May give instruction to a preacher.

FAUST

Ay, if your priest should be an actor too,
As not improbably may come to pass.

WAGNER

When in his study pent the whole year through,
Man views the world, as through an optic glass,
On a chance holiday, and scarcely then,
How by persuasion can he govern men?

FAUST

If feeling prompt not, if it doth not flow
Fresh from the spirit's depths, with strong control
Swaying to rapture every listener's soul,
Idle your toil; the chase you may forego!
Brood o'er your task! Together glue,
Cook from another's feast your own ragout,
Still prosecute your paltry game,
And fan your ash-heaps into flame!
Thus children's wonder you'll excite,
And apes', if such your appetite;

But that which issues from the heart alone,
Will bend the hearts of others to your own.

WAGNER

The speaker in delivery will find
Success alone; I still am far behind.

FAUST

A worthy object still pursue!
Be not a hollow tinkling fool!
Sound understanding, judgment true,
Find utterance without art or rule;
And when in earnest you are moved to speak,
Then is it needful cunning words to seek?
Your fine harangues, so polish'd in their kind,
Wherein the shreds of human thought ye twist,
Are unrefreshing as the empty wind,
Whistling through wither'd leaves and autumn mist!

WAGNER

Oh God! How long is art,
Our life how short! With earnest zeal
Still as I ply the critic's task, I feel
A strange oppression both of head and heart.
The very means how hardly are they won,
By which we to the fountains rise!
And haply, ere one half the course is run,
Check'd in his progress, the poor devil dies.

FAUST

Parchment, is that the sacred fount whence roll
Waters, he thirsteth not who once hath quaffed?
Oh, if it gush not from thine inmost soul,
Thou has not won the life-restoring draught.

WAGNER

Your pardon! 'tis delightful to transport
Oneself into the spirit of the past,
To see in times before us how a wise man thought,
And what a glorious height we have achieved at last.

FAUST

Ay truly! even to the loftiest star!
To us, my friend, the ages that are pass'd
A book with seven seals, close-fasten'd, are;
And what the spirit of the times men call,
Is merely their own spirit after all,
Wherein, distorted oft, the times are glass'd.
Then truly, 'tis a sight to grieve the soul!
'At the first glance we fly it in dismay;
'A very lumber-room, a rubbish-hole;
'At best a sort of mock-heroic play,
With saws pragmatical, and maxims sage,
To suit the puppets and their mimic stage.

WAGNER

But then the world and man, his heart and brain!
Touching these things all men would something know.

FAUST

Ay! what 'mong men as knowledge doth obtain!
Who on the child its true name dares bestow?
The few who somewhat of these things have known,
Who their full hearts unguardedly reveal'd,
Nor thoughts, nor feelings, from the mob conceal'd,
Have died on crosses, or in flames been thrown.—
Excuse me, friend, far now the night is spent,
For this time we must say adieu.

WAGNER

Still to watch on I had been well content,
Thus to converse so learnedly with you.
But as to-morrow will be Easter-day,
Some further questions grant, I pray;
With diligence to study still I fondly cling;
Already I know much, but would know everything.

(*Exit.*)

FAUST (*alone*)

How him alone all hope abandons never,
To empty trash who clings, with zeal untired,

With greed for treasure gropes, and, joy-inspir'd,
Exults if earth-worms second his endeavour.

And dare a voice of merely human birth,
E'en here, where shapes immortal throng'd, intrude?
Yet ah! thou poorest of the sons of earth,
For once, I e'en to thee feel gratitude.
Despair the power of sense did well-nigh blast,
And thou didst save me ere I sank dismay'd,
So giant-like the vision seem'd, so vast,
I felt myself shrink dwarf'd as I survey'd!

I, God's own image, from this toil of clay
Already freed, with eager joy who hail'd
The mirror of eternal truth unveil'd,
Mid light effulgent and celestial day:—
I, more than cherub, whose unfetter'd soul
With penetrative glance aspir'd to flow
Through nature's veins, and, still creating, know
The life of gods,—how am I punish'd now!
One thunder-word hath hurl'd me from the goal!

Spirit! I dare not lift me to thy sphere.
What though my power compell'd thee to appear,
My art was powerless to detain thee here.
In that great moment, rapture-fraught,
I felt myself so small, so great;
Fiercely didst thrust me from the realm of thought
Back on humanity's uncertain fate!
Who'll teach me now? What ought I to forego?
Ought I that impulse to obey?
Alas! our every deed, as well as every woe,
Impedes the tenor of life's onward way!

E'en to the noblest by the soul conceiv'd,
Some feelings cling of baser quality;
And when the goods of this world are achiev'd,
Each nobler aim is termed a cheat, a lie.
Our aspirations, our soul's genuine life,
Grow torpid in the din of earthly strife.

Though youthful phantasy, while hope inspires,
Stretch o'er the infinite her wing sublime,
A narrow compass limits her desires,
When wreck'd our fortunes in the gulf of time.
In the deep heart of man care builds her nest,
O'er secret woes she broodeth there,
Sleepless she rocks herself and scareth joy and rest;
Still is she wont some new disguise to wear,
She may as house and court, as wife and child appear,
As dagger, poison, fire and flood;
Imagined evils chill thy blood,
And what thou ne'er shall lose, o'er that dost shed the
    tear.
I am not like the gods! Feel it I must;
I'm like the earth-worm, writhing in the dust,
Which, as on dust it feeds, its native fare,
Crushed 'neath the passer's tread, lies buried there.

Is it not dust, wherewith this lofty wall,
With hundred shelves, confines me round;
Rubbish, in thousand shapes, may I not call
What in this moth-world doth my being bound?
Here, what doth fail me, shall I find?
Read in a thousand tomes that, everywhere,
Self-torture is the lot of human-kind,
With but one mortal happy, here and there?
Thou hollow skull, that grin, what should it say,
But that thy brain, like mine, of old perplexed,
Still yearning for the truth, hath sought the light of day.
And in the twilight wandered, sorely vexed?
Ye instruments, forsooth, ye mock at me,—
With wheel, and cog, and ring, and cylinder;
To nature's portals ye should be the key;
Cunning your wards, and yet the bolts ye fail to stir.
Inscrutable in broadest light,
To be unveil'd by force she doth refuse,
What she reveals not to thy mental sight,
Thou wilt not wrest me from her with levers and with screws.
Old useless furnitures, yet stand ye here,
Because my sire ye served, now dead and gone.

Old scroll, the smoke of years dost wear,
So long as o'er this desk the sorry lamp hath shone.
Better my little means hath squandered quite away,
Than burden'd by that little here to sweat and groan!
Wouldst thou possess thy heritage, essay,
By use to render it thine own!
What we employ not, but impedes our way,
That which the hour creates, that can it use alone!

But wherefore to yon spot is riveted my gaze?
Is yonder flasket there a magnet to my sight?
Whence this mild radiance that around me plays,
As when, 'mid forest gloom, reigneth the moon's soft
    light?

Hail precious phial! Thee, with reverent awe,
Down from thine old receptacle I draw!
Science in thee I hail and human art.
Essence of deadliest powers, refin'd and sure,
Of soothing anodynes abstraction pure,
Now in thy master's need thy grace impart!
I gaze on thee, my pain is lull'd to rest;
I grasp thee, calm'd the tumult in my breast;
The flood-tide of my spirit ebbs away;
Onward I'm summon'd o'er a boundless main,
Calm at my feet expands the glassy plain,
To shores unknown allures a brighter day.

Lo, where a car of fire, on airy pinion,
Comes floating towards me! I'm prepar'd to fly
By a new track through ether's wide dominion,
To distant spheres of pure activity.
This life intense, this godlike ecstasy—
Worm that thou art such rapture canst thou earn?
Only resolve with courage stern and high,
Thy visage from the radiant sun to turn!
Dare with determin'd will to burst the portals
Past which in terror others fain would steal!
Now is the time, through deeds, to show that mortals
The calm sublimity of gods can feel;

To shudder not at yonder dark abyss,
Where phantasy creates her own self-torturing brood,
Right onward to the yawning gulf to press,
Around whose narrow jaws rolleth hell's fiery flood;
With glad resolve to take the fatal leap,
Though danger threaten thee, to sink in endless sleep!

Pure crystal goblet! forth I draw thee now,
From out thine antiquated case, where thou
Forgotten hast reposed for many a year!
Oft at my father's revels thou didst shine,
To glad the earnest guests was thine,
As each to other passed the generous cheer.
The gorgeous brede of figures, quaintly wrought,
Which he who quaff'd must first in rhyme expound,
Then drain the goblet at one draught profound,
Hath nights of boyhood to fond memory brought.
I to my neighbour shall not reach thee now,
Nor on thy rich device shall I my cunning show.
Here is a juice, makes drunk without delay;
Its dark brown flood thy crystal round doth fill;
Let this last draught, the product of my skill,
My own free choice, be quaff'd with resolute will,
A solemn festive greeting, to the coming day!

(He places the goblet to his mouth.)
(The ringing of bells, and choral voices.)

Chorus of Angels

Christ is arisen!
Mortal, all hail to thee,
Thou whom mortality,
Earth's sad reality,
Held as in prison.

Faust

What hum melodious, what clear silvery chime
Thus draws the goblet from my lips away?

Ye deep-ton'd bells, do ye with voice sublime,
Announce the solemn dawn of Easter-day?
Sweet choir! are ye the hymn of comfort singing,
Which once around the darkness of the grave,
From seraph-voices, in glad triumph ringing,
Of a new covenant assurance gave?

CHORUS OF WOMEN

We, his true-hearted,
With spices and myrrh,
Embalmed the departed,
And swathed him with care;
Here we conveyed Him,
Our Master, so dear;
Alas! Where we laid Him,
The Christ is not here.

CHORUS OF ANGELS

Christ is arisen!
Blessèd the loving one,
Who from earth's trial throes,
Healing and strengthening woes,
Soars as from prison.

FAUST

Wherefore, ye tones celestial, sweet and strong,
Come ye a dweller in the dust to seek?
Ring out your chimes believing crowds among,
The message well I hear, my faith alone is weak;
From faith her darling, miracle, hath sprung.
Aloft to yonder spheres I dare not soar,
Whence sound the tidings of great joy;
And yet, with this sweet strain familiar when a boy,
Back it recalleth me to life once more.
Then would celestial love, with holy kiss,
Come o'er me in the Sabbath's stilly hour,
While, fraught with solemn meaning and mysterious
    power,

Chim'd the deep-sounding bell, and prayer was bliss;
A yearning impulse, undefin'd yet dear,
Drove me to wander on through wood and field;
With heaving breast and many a burning tear,
I felt with holy joy a world reveal'd.
Gay sports and festive hours proclaim'd with joyous
    pealing,
This Easter hymn in days of old;
And fond remembrance now doth me, with childlike
    feeling,
Back from the last, the solemn step, withhold.
O still sound on, thou sweet celestial strain!
The tear-drop flows,—Earth, I am thine again!

Chorus of Disciples

He whom we mourned as dead,
Living and glorious,
From the dark grave hath fled,
O'er death victorious;
Almost creative bliss
Waits on his growing powers;
Ah! Him on earth we miss;
Sorrow and grief are ours.
Yearning he left his own,
Mid sore annoy;
Ah! we must needs bemoan.
Master, thy joy!

Chorus of Angels

Christ is arisen,
Redeem'd from decay.
The bonds which imprison
Your souls, rend away!
Praising the Lord with zeal,
By deeds that love reveal,
Like brethren true and leal
Sharing the daily meal,
To all that sorrow feel
Whisp'ring of heaven's weal,

Still is the master **near,**
Still is he here!

BEFORE THE GATE
Promenaders of all sorts pass out.

ARTISANS

Why choose ye that direction, pray?

OTHERS

To the hunting-lodge we're on our way.

THE FIRST

We towards the mill are strolling on.

A MECHANIC

A walk to Wasserhof were best.

A SECOND

The road is not a pleasant one.

THE OTHERS

What will you do?

A THIRD

     I'll join the **rest.**

A FOURTH

Let's up to Burghof, there you'll find good cheer,
The prettiest maidens and the best of beer,
And brawls of a prime sort.

A FIFTH

          You scapegrace! How,
Your skin still itching for a row?
Thither I will not go, I loathe the place.

SERVANT GIRL

No, no! I to the town my steps retrace.

ANOTHER

Near yonder poplars he is sure to be.

THE FIRST

And if he is, what matters it to me!
With you he'll walk, he'll dance with none but you,
And with your pleasures what have I to do?

THE SECOND

To-day he will not be alone, he said
His friend would be with him, the curly-head.

STUDENT

Why how those buxom girls step on!
Come, brother, we will follow them anon.
Strong beer, a damsel smartly dress'd,
Stinging tobacco,—these I love the best.

BURGHER'S DAUGHTER

Look at those handsome fellows there!
'Tis really shameful, I declare,
The very best society they shun,
After those servant girls forsooth, to run.

SECOND STUDENT (*to the first*)

Not quite so fast! for in our rear,
Two girls, well-dress'd, are drawing near;
Not far from us the one doth dwell,
And sooth to say, I like her well.
They walk demurely, yet you'll see,
That they will let us join them presently.

THE FIRST

Not I! restraints of all kinds I detest.
Quick! let us catch the wild-game ere it flies,
The hand on Saturday the mop that plies,
Will on the Sunday fondle you the best.

Burgher

No, this new Burgomaster, I like him not, God knows,
Now, he's in office, daily more arrogant he grows;
And for the town, what doth he do for it?
Are not things worse from day to day?
To more restraints we must submit;
And taxes more than ever pay.

Beggar (*sings*).

Kind gentleman and ladies fair,
So rosy-cheek'd and trimly dress'd,
Be pleas'd to listen to my prayer,
Relieve and pity the distress'd.
Let me not vainly sing my lay!
His heart's most glad whose hand is free.
Now when all men keep holiday,
Should be a harvest-day to me.

Another Burgher

On holidays and Sundays naught know I more inviting
Than chatting about war and war's alarms,
When folk in Turkey, up in arms,
Far off, are 'gainst each other fighting.
We at the window stand, our glasses drain,
And watch adown the stream the painted vessels gliding,
Then joyful we at eve come home again,
And peaceful times we bless, peace long-abiding.

Third Burgher

Ay, neighbour! So let matters stand for me!
There they may scatter one another's brains,
And wild confusion round them see—
So here at home in quiet all remains!

Old Woman (*to the* Burghers' Daughters)

Heyday! How smart! The fresh young blood!
Who would not fall in love with you?

Not quite so proud! 'Tis well and good!
And what you wish, that I could help you to.

BURGHER'S DAUGHTER

Come, Agatha! I care not to be seen
Walking in public with these witches. True,
My future lover, last St. Andrew's E'en,
In flesh and blood she brought before my view.

ANOTHER

And mine she show'd me also in the glass,
A soldier's figure, with companions bold;
I look around, I seek him as I pass,
In vain, his form I nowhere can behold.

SOLDIERS

Fortress with turrets
And walls high in air,
Damsel disdainful,
Haughty and fair,
These be my prey!
Bold is the venture,
Costly the pay!

Hark how the trumpet
Thither doth call us,
Where either pleasure
Or death may befall us.
Hail to the tumult!
Life's in the field!
Damsel and fortress
To us must yield.
Bold is the venture,
Costly the pay!
Gaily the soldier
Marches away.

Faust and Wagner

Faust

Loosed from their fetters are streams and rills
Through the gracious spring-tide's all-quickening glow;
Hope's budding joy in the vale doth blow;
Old Winter back to the savage hills
Withdraweth his force, decrepid now.
Thence only impotent icy grains
Scatters he as he wings his flight,
Striping with sleet the verdant plains;
But the sun endureth no trace of white;
Everywhere growth and movement are rife,
All things investing with hues of life:
Though flowers are lacking, varied of dye,
Their colours the motly throng supply.
Turn thee around, and from this height,
Back to the town direct thy sight.
Forth from the hollow, gloomy gate,
Stream forth the masses, in bright array.
Gladly seek they the sun to-day;
The Lord's Resurrection they celebrate:
For they themselves have risen, with joy,
From tenement sordid, from cheerless room,
From bonds of toil, from care and annoy,
From gable and roof's o'er-hanging gloom,
From crowded alley and narrow street,
And from the churches' awe-breathing night,
All now have come forth into the light.
Look, only look, on nimble feet,
Through garden and field how spread the throng,
How o'er the river's ample sheet,
Many a gay wherry glides along;
And see, deep sinking in the tide,
Pushes the last boat now away.
E'en from yon far hill's path-worn side,
Flash the bright hues of garments gay.
Hark! Sounds of village mirth arise;
This is the people's paradise.

Both great and small send up a cheer;
Here am I man, I feel it here.

WAGNER

Sir Doctor, in a walk with you
There's honour and instruction too;
Yet here alone I care not to resort,
Because I coarseness hate of every sort.
This fiddling, shouting, skittling, I detest;
I hate the tumult of the vulgar throng;
They roar as by the evil one possess'd,
And call it pleasure, call it song.

PEASANTS (*under the linden-tree*)
Dance and song

The shepherd for the dance was dress'd,
With ribbon, wreath, and coloured vest,
A gallant show displaying.
And round about the linden-tree,
They footed it right merrily.
Juchhe! Juchhe!
Juchheisa! Heisa! He!
So fiddle-bow was braying.

Our swain amidst the circle press'd,
He push'd a maiden trimly dress'd,
And jogg'd her with his elbow;
The buxom damsel turn'd her head,
"Now that's a stupid trick!" she said,
Juchhe! Juchhe!
Juchhesia! Heisa! He!
Don't be so rude, good fellow!

Swift in the circle they advanced,
They danced to right, to left they danced,
And all the skirts were swinging.
And they grew red, and they grew warm,
Panting, they rested arm in arm,
Juchhe! Juchhe!
Juchheisa! Heisa! He!
To hip their elbow bringing.

Don't make so free! How many a maid
Has been betroth'd and then betray'd;
And has repented after!
Yet still he flatter'd her aside,
And from the linden, far and wide,
     Juchhe! Juchhe!
     Juchheisa! Heisa! He!
Rang fiddle-bow and laughter.

OLD PEASANT

Doctor, 'tis really kind of you,
To condescend to come this way,
A highly learned man like you,
To join our mirthful throng to-day.
Our fairest cup I offer you,
Which we with sparkling drink have crown'd,
And pledging you, I pray aloud,
That every drop within its round,
While it your present thirst allays,
May swell the number of your days.

FAUST

I take the cup you kindly reach,
Thanks and prosperity to each!
         (*The crowd gather round in a circle.*)

OLD PEASANT

Ay, truly! 'tis well done, that you
Our festive meeting thus attend;
You, who in evil days of yore,
So often show'd yourself our friend!
Full many a one stands living here,
Who from the fever's deadly blast,
Your father rescu'd, when his skill
The fatal sickness stay'd at last.
A young man then, each house you sought,
Where reign'd the mortal pestilence.
Corpse after corpse was carried forth,
But still unscath'd you issued thence.

Sore then your trials and severe;
The Helper yonder aids the helper here.

ALL

Heaven bless the trusty friend, and long
To help the poor his life prolong!

FAUST

To Him above in homage bend,
Who prompts the helper and Who help doth send.
(He proceeds with WAGNER.)

WAGNER

What feelings, great man, must thy breast inspire,
At homage paid thee by this crowd! Thrice blest
Who from the gifts by him possessed
Such benefit can draw! The sire
Thee to his boy with reverence shows;
They press around, inquire, advance,
Hush'd is the fiddle, check'd the dance.
Where thou dost pass they stand in rows,
And each aloft his bonnet throws,
But little fails and they to thee,
As though the Host came by, would bend the knee.

FAUST

A few steps further, up to yonder stone!
Here rest we from our walk. In times long past,
Absorb'd in thought, here oft I sat alone,
And disciplin'd myself with prayer and fast.
Then rich in hope, with faith sincere,
With sighs, and hands in anguish press'd,
The end of that sore plague, with many a tear,
From heaven's dread Lord, I sought to wrest.
The crowd's applause assumes a scornful tone.
Oh, could'st thou in my inner being read,
How little either sire or son,
Of such renown deserves the meed!
My sire, of good repute, and sombre mood,
O'er nature's powers and every mystic zone,

With honest zeal, but methods of his own,
With toil fantastic loved to brood;
His time in dark alchemic cell,
With brother adepts he would spend,
And there antagonists compel,
Through numberless receipts to blend.
A ruddy lion there, a suitor bold,
In tepid bath was with the lily wed.
Thence both, while open flames around them roll'd,
Were tortur'd to another bridal bed.
Was then the youthful queen descried
With varied colours in the flask;—
This was our medicine; the patients died,
" Who were restored? " none cared to ask.
With our infernal mixture thus, ere long,
These hills and peaceful vales among,
We rag'd more fiercely than the pest;
Myself the deadly poison did to thousands give;
They pined away, I yet must live,
To hear the reckless murderers blest.

Wagner

Why let this thought your soul o'ercast?
Can man do more than with nice skill,
With firm and conscientious will,
Practise the art transmitted from the past?
If thou thy sire dost honour in thy youth,
His lore thou gladly wilt receive;
In manhood, dost thou spread the bounds of truth,
Then may thy son a higher goal achieve.

Faust

How blest, in whom the fond desire
From error's sea to rise, hope still renews!
What a man knows not, that he doth require,
And what he knoweth, that he cannot use.
But let not moody thoughts their shadow throw
O'er the calm beauty of this hour serene!
In the rich sunset see how brightly glow

Yon cottage homes, girt round with verdant green!
Slow sinks the orb, the day is now no more;
Yonder he hastens to diffuse new life.
Oh for a pinion from the earth to soar,
'And after, ever after him to strive!
Then should I see the world below,
Bathed in the deathless evening-beams,
The vales reposing, every height a-glow,
The silver brooklets meeting golden streams.
The savage mountain, with its cavern'd side,
Bars not my godlike progress. Lo, the ocean,
Its warm bays heaving with a tranquil motion,
To my rapt vision opes its ample tide!
But now at length the god appears to sink;
A new-born impulse wings my flight,
Onward I press, his quenchless light to drink,
The day before me, and behind the night,
The pathless waves beneath, and over me the skies.
Fair dream, it vanish'd with the parting day!
Alas! that when on spirit-wing we rise,
No wing material lifts our mortal clay.
But 'tis our inborn impulse, deep and strong,
Upwards and onwards still to urge our flight,
When far above us pours its thrilling song
The sky-lark, lost in azure light,
When on extended wing amain
O'er pine-crown'd height the eagle soars,
'And over moor and lake, the crane
Still striveth towards its native shores.

WAGNER

To strange conceits oft I myself must own,
'But impulse such as this I ne'er have known:
'Nor woods, nor fields, can long our thoughts engage,
Their wings I envy not the feather'd kind;
Far otherwise the pleasures of the mind,
Bear us from book to book, from page to page!
Then winter nights grow cheerful; keen delight
Warms every limb; and ah! when we unroll

Some old and precious parchment, at the sight
All heaven itself descends upon the soul.

Faust

Thy heart by one sole impulse is possess'd;
Unconscious of the other still remain!
Two souls, alas! are lodg'd within my breast,
Which struggle there for undivided reign:
One to the world, with obstinate desire,
And closely-cleaving organs, still adheres;
Above the mist, the other doth aspire,
With sacred vehemence, to purer spheres.
Oh, are there spirits in the air,
Who float 'twixt heaven and earth dominion wielding,
Stoop hither from your golden atmosphere,
Lead me to scenes, new life and fuller yielding!
A magic mantle did I but possess,
Abroad to waft me as on viewless wings,
I'd prize it far beyond the costliest dress,
Nor would I change it for the robe of kings.

Wagner

Call not the spirits who on mischief wait!
Their troop familiar, streaming through the air,
From every quarter threaten man's estate,
And danger in a thousand forms prepare!
They drive impetuous from the frozen north,
With fangs sharp-piercing, and keen arrowy tongues;
From the ungenial east they issue forth,
And prey, with parching breath, upon thy lungs;
If, waft'd on the desert's flaming wing,
They from the south heap fire upon the brain,
Refreshment from the west at first they bring,
Anon to drown thyself and field and plain.
In wait for mischief, they are prompt to hear;
With guileful purpose our behests obey;
Like ministers of grace they oft appear,
And lisp like angels, to betray.
But let us hence! Grey eve doth all things blend,

The air grows chill, the mists descend!
'Tis in the evening first our home we prize—
Why stand you thus, and gaze with wondering eyes?
What in the gloom thus moves you?

FAUST

                                Yon black hound
See'st thou, through corn and stubble scampering
    round?

WAGNER

I've mark'd him long, naught strange in him I see!

FAUST

Note him! What takest thou the brute to be?

WAGNER

But for a poodle, whom his instinct serves
His master's track to find once more.

FAUST

Dost mark how round us, with wide spiral curves,
He wheels, each circle closer than before?
And, if I err not, he appears to me
A line of fire upon his track to leave.

WAGNER

Naught but a poodle black of hue I see;
'Tis some illusion doth your sight deceive.

FAUST

Methinks a magic coil our feet around,
He for a future snare doth lightly spread.

WAGNER

Around us as in doubt I see him shyly bound,
Since he two strangers seeth in his master's stead.

FAUST

The circle narrows, he's already near!

WAGNER

A dog dost see, no spectre have we here;
He growls, doubts, lays him on his belly, too,
And wags his tail—as dogs are wont to do.

FAUST

Come hither, Sirrah! join our company!

WAGNER

A very poodle, he appears to be!
Thou standest still, for thee he'll wait;
Thou speak'st to him, he fawns upon thee straight;
Aught thou mayst lose, again he'll bring,
And for thy stick will into water spring.

FAUST

Thou'rt right indeed; no traces now I see
Whatever of a spirit's agency.
'Tis training—nothing more.

WAGNER

      A dog well taught
E'en by the wisest of us may be sought.
Ay, to your favour he's entitled too,
Apt scholar of the students, 'tis his due!
    (*They enter the gate of the town.*

STUDY

FAUST (*entering with the poodle*)

Now field and meadow I've forsaken;
O'er them deep night her veil doth draw;
In us the better soul doth waken,
With feelings of foreboding awe,
All lawless promptings, deeds unholy,

Now slumber, and all wild desires;
The love of man doth sway us wholly,
And love to God the soul inspires.

Peace, poodle, peace! Scamper not thus; obey me!
Why at the threshold snuffest thou so?
Behind the stove now quietly lay thee,
My softest cushion to thee I'll throw.
As thou, without, didst please and amuse me
Running and frisking about on the hill,
So tendance now I will not refuse thee;
A welcome guest, if thou'lt be still.

Ah! when the friendly taper gloweth,
Once more within our narrow cell,
Then in the heart itself that knoweth,
A light the darkness doth dispel.
Reason her voice resumes; returneth
Hope's gracious bloom, with promise rife;
For streams of life the spirit yearneth,
Ah! for the very fount of life.

Poodle, snarl not! with the tone that arises,
Hallow'd and peaceful, my soul within,
Accords not thy growl, thy bestial din.
We find it not strange, that man despises
What he conceives not;
That he the good and fair misprizes—
Finding them often beyond his ken;
Will the dog snarl at them like men?

But ah! Despite my will, it stands confessed,
Contentment welleth up no longer in my breast.
Yet wherefore must the stream, alas, so soon be dry,
That we once more athirst should lie?
Full oft this sad experience hath been mine;
Nathless the want admits of compensation;
For things above the earth we learn to pine,
Our spirits yearn for revelation,
Which nowhere burns with purer beauty blent,

Than here in the New Testament.
To ope the ancient text an impulse strong
Impels me, and its sacred lore,
With honest purpose to explore,
And render into my loved German tongue.
           (*He opens a volume, and applies himself to it.*)
'Tis writ, "In the beginning was the Word!"
I pause, perplex'd! Who now will help afford?
I cannot the mere Word so highly prize;
I must translate it otherwise,
If by the spirit guided as I read.
"In the beginning was the Sense!" Take heed,
The import of this primal sentence weigh,
Lest thy too hasty pen be led astray!
Is force creative then of Sense the dower?
"In the beginning was the Power!"
Thus should it stand: yet, while the line I trace,
A something warns me, once more to efface.
The spirit aids! from anxious scruples freed,
I write, "In the beginning was the Deed!"

       Am I with thee my room to share,
       Poodle, thy barking now forbear,
       Forbear thy howling!
       Comrade so noisy, ever growling,
       I cannot suffer here to dwell.
       One or the other, mark me well,
       Forthwith must leave the cell.
       I'm loath the guest-right to withhold;
       The door's ajar, the passage clear;
       But what must now mine eyes behold!
       Are nature's laws suspended here?
       Real is it, or a phantom show?
       In length and breadth how doth my poodle grow!
       He lifts himself with threat'ning mien,
       In likeness of a dog no longer seen!
       What spectre have I harbour'd thus!
       Huge as a hippopotamus,
       With fiery eye, terrific tooth!
       Ah! now I know thee, sure enough!

For such a base, half-hellish brood,
The key of Solomon is good.

SPIRITS (*without*)
Captur'd there within is one!
Stay without and follow none!
Like a fox in iron snare,
Hell's old lynx is quaking there,
    But take heed!
Hover round, above, below,
    To and fro,
Then from durance is he freed!
Can ye aid him, spirits all,
Leave him not in mortal thrall!
Many a time and oft hath he
Served us, when at liberty.

FAUST
The monster to confront, at first,
The spell of Four must be rehears'd;

Salamander shall kindle,
Writhe nymph of the wave,
In air sylph shall dwindle,
And Kobold shall slave.

Who doth ignore
The primal Four,
Nor knows aright
Their use and might,
O'er spirits will he
Ne'er master be!

Vanish in the fiery glow,
Salamander!
Rushingly together flow.
Undine!
Shimmer in the meteor's gleam,
Sylphide!
Hither bring thine homely aid,

Incubus! Incubus!
Step forth! I do adjure thee thus!
None of the Four
Lurks in the beast:
He grins at me, untroubled as before;
I have not hurt him in the least.
A spell of fear
Thou now shalt hear.
> Art thou, comrade fell,
> Fugitive from Hell?
> See then this sign,
> Before which incline
> The murky troops of Hell!

With bristling hair now doth the creature swell

> Canst thou, reprobate,
> Read the uncreate,
> Unspeakable, diffused
> Throughout the heavenly sphere,
> Shamefully abused,
> Transpierced with nail and spear!

Behind the stove, tam'd by my spells,
Like an elephant he swells;
Wholly now he fills the room,
He into mist will melt away.
Ascend not to the ceiling! Come,
Thyself at the master's feet now lay!
Thou seest that mine is no idle threat.
With holy fire I will scorch thee yet!
Wait not the might
That lies in the triple-glowing light!
Wait not the might
Of all my arts in fullest measure!

MEPHISTOPHELES

*(As the mist sinks, comes forward from behind the
stove, in the dress of a travelling scholar)*
Why all this uproar? What's the master's pleasure?

FAUST

This then the kernel of the brute!
A travelling scholar? Why I needs must smile.

MEPHISTOPHELES

Your learned reverence humbly I salute!
You've made me swelter in a pretty style.

FAUST

Thy name?

MEPHISTOPHELES

      The question trifling seems from one,
Who it appears the Word doth rate so low;
Who, undeluded by mere outward show,
To Being's depths would penetrate alone.

FAUST

With gentlemen like you indeed
The inward essence from the name we read,
As all too plainly it doth appear,
When Beelzebub, Destroyer, Liar, meets the ear.
Who then art thou?

MEPHISTOPHELES

      Part of that power which still
Produceth good, whilst ever scheming ill.

FAUST

What hidden mystery in this riddle lies?

MEPHISTOPHELES

The spirit I, which evermore denies!
And justly; for whate'er to light is brought
Deserves again to be reduced to naught;
Then better 'twere that naught should be.
Thus all the elements which ye

Destruction, Sin, or briefly, Evil, name,
As my peculiar element I claim.

FAUST

Thou nam'st thyself a part, and yet a whole I see.

MEPHISTOPHELES

The modest truth I speak to thee.
Though folly's microcosm, man, it seems,
Himself to be a perfect whole esteems:
Part of the part am I, which at the first was all,
A part of darkness, which gave birth to light,
Proud light, who now his mother would enthrall,
Contesting space and ancient rank with night.
Yet he succeedeth not, for struggle as he will,
To forms material he adhereth still;
From them he streameth, them he maketh fair,
And still the progress of his beams they check;
And so, I trust, when comes the final wreck,
Light will, ere long, the doom of matter share.

FAUST

Thy worthy avocation now I guess!
Wholesale annihilation won't prevail,
So thou'rt beginning on a smaller scale.

MEPHISTOPHELES

And, to say truth, as yet with small success.
Oppos'd to naught, this clumsy world,
The something—it subsisteth still;
Not yet is it to ruin hurl'd,
Despite the efforts of my will.
Tempests and earthquakes, fire and flood, I've tried;
Yet land and ocean still unchang'd abide!
And then of humankind and beasts, the accursed
        brood,—
Neither o'er them can I extend my sway.
What countless myriads have I swept away!
Yet ever circulates the fresh young blood.

It is enough to drive me to despair!
As in the earth, in water, and in air,
A thousand germs burst forth spontaneously;
In moisture, drought, heat, cold, they still appear!
Had I not flame selected as my sphere
Nothing apart had been reserved for me.

Faust

So thou with thy cold devil's fist
Still clench'd in malice impotent
Dost the creative power resist,
The active, the beneficent!
Henceforth some other task essay,
Of Chaos thou the wondrous son!

Mephistopheles

We will consider what you say,
And talk about it more anon!
For this time have I leave to go?

Faust

Why thou shouldst ask, I cannot see.
Since thee I now have learned to know,
At thy good pleasure, visit me.
Here is the window, here the door,
The chimney, too, may serve thy need.

Mephistopheles

I must confess, my stepping o'er
Thy threshold a slight hindrance doth impede;
The wizard-foot doth me retain.

Faust

The pentagram thy peace doth mar?
To me, thou son of hell, explain,
How camest thou in, if this thine exit bar?
Could such a spirit aught ensnare?

MEPHISTOPHELES

Observe it well, it is not drawn with care,
One of the angles, that which points without,
Is, as thou seest, not quite closed.

FAUST

Chance hath the matter happily dispos'd!
So thou my captive art?　No doubt!
By accident thou thus art caught!

MEPHISTOPHELES

In sprang the dog, indeed, observing naught;
Things now assume another shape,
The devil's in the house and can't escape.

FAUST

Why through the window not withdraw?

MEPHISTOPHELES

For ghosts and for the devil 'tis a law.
Where they stole in, there they must forth.　We're free
The first to choose; as to the second, slaves are we.

FAUST

E'en hell hath its peculiar laws, I see!
I'm glad of that! a pact may then be made,
The which you gentlemen will surely keep?

MEPHISTOPHELES

What e'er therein is promised thou shalt reap,
No tittle shall remain unpaid.
But such arrangements time require;
We'll speak of them when next we meet;
Most earnestly I now entreat,
This once permission to retire.

Faust

Another moment prithee here remain,
Me with some happy word to pleasure.

Mephistopheles

Now let me go! ere long I'll come again,
Then thou may'st question at thy leisure.

Faust

'Twas not my purpose thee to lime;
The snare hast entered of thine own free will:
Let him who holds the devil, hold him still!
So soon he'll catch him not a second time.

Mephistopheles

If it so please thee, I'm at thy command;
Only on this condition, understand;
That worthily thy leisure to beguile,
I here may exercise my arts awhile.

Faust

Thou'rt free to do so! Gladly I'll attend;
But be thine art a pleasant one!

Mephistopheles

My friend,

This hour enjoyment more intense,
Shall captivate each ravish'd sense,
Than thou could'st compass in the bound
Of the whole year's unvarying round;
And what the dainty spirits sing,
The lovely images they bring,
Are no fantastic sorcery.
Rich odours shall regale your smell,
On choicest sweets your palate dwell,
Your feelings thrill with ecstasy.

No preparation do we need,
Here we together are. Proceed.

SPIRITS

Hence overshadowing gloom,
Vanish from sight!
O'er us thine azure dome,
Bend, beauteous light!
Dark clouds that o'er us spread,
Melt in thin air!
Stars, your soft radiance shed,
Tender and fair.
Girt with celestial might,
Winging their airy flight,
Spirits are thronging.
Follows their forms of light
Infinite longing!
Flutter their vestures bright
O'er field and grove!
Where in their leafy bower
Lovers the livelong hour
Vow deathless love.
Soft bloometh bud and bower!
Bloometh the grove!
Grapes from the spreading vine
Crown the full measure;
Fountains of foaming wine
Gush from the pressure.
Still where the currents wind,
Gems brightly gleam.
Leaving the hills behind
On rolls the stream;
Now into ample seas,
Spreadeth the flood;
Laving the sunny leas,
Mantled with wood.
Rapture the feather'd throng,
Gaily careering,
Sip as they float along;
Sunward they're steering;

On towards the isles of light
Winging their way,
That on the waters bright
Dancingly play.
Hark to the choral strain,
Joyfully ringing!
While on the grassy plain
Dancers are springing;
Climbing the steep hill's side,
Skimming the glassy tide,
Wander they there;
Others on pinions wide
Wing the blue air;
All lifeward tending, upward still wending,
Towards yonder stars that gleam,
Far, far above;
Stars from whose tender beam
Rains blissful love.

MEPHISTOPHELES

Well done, my dainty spirits! now he slumbers!
Ye have entranc'd him fairly with your numbers!
This minstrelsy of yours I must repay,—
Thou art not yet the man to hold the devil fast!—
With fairest shapes your spells around him cast,
And plunge him in a sea of dreams!
But that this charm be rent, the threshold passed,
Tooth of rat the way must clear.
I need not conjure long it seems,
One rustles hitherward, and soon my voice will hear.
The master of the rats and mice,
Of flies and frogs, of bugs and lice,
Commands thy presence; without fear
Come forth and gnaw the threshold here,
Where he with oil has smear'd it.—Thou
Com'st hopping forth already! Now
To work! The point that holds me bound
Is in the outer angle found.
Another bite—so—now 'tis done—
Now, Faustus, till we meet again, dream on.

FAUST (*awaking*)

Am I once more deluded! must I deem
That thus the throng of spirits disappear?
The devil's presence, was it but a dream?
Hath but a poodle scap'd and left me here?

STUDY

FAUST.   MEPHISTOPHELES

FAUST

A knock? Come in! Who now would break my rest?

MEPHISTOPHELES

'Tis I!

FAUST

Come in!

MEPHISTOPHELES

Thrice be the words express'd.

FAUST

Then I repeat, Come in!

MEPHISTOPHELES

'Tis well,
I hope that we shall soon agree!
For now your fancies to expel,
Here, as a youth of high degree,
I come in gold-lac'd scarlet vest,
And stiff-silk mantle richly dress'd,
A cock's gay feather for a plume,
A long and pointed rapier, too;
And briefly I would counsel you
To don at once the same costume,
And, free from trammels, speed away,
That what life is you may essay.

FAUST

In every garb I needs must feel oppress'd,
My heart to earth's low cares a prey.
Too old the trifler's part to play,
Too young to live by no desire possess'd.
What can the world to me afford?
Renounce! renounce! is still the word;
This is the everlasting song
In every ear that ceaseless rings,
And which, alas, our whole life long,
Hoarsely each passing moment sings.
But to new horror I awake each morn,
And I could weep hot tears, to see the sun
Dawn on another day, whose round forlorn
Accomplishes no wish of mine—not one.
Which still, with froward captiousness, impairs
E'en the presentiment of every joy,
While low realities and paltry cares
The spirit's fond imaginings destroy.
Then must I too, when falls the veil of night,
Stretch'd on my pallet languish in despair,
Appalling dreams my soul affright;
No rest vouchsafed me even there.
The god, who throned within my breast resides,
Deep in my soul can stir the springs;
With sovereign sway my energies he guides,
He cannot move external things;
And so existence is to me a weight.
Death fondly I desire, and life I hate.

MEPHISTOPHELES

And yet, methinks, by most 'twill be confess'd
That Death is never quite a welcome guest.

FAUST

Happy the man around whose brow he binds
The bloodstain'd wreath in conquest's dazzling hour;
Or whom, excited by the dance, he finds

Dissolv'd in bliss, in love's delicious bower!
O that before the lofty spirit's might,
Enraptured, I had rendered up my soul!

MEPHISTOPHELES

Yet did a certain man refrain one night,
Of its brown juice to drain the crystal bowl.

FAUST

To play the spy diverts you then?

MEPHISTOPHELES

          I own,
Though not omniscient, much to me is known.

FAUST

If o'er my soul the tone familiar, stealing,
Drew me from harrowing thought's bewild'ring maze,
Touching the ling'ring chords of childlike feeling,
With sweet harmonies of happier days:
So curse I all, around the soul that windeth
Its magic and alluring spell,
And with delusive flattery bindeth
Its victim to this dreary cell!
Curs'd before all things be the high opinion,
Wherewith the spirit girds itself around!
Of shows delusive curs'd be the dominion,
Within whose mocking sphere our sense is bound!
Accurs'd of dreams the treacherous wiles,
The cheat of glory, deathless fame!
Accurs'd what each as property beguiles,
Wife, child, slave, plough, whate'er its name!
Accurs'd be mammon, when with treasure
He doth to daring deeds incite:
Or when to steep the soul in pleasure,
He spreads the couch of soft delight!
Curs'd be the grape's balsamic juice!
Accurs'd love's dream, of joys the first!

Accurs'd be hope! accurs'd be faith!
And more than all, be patience curs'd!

Chorus of Spirits (*invisible*)

Woe! woe!
Thou hast destroy'd
The beautiful world
With violent blow;
'Tis shiver'd! 'tis shatter'd!
The fragments abroad by a demigod scatter'd!
Now we sweep
The wrecks into nothingness!
Fondly we weep
The beauty that's gone!
Thou, 'mongst the sons of earth,
Lofty and mighty one,
Build it once more!
In thine own bosom the lost world restore!
Now with unclouded sense
Enter a new career;
Songs shall salute thine ear,
Ne'er heard before!

Mephistopheles

My little ones these spirits be.
Hark! with shrewd intelligence,
How they recommend to thee
Action, and the joys of sense!
In the busy world to dwell,
Fain they would allure thee hence:
For within this lonely cell,
Stagnate sap of life and sense.

Forbear to trifle longer with thy grief,
Which, vulture-like, consumes thee in this den.
The worst society is some relief,
Making thee feel thyself a man with men.
Nathless, it is not meant, I trow,
To thrust thee 'mid the vulgar throng.

I to the upper ranks do not belong;
Yet if, by me companion'd, thou
Thy steps through life forthwith wilt take,
Upon the spot myself I'll make
Thy comrade;—
Should it suit thy need,
I am thy servant, am thy slave indeed!

FAUST

And how must I thy services repay?

MEPHISTOPHELES

Thereto thou lengthen'd respite hast!

FAUST

                                    No! No!
The devil is an egoist I know:
And, for Heaven's sake, 'tis not his way
Kindness to any one to show.
Let the condition plainly be exprest!
Such a domestic is a dangerous guest.

MEPHISTOPHELES

I'll pledge myself to be thy servant *here,*
Still at thy back alert and prompt to be;
But when together *yonder* we appear,
Then shalt thou do the same for me.

FAUST

But small concern I feel for yonder world;
Hast thou this system into ruin hurl'd,
Another may arise the void to fill.
This earth the fountain whence my pleasures flow,
This sun doth daily shine upon my woe,
And if this world I must forego,
Let happen then,—what can and will.
I to this theme will close mine ears,
If men hereafter hate and love,

And if there be in yonder spheres
A depth below or height above.

MEPHISTOPHELES

In this mood thou mayst venture it. But make
The compact! I at once will undertake
To charm thee with mine arts. I'll give thee more
Than mortal eye hath e'er beheld before.

FAUST

What, sorry Devil, hast thou to bestow?
Was ever mortal spirit, in its high endeavour,
Fathom'd by Being such as thou?
Yet food thou hast which satisfieth never,
Hast ruddy gold, that still doth flow
Like restless quicksilver away,
A game thou hast, at which none win who play,
A girl who would, with amorous eyen,
E'en from my breast, a neighbour snare,
Lofty ambition's joy divine, ,
That, meteor-like, dissolves in air.
Show me the fruit that, ere 'tis pluck'd, doth rot,
And trees. whose verdure daily buds anew!

MEPHISTOPHELES

Such a commission scares me not,
I can provide such treasures, it is true;
But, my good friend, a season will come round,
When on what's good we may regale in peace.

FAUST

If e'er upon my couch, stretched at my ease, I'm found,
Then may my life that instant cease!
Me canst thou cheat with glozing wile
Till self-reproach away I cast,—
Me with joy's lure canst thou beguile;—
Let that day be for me the last!
Be this our wager!

MEPHISTOPHELES

Settled!

FAUST

Sure and fast!

When to the moment I shall say,
"Linger awhile! so fair thou art!"
Then mayst thou fetter me straightway,
Then to the abyss will I depart!
Then may the solemn death-bell sound,
Then from thy service thou art free,
The index then may cease its round,
And time be never more for me!

MEPHISTOPHELES

I shall remember: pause, ere 'tis too late.

FAUST

Thereto a perfect right hast thou.
My strength I do not rashly overrate.
Slave am I here, at any rate,
If thine, or whose, it matters not, I trow.

MEPHISTOPHELES

At thine inaugural feast I will this day
Attend, my duties to commence.—
But one thing!—Accidents may happen, hence
A line or two in writing grant, I pray.

FAUST

A writing, Pedant! dost demand from me?
Man, and man's plighted word, are these unknown to
    thee?
Is't not enough, that by the word I gave,
My doom for evermore is cast?
Doth not the world in all its currents rave,
And must a promise hold me fast?
Yet fixed is this delusion in our heart;

Who, of his own free will, therefrom would part?
How blest within whose breast truth reigneth pure!
No sacrifice will he repent when made!
A formal deed, with seal and signature,
A spectre this from which all shrink afraid.
The word its life resigneth in the pen,
Leather and wax usurp the mastery then.
Spirits of evil! what dost thou require?
Brass, marble, parchment, paper, dost desire?
Shall I with chisel, pen, or graver write?
Thy choice is free; to me 'tis all the same.

MEPHISTOPHELES

Wherefore thy passion so excite
And thus thine eloquence inflame?
A scrap is for our compact good.
Thou under-signest merely with a drop of blood.

FAUST

If this will satisfy thy mind,
Thy whim I'll gratify, howe'er absurd.

MEPHISTOPHELES

Blood is a juice of very special kind.

FAUST

Be not afraid that I shall break my word!
The scope of all my energy
Is in exact accordance with my vow.
Vainly I have aspired too high;
I'm on a level but with such as thou;
Me the great spirit scorn'd, defied;
Nature from me herself doth hide;
Rent is the web of thought; my mind
Doth knowledge loathe of every kind.
In depths of sensual pleasure drown'd,
Let us our fiery passions still!
Enwrapp'd in magic's veil profound,
Let wondrous charms our senses thrill!

Plunge we in time's tempestuous flow,
Stem we the rolling surge of chance!
There may alternate weal and woe,
Success and failure, as they can,
Mingle and shift in changeful dance!
Excitement is the sphere for man.

MEPHISTOPHELES

Nor goal, nor measure is prescrib'd to you,
If you desire to taste of every thing,
To snatch at joy while on the wing,
May your career amuse and profit too!
Only fall to and don't be over coy!

FAUST

Hearken! The end I aim at is not joy;
I crave excitement, agonizing bliss,
Enamour'd hatred, quickening vexation.
Purg'd from the love of knowledge, my vocation,
The scope of all my powers henceforth be this,
To bare my breast to every pang,—to know
In my heart's core all human weal and woe,
To grasp in thought the lofty and the deep,
Men's various fortunes on my breast to heap,
And thus to theirs dilate my individual mind,
And share at length with them the shipwreck of
　　　　mankind.

MEPHISTOPHELES

Oh, credit me, who still as ages roll,
Have chew'd this bitter fare from year to year,
No mortal, from the cradle to the bier,
Digests the ancient leaven! Know, this Whole
Doth for the Deity alone subsist!
He in eternal brightness doth exist,
Us unto darkness he hath brought, and here
Where day and night alternate, is your sphere.

FAUST

But 'tis my will!

MEPHISTOPHELES

   Well spoken, I admit!
But one thing puzzles me, my friend;
Time's short, art long; methinks 'twere fit
That you to friendly counsel should attend.
A poet choose as your ally!
Let him thought's wide dominion sweep,
Each good and noble quality,
Upon your honoured brow to heap;
The lion's magnanimity,
The fleetness of the hind,
The fiery blood of Italy,
The Northern's stedfast mind.
Let him to you the mystery show
To blend high aims and cunning low;
And while youth's passions are aflame
To fall in love by rule and plan!
I fain would meet with such a man;
Would him Sir Microcosmus name.

FAUST

What then am I, if I aspire in vain
The crown of our humanity to gain,
Towards which my every sense doth strain?

MEPHISTOPHELES

Thou'rt after all—just what thou art.
Put on thy head a wig with countless locks,
And to a cubit's height upraise thy socks,
Still thou remainest ever, what thou art.

FAUST

I feel it, I have heap'd upon my brain
The gather'd treasure of man's thought in vain;
And when at length from studious toil I rest,

No power, new-born, springs up within my breast;
A hair's breadth is not added to my height,
I am no nearer to the infinite.

MEPHISTOPHELES

Good sir, these things you view indeed,
Just as by other men they're view'd;
We must more cleverly proceed,
Before life's joys our grasp elude.
The devil! thou hast hands and feet,
And head and heart are also thine;
What I enjoy with relish sweet,
Is it on that account less mine?
If for six stallions I can pay,
Do I not own their strength and speed?
A proper man I dash away,
As their two dozen legs were mine indeed.
Up then, from idle pondering free,
And forth into the world with me!
I tell you what;—your speculative churl
Is like a beast which some ill spirit leads,
On barren wilderness, in ceaseless whirl,
While all around lie fair and verdant meads.

FAUST

But how shall we begin?

MEPHISTOPHELES

            We will go hence with speed,
A place of torment this indeed!
A precious life, thyself to bore,
And some few youngsters evermore!
Leave that to neighbour Paunch!—withdraw,
Why wilt thou plague thyself with thrashing straw?
The very best that thou dost know
Thou dar'st not to the striplings show.
One in the passage now doth wait!

FAUST

I'm in no mood to see him now.

MEPHISTOPHELES

Poor lad! He must be tired, I trow;
He must not go disconsolate.
Hand me thy cap and gown; the mask
Is for my purpose quite first rate.

(He changes his dress.)

Now leave it to my wit! I ask
But quarter of an hour; meanwhile equip,
And make all ready for our pleasant trip!

(Exit FAUST.)

MEPHISTOPHELES (*in* FAUST'S *long gown*)

Mortal! the loftiest attributes of men,
Reason and Knowledge, only thus contemn,
Still let the Prince of lies, without control,
With shows, and mocking charms delude thy soul,
I have thee unconditionally then!
Fate hath endow'd him with an ardent mind,
Which unrestrain'd still presses on for ever,
And whose precipitate endeavour
Earth's joys o'erleaping, leaveth them behind.
Him will I drag through life's wild waste,
Through scenes of vapid dulness, where at last
Bewilder'd, he shall falter, and stick fast;
And, still to mock his greedy haste,
Viands and drink shall float his craving lips beyond—
Vainly he'll seek refreshment, anguish-tost,
And were he not the devil's by his bond,
Yet must his soul infallibly be lost!

A STUDENT *enters*

STUDENT

But recently I've quitted home,
Full of devotion am I come
A man to know and hear, whose name
With reverence is known to fame.

Mephistopheles

Your courtesy much flatters me!
A man like other men you see;
Pray have you yet applied elsewhere?

Student

I would entreat your friendly care!
I've youthful blood and courage high;
Of gold I bring a fair supply;
To let me go my mother was not fain;
But here I longed true knowledge to attain.

Mephistopheles

You've hit upon the very place.

Student

And yet my steps I would retrace.
These walls, this melancholy room,
O'erpower me with a sense of gloom;
The space is narrow, nothing green,
No friendly tree is to be seen:
And in these halls, with benches filled, distraught,
Sight, hearing fail me, and the power of thought.

Mephistopheles

It all depends on habit. Thus at first
The infant takes not kindly to the breast,
But before long, its eager thirst
Is fain to slake with hearty zest:
Thus at the breasts of wisdom day by day
With keener relish you'll your thirst allay.

Student

Upon her neck I fain would hang with joy;
To reach it, say, what means must I employ?

MEPHISTOPHELES

Explain, ere further time we lose,
What special faculty you choose?

STUDENT

Profoundly learned I would grow,
What heaven contains would comprehend,
O'er earth's wide realm my gaze extend,
Nature and science I desire to know.

MEPHISTOPHELES

You are upon the proper track, I find;
Take heed, let nothing dissipate your mind.

STUDENT

My heart and soul are in the chase!
Though to be sure I fain would seize,
On pleasant summer holidays,
A little liberty and careless ease.

MEPHISTOPHELES

Use well your time, so rapidly it flies;
Method will teach you time to win;
Hence, my young friend, I would advise,
With college logic to begin!
Then will your mind be so well braced,
In Spanish boots so tightly laced,
That on 'twill circumspectly creep,
Thought's beaten track securely keep,
Nor will it, ignis-fatuus like,
Into the path of error strike.
Then many a day they'll teach you how
The mind's spontaneous acts, till now
As eating and as drinking free,
Require a process;—one! two! three!
In truth the subtle web of thought
Is like the weaver's fabric wrought:
One treadle moves a thousand lines,

Swift dart the shuttles to and fro,
Unseen the threads together flow,
A thousand knots one stroke combines.
Then forward steps your sage to show,
And prove to you, it must be so;
The first being so, and so the second,
The third and fourth deduc'd we see;
And if there were no first and second,
Nor third nor fourth would ever be.
This, scholars of all countries prize,—
Yet 'mong themselves no weavers rise.—
He who would know and treat of aught alive,
Seeks first the living spirit thence to drive:
Then are the lifeless fragments in his hand,
There only fails, alas! the spirit-band.
This process, chemists name, in learned thesis,
Mocking themselves, *Naturæ encheiresis.*

STUDENT

Your words I cannot fully comprehend.

MEPHISTOPHELES

In a short time you will improve, my friend,
When of scholastic forms you learn the use;
And how by method all things to reduce.

STUDENT

So doth all this my brain confound,
As if a mill-wheel there were turning round.

MEPHISTOPHELES

And next, before aught else you learn,
You must with zeal to metaphysics turn!
There see that you profoundly comprehend,
What doth the limit of man's brain transcend;
For that which is or is not in the head
A sounding phrase will serve you in good stead.
But before all strive this half year
From one fix'd order ne'er to swerve!

Five lectures daily you must hear;
The hour still punctually observe!
Yourself with studious zeal prepare,
And closely in your manual look,
Hereby may you be quite aware
That all he utters standeth in the book;
Yet write away without cessation,
As at the Holy Ghost's dictation!

STUDENT

This, Sir, a second time you need not say!
Your counsel I appreciate quite;
What we possess in black and white,
We can in peace and comfort bear away.

MEPHISTOPHELES

A faculty I pray you name.

STUDENT

For jurisprudence, some distaste I own.

MEPHISTOPHELES

To me this branch of science is well known,
And hence I cannot your repugnance blame.
Customs and laws in every place,
Like a disease, an heir-loom dread,
Still trail their curse from race to race,
And furtively abroad they spread.
To nonsense, reason's self they turn;
Beneficence becomes a pest;
Woe unto thee, that thou'rt a grandson born!
As for the law born with us, unexpressed;—
That law, alas, none careth to discern.

STUDENT

You deepen my dislike. The youth
Whom you instruct, is blest in sooth!
To try theology I feel inclined.

MEPHISTOPHELES

I would not lead you willingly astray,
But as regards this science, you will find
So hard it is to shun the erring way,
And so much hidden poison lies therein,
Which scarce can you discern from medicine.
Here too it is the best, to listen but to one,
And by the master's words to swear alone.
To sum up all—To words hold fast!
Then the safe gate securely pass'd,
You'll reach the fane of certainty at last.

STUDENT

But then some meaning must the words convey.

MEPHISTOPHELES

Right! But o'er-anxious thought, you'll find of no
    avail,
For there precisely where ideas fail,
A word comes opportunely into play
Most admirable weapons words are found,
On words a system we securely ground,
In words we can conveniently believe,
Nor of a single jot can we a word bereave.

STUDENT

Your pardon for my importunity;
Yet once more must I trouble you:
On medicine, I'll thank you to supply
A pregnant utterance or two!
Three years! how brief the appointed tide!
The field, heaven knows, is all too wide!
If but a friendly hint be thrown,
'Tis easier then to feel one's way.

MEPHISTOPHELES (*aside*)

I'm weary of the dry pedantic tone,
And must again the genuine devil play.

(Aloud)

Of medicine the spirit's caught with ease,
The great and little world you study through,
That things may then their course pursue,
As heaven may please.
In vain abroad you range through science' ample
    space,
Each man learns only that which learn he can;
Who knows the moment to embrace,
He is your proper man.
In person you are tolerably made,
Nor in assurance will you be deficient:
Self-confidence acquire, be not afraid,
Others will then esteem you a proficient.
Learn chiefly with the sex to deal!
Their thousands ahs and ohs,
These the sage doctor knows,
He only from one point can heal.
Assume a decent tone of courteous ease,
You have them then to humour as you please.
First a diploma must belief infuse,
That you in your profession take the lead:
You then at once those easy freedoms use
For which another many a year must plead;
Learn how to feel with nice address
The dainty wrist;—and how to press,
With ardent furtive glance, the slender waist,
To feel how tightly it is laced.

STUDENT

There is some sense in that! one sees the how and why.

MEPHISTOPHELES

Grey is, young friend, all theory:
And green of life the golden tree.

STUDENT

I swear it seemeth like a dream to me.
May I some future time repeat my visit,
To hear on what your wisdom grounds your views?

MEPHISTOPHELES

Command my humble service when you choose.

STUDENT

Ere I retire, one boon I must solicit:
Here is my album, do not, Sir, deny
This token of your favour!

MEPHISTOPHELES

Willingly!
(*He writes and returns the book.*)

STUDENT (*reads*)

ERITIS SICUT DEUS, SCIENTES BONUM ET MALUM
(*He reverently closes the book and retires.*)

MEPHISTOPHELES

Let but this ancient proverb be your rule,
My cousin follow still, the wily snake,
And with your likeness to the gods, poor fool,
Ere long be sure your poor sick heart will quake!

FAUST (*enters*)

Whither away?

MEPHISTOPHELES

'Tis thine our course to steer.
The little world, and then the great we'll view.
With what delight, what profit too,
Thou'lt revel through thy gay career!

FAUST

Despite my length of beard I need
The easy manners that insure success;
Th' attempt I fear can ne'er succeed;
To mingle in the world I want address;
I still have an embarrass'd air, and then
I feel myself so small with other men.

MEPHISTOPHELES

Time, my good friend, will all that's needful give;
Be only self-possessed, and thou hast learn'd to live.

FAUST

But how are we to start, I pray?
Steeds, servants, carriage, where are they?

MEPHISTOPHELES

We've but to spread this mantle wide,
'Twill serve whereon through air to ride,
No heavy baggage need you take,
When we our bold excursion make,
A little gas, which I will soon prepare,
Lifts us from earth; aloft through air,
Light laden, we shall swiftly steer;—
I wish you joy of your new life-career.

AUERBACH'S CELLAR IN LEIPZIG

A Drinking Party

FROSCH

No drinking? Naught a laugh to raise?
None of your gloomy looks, I pray!
You, who so bright were wont to blaze,
Are dull as wetted straw to-day.

BRANDER

'Tis all your fault; your part you do not bear,
No beastliness, no folly.

FROSCH

(*pours a glass of wine over his head*)

There,

You have them both!

BRANDER

You double beast!

FROSCH

'Tis what you ask'd me for, at least!

SIEBEL

Whoever quarrels, turn him out!
With open throat drink, roar, and shout.
Hollo! Hollo! Ho!

ALTMAYER

Zounds, fellow, cease your deaf'ning cheers!
Bring cotton-wool! He splits my ears.

SIEBEL

'Tis when the roof rings back the tone,
Then first the full power of the bass is known.

FROSCH

Right! out with him who takes offence!
A! tara lara da!

ALTMAYER

A! tara lara da!

FROSCH

Our throats are tuned. Come let's commence!

(*Sings*)
The holy Roman empire now,
How holds it still together?

BRANDER

An ugly song! a song political!
A song offensive! Thank God, every morn
To rule the Roman empire, that you were not born!
I bless my stars at least that mine is not
Either a kaiser's or a chancellor's lot.
Yet 'mong ourselves should one still lord it o'er the rest;
That we elect a pope I now suggest.
Ye know, what quality ensures
A man's success, his rise secures.

FROSCH (*sings*)
Bear, lady nightingale above,
Ten thousand greetings to my love.

SIEBEL

No greetings to a sweetheart! No love-songs shall
there be!

FROSCH

Love-greetings and love-kisses! Thou shalt not hinder
me!
(*Sings*)
Undo the bolt! in silly night,
Undo the bolt! the lover wakes.
Shut to the bolt! when morning breaks.

SIEBEL

Ay, sing, sing on, praise her with all thy might!
My turn to laugh will come some day.
Me hath she jilted once, you the same trick she'll play.
Some gnome her lover be! where cross-roads meet,

With her to play the fool; or old he-goat,
From Blocksberg coming in swift gallop, bleat
A good night to her, from his hairy throat!
A proper lad of genuine flesh and blood,
Is for the damsel far too good;
The greeting she shall have from me,
To smash her window-panes will be!

BRANDER (*striking on the table*)

Silence! Attend! to me give ear!
Confess, sirs, I know how to live:
Some love-sick folk are sitting here!
Hence, 'tis but fit, their hearts to cheer,
That I a good-night strain to them should give.
Hark! of the newest fashion is my song!
Strike boldly in the chorus, clear and strong!

(*He sings*)

Once in a cellar lived a rat,
He feasted there on butter,
Until his paunch became as fat
As that of Doctor Luther.
The cook laid poison for the guest,
Then was his heart with pangs oppress'd,
As if his frame love wasted.

CHORUS (*shouting*)

As if his frame love wasted.

BRANDER

He ran around, he ran abroad,
Of every puddle drinking.
The house with rage he scratch'd and gnaw'd,
In vain,—he fast was sinking;
Full many an anguish'd bound he gave,
Nothing the hapless brute could save,
As if his frame love wasted.

CHORUS

As if his frame love wasted.

BRANDER

By torture driven, in open day,
The kitchen he invaded,
Convulsed upon the hearth he lay,
With anguish sorely jaded;
The poisoner laugh'd, Ha! ha! quoth she,
His life is ebbing fast, I see,
As if his frame love wasted.

CHORUS

As if his frame love wasted.

SIEBEL

How the dull boors exulting shout!
Poison for the poor rats to strew
A fine exploit it is no doubt.

BRANDER

They, as it seems, stand well with you!

ALTMAYER

Old bald-pate! with the paunch profound!
The rat's mishap hath tamed his nature;
For he his counterpart hath found
Depicted in the swollen creature.

FAUST AND MEPHISTOPHELES

MEPHISTOPHELES

I now must introduce to you
Before aught else, this jovial crew,
To show how lightly life may glide away;
With the folk here each day's a holiday.
With little wit and much content,

Each on his own small round intent,
Like sportive kitten with its tail;
While no sick-headache they bewail,
And while their host will credit give,
Joyous and free from care they live.

BRANDER

They're off a journey, that is clear,—
From their strange manners; they have scarce been here
An hour.

FROSCH

      You're right! Leipzig's the place for me!
'Tis quite a little Paris; people there
Acquire a certain easy finish'd air.

SIEBEL

What take you now these travellers to be?

FROSCH

Let me alone! O'er a full glass you'll see,
As easily I'll worm their secret out,
As draw an infant's tooth. I've not a doubt
That my two gentlemen are nobly born,
They look dissatisfied and full of scorn.

BRANDER

They are but mountebanks, I'll lay a bet!

ALTMAYER

Most like.

FROSCH

      Mark me, I'll screw it from them yet!

MEPHISTOPHELES (*to* FAUST)

These fellows would not scent the devil out,
E'en though he had them by the very throat!

FAUST

Good-morrow, gentlemen!

SIEBEL

Thanks for your fair salute.
(Aside, glancing at MEPHISTOPHELES.*)*
How! goes the fellow on a halting foot?

MEPHISTOPHELES

Is it permitted here with you to sit?
Then though good wine is not forthcoming here,
Good company at least our hearts will cheer.

ALTMAYER

A dainty gentleman, no doubt of it.

FROSCH

You're doubtless recently from Rippach? Pray,
Did you with Master Hans there chance to sup?

MEPHISTOPHELES

To-day we pass'd him, but we did not stop!
When last we met him he had much to say
Touching his cousins, and to each he sent
Full many a greeting and kind compliment.
(With an inclination towards FROSCH.*)*

ALTMAYER *(aside to* FROSCH)
You have it there!

SIEBEL

Faith! he's a knowing one!

FROSCH

Have patience! I will show him up anon!

MEPHISTOPHELES

We heard erewhile, unless I'm wrong,
Voices well trained in chorus pealing?

Certes, most choicely here must song
Re-echo from this vaulted ceiling!

FROSCH

That you're an amateur one plainly sees!

MEPHISTOPHELES

Oh no, though strong the love, I cannot boast much skill.

ALTMAYER

Give us a song!

MEPHISTOPHELES

As many as you will.

SIEBEL

But be it a brand new one, if you please!

MEPHISTOPHELES

But recently returned from Spain are we,
The pleasant land of wine and minstrelsy.

(*Sings*)

A king there was once reigning,
Who had a goodly flea—

FROSCH

Hark! did you rightly catch the words? a flea!
An odd sort of a guest he needs must be.

MEPHISTOPHELES (*sings*)

A king there was once reigning,
Who had a goodly flea,
Him loved he without feigning,
As his own son were he!
His tailor then he summon'd,
The tailor to him goes:
Now measure me the youngster
For jerkin and for hose!

BRANDER

Take proper heed, the tailor strictly charge,
The nicest measurement to take,
And as he loves his head, to make
The hose quite smooth and not too large!

MEPHISTOPHELES

In satin and in velvet,
Behold the yonker dressed;
Bedizen'd o'er with ribbons,
A cross upon his breast.
Prime minister they made him,
He wore a star of state;
And all his poor relations
Were courtiers, rich and great.

The gentlemen and ladies
At court were sore distressed;
The queen and all her maidens
Were bitten by the pest,
And yet they dared not scratch them,
Or chase the fleas away.
If we are bit, we catch them,
And crack without delay.

CHORUS (shouting)

If we are bit, &c.

FROSCH

Bravo! That's the song for me!

SIEBEL

Such be the fate of every flea!

BRANDER

With clever finger catch and kill!

ALTMAYER

Hurrah for wine and freedom still!

MEPHISTOPHELES

Were but your wine a trifle better, friend,
A glass to freedom I would gladly drain.

SIEBEL

You'd better not repeat those words again!

MEPHISTOPHELES

I am afraid the landlord to offend;
Else freely I would treat each worthy guest
From our own cellar to the very best.

SIEBEL

Out with it then! Your doings I'll defend.

FROSCH

Give a good glass, and straight we'll praise you, one and
     all.
Only let not your samples be too small;
For if my judgment you desire,
Certes, an ample mouthful I require.

ALTMAYER (*aside*)

I guess they're from the Rhenish land.

MEPHISTOPHELES

Fetch me a gimlet here!

BRANDER

               Say, what therewith to bore?
You cannot have the wine-casks at the door?

ALTMAYER

Our landlord's tool-basket behind doth yonder stand.

MEPHISTOPHELES (*takes the gimlet*)

(*To* FROSCH)
Now only say! what liquor will you take?

FROSCH
How mean you that? have you of every sort?

MEPHISTOPHELES
Each may his own selection make.

ALTMAYER (*to* FROSCH)
Ha! Ha! You lick your lips already at the thought.

FROSCH
Good, if I have my choice, the Rhenish I propose;
For still the fairest gifts the fatherland bestows.

MEPHISTOPHELES
(*boring a hole in the edge of the table opposite to
where* FROSCH *is sitting*)

Give me a little wax—and make some stoppers—quick!

ALTMAYER
Why, this is nothing but a juggler's trick!

MEPHISTOPHELES (*to* BRANDER)
And you?

BRANDER
Champagne's the wine for me;
Right brisk, and sparkling let it be!

(MEPHISTOPHELES *bores; one of the party has
in the meantime prepared the wax-stop-
pers and stopped the holes.*)

BRANDER

What foreign is one always can't decline,
What's good is often scatter'd far apart.
The French your genuine German hates with all his
      heart,
Yet has a relish for their wine.

SIEBEL

(*as* MEPHISTOPHELES *approaches him*)

I like not acid wine, I must allow,
Give me a glass of genuine sweet!

MEPHISTOPHELES (*bores*)

                         Tokay
Shall, if you wish it, flow without delay.

ALTMAYER

Come! look me in the face! no fooling now!
You are but making fun of us, I trow.

MEPHISTOPHELES

Ah! ah! that would indeed be making free
With such distinguished guests. Come, no delay;
What liquor can I serve you with, I pray?

ALTMAYER

Only be quick, it matters not to me.
            (*After the holes are bored and stopped.*)

MEPHISTOPHELES (*with strange gestures*)

Grapes the vine-stock bears,
Horns the buck-goat wears!
Wine is sap, the vine is wood,
The wooden board yields wine as good.
With a deeper glance and true
The mysteries of nature view!
Have faith and here's a miracle!
Your stoppers draw and drink your fill!

ALL
(*as they draw the stoppers and the wine chosen by
each runs into his glass*)
Oh beauteous spring, which flows so far!

MEPHISTOPHELES
Spill not a single drop, of this beware!
(*They drink repeatedly.*)

ALL (*sing*)
Happy as cannibals are we,
Or as five hundred swine.

MEPHISTOPHELES
They're in their glory, mark their elevation!

FAUST
Let's hence, nor here our stay prolong.

MEPHISTOPHELES
Attend, of brutishness ere long
You'll see a glorious revelation.

SIEBEL
(*drinks carelessly; the wine is spilt upon the ground,
and turns to flame*)
Help! fire! help! Hell is burning!

MEPHISTOPHELES
(*addressing the flames*)

Stop,
Kind element, be still, I say!
(*To the Company.*)
Of purgatorial fire as yet 'tis but a drop.

SIEBEL

What means the knave! For this you'll dearly pay!
Us, it appears, you do not know.

FROSCH

Such tricks a second time he'd better show!

ALTMAYER

Methinks 'twere well we pack'd him quietly away.

SIEBEL

What, sir! with us your hocus-pocus play!

MEPHISTOPHELES

Silence, old wine-cask!

SIEBEL

              How! add insult, too!
Vile broomstick!

BRANDER

Hold, or blows shall rain on you!

ALTMAYER

(*draws a stopper out of the table; fire springs out
against him*)
I burn! I burn!

SIEBEL

              'Tis sorcery, I vow!
Strike home! The fellow is fair game, I trow!
(*They draw their knives and attack* MEPHISTOPHELES.)

MEPHISTOPHELES (*with solemn gestures*)
        Visionary scenes appear!

Words delusive cheat the ear!
Be ye there, and be ye here!
(*They stand amazed and gaze at each other.*)

ALTMAYER

Where am I? What a beauteous land!

FROSCH

Vineyards! unless my sight deceives?

SIEBEL

And clust'ring grapes too, close at hand!

BRANDER

And underneath the spreading leaves,
What stems there be! What grapes I see!
(*He seizes* SIEBEL *by the nose. The others recipro-
cally do the same, and raise their knives.*)

MEPHISTOPHELES (*as above*)

Delusion, from their eyes the bandage take!
Note how the devil loves a jest to break!
(*He disappears with* FAUST; *the fellows draw back
from one another.*)

SIEBEL

What was it?

ALTMAYER
How?

FROSCH
Was that your nose?

BRANDER (*to* SIEBEL)

And look, my hand doth thine enclose!

ALTMAYER

I felt a shock, it went through every limb!
A chair! I'm fainting! All things swim!

FROSCH

Say what has happened, what's it all about?

SIEBEL

Where is the fellow? Could I scent him out,
His body from his soul I'd soon divide!

ALTMAYER

With my own eyes, upon a cask astride,
Forth through the cellar-door I saw him ride—
Heavy as lead my feet are growing.
                            (*Turning to the table.*)
I wonder is the wine still flowing!

SIEBEL

'Twas all delusion, cheat and lie.

FROSCH

'Twas wine I drank, most certainly.

BRANDER

But with the grapes how was it, pray?

ALTMAYER

That none may miracles believe, who now will say?

WITCHES' KITCHEN

*A large caldron hangs over the fire on a low hearth; various
figures appear in the vapour rising from it. A* FEMALE
MONKEY *sits beside the caldron to skim it, and watch that
it does not boil over. The* MALE MONKEY *with the young*

one's is seated near, warming himself. The walls and ceiling are adorned with the strangest articles of witch-furniture.

FAUST, MEPHISTOPHELES

FAUST

This senseless, juggling witchcraft I detest!
Dost promise that in this foul nest
Of madness, I shall be restored?
Must I seek counsel from an ancient dame?
And can she, by these rites abhorred,
Take thirty winters from my frame?
Woe's me, if thou naught better canst suggest!
Hope has already fled my breast.
Has neither nature nor a noble mind
A balsam yet devis'd of any kind?

MEPHISTOPHELES

My friend, you now speak sensibly. In truth,
Nature a method giveth to renew thy youth:
But in another book the lesson's writ;—
It forms a curious chapter, I admit.

FAUST

I fain would know it.

MEPHISTOPHELES

     Good! A remedy
Without physician, gold, or sorcery:
Away forthwith, and to the fields repair,
Begin to delve, to cultivate the ground,
Thy senses and thyself confine
Within the very narrowest round,
Support thyself upon the simplest fare,
Live like a very brute the brutes among,
Neither esteem it robbery
The acre thou dost reap, thyself to dung;
This is the best method, credit me,
Again at eighty to grow hale and young.

FAUST

I am not used to it, nor can myself degrade
So far, as in my hand to take the spade.
This narrow life would suit me not at all.

MEPHISTOPHELES

Then we the witch must summon after all.

FAUST

Will none but this old beldame do?
Canst not thyself the potion brew?

MEPHISTOPHELES

A pretty play our leisure to beguile!
A thousand bridges I could build meanwhile.
Not science only and consummate art,
Patience must also bear her part.
A quiet spirit worketh whole years long;
Time only makes the subtle ferment strong.
And all things that belong thereto,
Are wondrous and exceeding rare!
The devil taught her, it is true;
But yet the draught the devil can't prepare.
                    (*Perceiving the beasts.*)
Look yonder, what a dainty pair!
Here is the maid! the knave is there!
                    (*To the beasts*)
It seems your dame is not at home?

THE MONKEYS

Gone to carouse,
Out of the house,
Thro' the chimney and away?

MEPHISTOPHELES

How long is it her wont to roam?

THE MONKEYS

While we can warm our paws she'll stay.

MEPHISTOPHELES (*to* FAUST)

What think you of the charming creatures?

FAUST

I loathe alike their form and features!

MEPHISTOPHELES

Nay, such discourse, be it confessed,
Is just the thing that pleases me the best.

(*To the* MONKEYS)

Tell me, ye whelps, accursed crew!
What stir ye in the broth about?

MONKEYS

Coarse beggar's gruel here we stew.

MEPHISTOPHELES

Of customers you'll have a rout.

THE HE-MONKEY
(*approaching and fawning on* MEPHISTOPHELES)

Quick! quick! throw the dice,
Make me rich in a trice,
Oh give me the prize!
Alas, for myself!
Had I plenty of pelf,
I then should be wise.

MEPHISTOPHELES

How blest the ape would think himself, if he
Could only put into the lottery!

(In the meantime the young Monkeys *have been playing with a large globe, which they roll forwards)*

The He-Monkey

The world behold;
Unceasingly roll'd,
It riseth and falleth ever;
It ringeth like glass!
How brittle, alas!
'Tis hollow, and resteth never.
How bright the sphere,
Still brighter here!
Now living am I!
Dear son, beware!
Nor venture there!
Thou too must die!
It is of clay;
'Twill crumble away;
There fragments lie.

Mephistopheles

Of what use is the sieve?

The He-Monkey (*taking it down*)

The sieve would show,
If thou wert a thief or no?
(He runs to the She-Monkey, *and makes her look through it.)*

Look through the sieve!
Dost know him the thief,
And dar'st thou not call him so?

Mephistopheles (*approaching the fire*)

And then this pot?

The Monkeys

The half-witted sot!
He knows not the pot!
He knows not the kettle!

MEPHISTOPHELES

Unmannerly beast!
Be civil at least!

THE HE-MONKEY

Take the whisk and sit down in the settle!
(*He makes* MEPHISTOPHELES *sit down.*)

FAUST

(*who all this time has been standing before a looking-glass,
    now approaching, and now retiring from it*)

What do I see? what form, whose charms transcend
The loveliness of earth, is mirror'd here!
O Love, to waft me to her sphere,
To me the swiftest of thy pinions lend!
Alas! If I remain not rooted to this place,
If to approach more near I'm fondly lur'd,
Her image fades, in veiling mist obscur'd!—
Model of beauty both in form and face!
Is't possible? Hath woman charms so rare?
In this recumbent form, supremely fair,
The essence must I see of heavenly grace?
Can aught so exquisite on earth be found?

MEPHISTOPHELES

The six days' labour of a god, my friend,
Who doth himself cry bravo, at the end,
By something clever doubtless should be crown'd.
For this time gaze your fill, and when you please
Just such a prize for you I can provide;
How blest is he to whom kind fate decrees,
To take her to his home, a lovely bride!

(FAUST *continues to gaze into the mirror.* MEPHISTO-
    PHELES *stretching himself on the settle and playing
    with the whisk, continues to speak.*)

Here sit I, like a king upon his throne;
My sceptre this;—the crown I want alone.

THE MONKEYS

(*who have hitherto been making all sorts of strange gestures,
bring* MEPHISTOPHELES *a crown, with loud cries*)

Oh, be so good,
With sweat and with blood
The crown to lime!

(*They handle the crown awkwardly and break it in two
pieces, with which they skip about.*)

'Twas fate's decree!
We speak and see!
We hear and rhyme.

FAUST (*before the mirror*)

Woe's me! well-nigh distraught I feel!

MEPHISTOPHELES

(*pointing to the beasts*)
And even my own head almost begins to reel.

THE MONKEYS

If good luck attend,
If fitly things blend,
Our jargon with thought
And with reason is fraught!

FAUST (*as above*)

A flame is kindled in my breast!
Let us begone! nor linger here!

MEPHISTOPHELES

(*in the same position*)
It now at least must be confessed,
That poets sometimes are sincere.

(*The caldron which the* SHE-MONKEY *has neglected*

begins to boil over; a great flame arises, which streams up the chimney. The WITCH *comes down the chimney with horrible cries.*)

THE WITCH

Ough! ough! ough! ough!
Accursed brute! accursed sow!
The caldron dost neglect, for shame!
Accursed brute to scorch the dame!

(*Perceiving* FAUST *and* MEPHISTOPHELES)

Whom have we here?
Who's sneaking here?
Whence are ye come?
With what desire?
The plague of fire
Your bones consume!

(*She dips the skimming-ladle into the caldron and throws flames at* FAUST, MEPHISTOPHELES, *and the* MONKEYS. *The* MONKEYS *whimper.*)

MEPHISTOPHELES

(*twirling the whisk which he holds in his hand, and striking among the glasses and pots*)

Dash! Smash!
There lies the glass!
There lies the slime!
'Tis but a jest;
I but keep time,
Thou hellish pest,
To thine own chime!

(*While the* WITCH *steps back in rage and astonishment.*)

Dost know me! Skeleton! Vile scarecrow, thou!
Thy lord and master dost thou know?
What holds me, that I deal not now
Thee and thine apes a stunning blow?
No more respect to my red vest dost pay?

Does my cock's feather no allegiance claim?
Have I my visage masked to-day?
Must I be forced myself to name?

The Witch

Master, forgive this rude salute!
But I perceive no cloven foot.
And your two ravens, where are they?

Mephistopheles

This once I must admit your plea;—
For truly I must own that we
Each other have not seen for many a day.
The culture, too, that shapes the world, at last
Hath e'en the devil in its sphere embraced;
The northern phantom from the scene hath pass'd,
Tail, talons, horns, are nowhere to be traced!
As for the foot, with which I can't dispense,
'Twould injure me in company, and hence,
Like many a youthful cavalier,
False calves I now have worn for many a year.

The Witch (dancing)

I am beside myself with joy,
To see once more the gallant Satan here!

Mephistopheles

Woman, no more that name employ!

The Witch

But why? what mischief hath it done?

Mephistopheles

To fable-books it now doth appertain;
But people from the change have nothing won.
Rid of the evil one, the evil ones remain.
Lord Baron call thou me, so is the matter good;
Of other cavaliers the mien I wear.

Dost make no question of my gentle blood;
See here, this is the scutcheon that I bear!

>   (*He makes an unseemly gesture.*)

THE WITCH
(*laughing immoderately*)
Ha! Ha! Just like yourself! You are, I ween,
The same mad wag that you have ever been!

MEPHISTOPHELES (*to* FAUST)
My friend, learn this to understand, I pray!
To deal with witches this is still the way.

THE WITCH
Now tell me, gentlemen, what you desire?

MEPHISTOPHELES
Of your known juice a goblet we require.
But for the very oldest let me ask;
Double its strength with years doth grow.

THE WITCH
Most willingly! And here I have a flask,
From which I've sipp'd myself ere now;
What's more, it doth no longer stink;
To you a glass I joyfully will give.

>   (*Aside.*)

If unprepar'd, however, this man drink,
He hath not, as you know, an hour to live.

MEPHISTOPHELES
He's my good friend, with whom 'twill prosper well;
I grudge him not the choicest of thy store.
Now draw thy circle, speak thy spell,
And straight a bumper for him pour!
(*The* WITCH, *with extraordinary gestures, describes
a circle, and places strange things within it. The
glasses meanwhile begin to ring, the caldron to*

sound, and to make music. Lastly, she brings a
great book; places the MONKEYS *in the circle to*
serve her as a desk, and to hold the torches. She
beckons FAUST *to approach.)*

FAUST (*to* MEPHISTOPHELES)

Tell me, to what doth all this tend?
Where will these frantic gestures end?
This loathsome cheat, this senseless stuff
I've known and hated long enough.

MEPHISTOPHELES

Mere mummery, a laugh to raise!
Pray don't be so fastidious! She
But as a leech, her hocus-pocus plays,
That well with you her potion may agree.
         (*He compels* FAUST *to enter the circle.*)

(*The* WITCH, *with great emphasis, begins to de-*
claim the book.)
         This must thou ken:
         Of one make ten,
         Pass two, and then
         Make square the three,
         So rich thou'lt be.
         Drop out the four!
         From five and six,
         Thus says the witch,
         Make seven and eight.
         So all is straight!
         And nine is one,
         And ten is none,
         This is the witch's one-time-one!

FAUST

The hag doth as in fever rave.

MEPHISTOPHELES

To these will follow many a stave.
I know it well, so rings the book throughout;

Much time I've lost in puzzling o'er its pages,
For downright paradox, no doubt,
A mystery remains alike to fools and sages.
Ancient the art and modern too, my friend.
'Tis still the fashion as it used to be,
Error instead of truth abroad to send
By means of three and one, and one and three.
'Tis ever taught and babbled in the schools.
Who'd take the trouble to dispute with fools?
When words men hear, in sooth, they usually believe,
That there must needs therein be something to
        conceive.

THE WITCH (*continues*)
The lofty power
Of wisdom's dower,
From all the world conceal'd!
Who thinketh not,
To him I wot,
Unsought it is reveal'd.

FAUST

What nonsense doth the hag propound?
My brain it doth well-nigh confound.
A hundred thousand fools or more,
Methinks I hear in chorus roar.

MEPHISTOPHELES

Incomparable Sibyl cease, I pray!
Hand us thy liquor without more delay.
And to the very brim the goblet crown!
My friend he is, and need not be afraid;
Besides, he is a man of many a grade,
Who hath drunk deep already.
    (*The* WITCH, *with many ceremonies, pours the liquor
    into a cup; as* FAUST *lifts it to his mouth, a light
    flame arises.*)

MEPHISTOPHELES

           Gulp it down!
No hesitation! It will prove
A cordial, and your heart inspire!
What! with the devil hand and glove,
And yet shrink back afraid of fire?
(*The* WITCH *dissolves the circle.* FAUST *steps out.*)

MEPHISTOPHELES

Now forth at once! thou dar'st not rest.

WITCH

And much, sir, may the liquor profit you!

MEPHISTOPHELES (*to the* WITCH)

And if to pleasure thee I aught can do,
Pray on Walpurgis mention thy request.

WITCH

Here is a song, sung o'er, sometimes you'll see,
That 'twill a singular effect produce.

MEPHISTOPHELES (*to* FAUST)

Come, quick, and let thyself be led by me;
Thou must perspire, in order that the juice
Thy frame may penetrate through every part.
Then noble idleness I thee will teach to prize,
And soon with ecstasy thou'lt recognise
How Cupid stirs and gambols in thy heart.

FAUST

Let me but gaze one moment in the glass!
Too lovely was that female form!

MEPHISTOPHELES

                         Nay! nay!
A model which all women shall surpass,
In flesh and blood ere long thou shalt survey.
                               (*Aside.*)

As works the draught, thou presently shalt greet
A Helen in each woman thou dost meet.

A STREET
FAUST (MARGARET *passing by*)

FAUST
Fair lady, may I thus make free
To offer you my arm and company?

MARGARET
I am no lady, am not fair,
Can without escort home repair.
                    (*She disengages herself and exit.*)

FAUST
By heaven! This girl is fair indeed!
No form like hers can I recall.
Virtue she hath, and modest heed,
Is piquant too, and sharp withal.
Her cheek's soft light, her rosy lips,
No length of time will e'er eclipse!
Her downward glance in passing by,
Deep in my heart is stamp'd for aye;
How curt and sharp her answer too,
To ecstasy the feeling grew!
                    (MEPHISTOPHELES *enters.*)

FAUST
This girl must win for me! Dost hear?

MEPHISTOPHELES
Which?

FAUST
She who but now passed.

MEPHISTOPHELES
                    What! She?

She from confession cometh here,
From every sin absolved and free;
I crept near the confessor's chair.
All innocence her virgin soul,
For next to nothing went she there;
O'er such as she I've no control!

FAUST

She's past fourteen.

MEPHISTOPHELES

               You really talk
Like any gay Lothario,
Who every floweret from its stalk
Would pluck, and deems nor grace, nor truth,
Secure against his arts, forsooth!
This ne'er the less won't always do.

FAUST

Sir Moralizer, prithee, pause;
Nor plague me with your tiresome laws!
To cut the matter short, my friend,
She must this very night be mine,—
And if to help me you decline,
Midnight shall see our compact end.

MEPHISTOPHELES

What may occur just bear in mind!
A fortnight's space, at least, I need,
A fit occasion but to find.

FAUST

With but seven hours I could succeed;
Nor should I want the devil's wile,
So young a creature to beguile.

MEPHISTOPHELES

Like any Frenchman now you speak,
But do not fret, I pray; why seek

To hurry to enjoyment straight?
The pleasure is not half so great,
As when at first around, above,
With all the fooleries of love,
The puppet you can knead and mould
As in Italian story oft is told.

FAUST

No such incentives do I need.

MEPHISTOPHELES

But now, without offence or jest!
You cannot quickly. I protest,
In winning this sweet child succeed.
By storm we cannot take the fort,
To stratagem we must resort.

FAUST

Conduct me to her place of rest!
Some token of the angel bring!
A kerchief from her snowy breast,
A garter bring me,—any thing!

MEPHISTOPHELES

That I my anxious zeal may prove,
Your pangs to sooth and aid your love,
A single moment will we not delay,
Will lead you to her room this very day.

FAUST

And shall I see her?—Have her?

MEPHISTOPHELES

                        No!
She to a neighbour's house will go;
But in her atmosphere alone,
The tedious hours meanwhile you may employ,
In blissful dreams of future joy.

FAUST

Can we go now?

MEPHISTOPHELES

'Tis yet too soon.

FAUST

Some present for my love procure! (*Exit.*)

MEPHISTOPHELES

Presents so soon! 'tis well! success is sure!
Full many a goodly place I know,
And treasures buried long ago;
I must a bit o'erlook them now. (*Exit.*)

EVENING. A SMALL AND NEAT ROOM

MARGARET
(braiding and binding up her hair)
I would give something now to know,
Who yonder gentleman could be!
He had a gallant air, I trow,
And doubtless was of high degree:
That written on his brow was seen—
Nor else would he so bold have been. (*Exit.*)

MEPHISTOPHELES

Come in! tread softly! be discreet!

FAUST (*after a pause*)
Begone and leave me, I entreat!

MEPHISTOPHELES (*looking round*)
Not every maiden is so neat. (*Exit.*)

FAUST (*gazing round*)

Welcome sweet twilight, calm and blest,
That in this hallow'd precinct reigns!
Fond yearning love, inspire my breast,
Feeding on hope's sweet dew thy blissful pains!
What stillness here environs me!
Content and order brood around.
What fulness in this poverty!
In this small cell what bliss profound!
    (*He throws himself on the leather arm-chair beside
                                        the bed*)
Receive me thou, who hast in thine embrace,
Welcom'd in joy and grief the ages flown!
How oft the children of a by-gone race
Have cluster'd round this patriarchal throne!
Haply she, also, whom I hold so dear,
For Christmas gift, with grateful joy possess'd,
Hath with the full round cheek of childhood, here,
Her grandsire's wither'd hand devoutly press'd.
Maiden! I feel thy spirit haunt the place,
Breathing of order and abounding grace.
As with a mother's voice it prompteth thee,
The pure white cover o'er the board to spread,
To strew the crisping sand beneath thy tread.
Dear hand! so godlike in its ministry!
The hut becomes a paradise through thee!
And here—   (*He raises the bed-curtain.*)
How thrills my pulse with strange delight!
Here could I linger hours untold;
Thou, Nature, didst in vision bright,
The embryo angel here unfold.
Here lay the child, her bosom warm
With life; while steeped in slumber's dew,
To perfect grace, her godlike form,
With pure and hallow'd weavings grew!

And thou! ah here what seekest thou?
How quails mine inmost being now!

What wouldst thou here? what makes thy heart so
    sore?
Unhappy Faust! I know thee now no more.

Do I a magic atmosphere inhale?
Erewhile, my passion would not brook delay!
Now in a pure love-dream I melt away.
Are we the sport of every passing gale?

Should she return and enter now,
How wouldst thou rue thy guilty flame!
Proud vaunter—thou wouldst hide thy brow,—
And at her feet sink down with shame.

MEPHISTOPHELES

Quick! quick! below I see her there.

FAUST

Away! I will return no more!

MEPHISTOPHELES

Here is a casket, with a store
Of jewels, which I got elsewhere.
Just lay it in the press; make haste!
I swear to you, 'twill turn her brain;
Therein some trifles I have placed,
Wherewith another to obtain.
But child is child, and play is play.

FAUST

I know not—shall I?

MEPHISTOPHELES

                Do you ask?
Perchance you would retain the treasure?
If such your wish, why then, I say,
Henceforth absolve me from my task.

Nor longer waste your hours of leisure.
I trust you're not by avarice led!
I rub my hands, I scratch my head,—
(*He places the casket in the press and closes the
lock.*)

Now quick! Away!
That soon the sweet young creature may
The wish and purpose of your heart obey;
Yet stand you there
As would you to the lecture-room repair,
As if before you stood,
Arrayed in flesh and blood,
Physics and metaphysics weird and grey!—
Away! (*Exeunt.*)

MARGARET (*with a lamp*)
Here 'tis so close, so sultry now,
(*She opens the window.*)
Yet out of doors 'tis not so warm.
I feel so strange, I know not how—
I wish my mother would come home.
Through me there runs a shuddering—
I'm but a foolish timid thing!
(*While undressing herself she begins to sing.*)
There was a king in Thule,
True even to the grave;
To whom his dying mistress
A golden beaker gave.

At every feast he drained it,
Naught was to him so dear,
And often as he drained it,
Gush'd from his eyes the tear.

When death came, unrepining
His cities o'er he told;
All to his heir resigning,
Except his cup of gold.

With many a knightly vassal
At a royal feast sat he,
In yon proud hall ancestral,
In his castle o'er the sea.

Up stood the jovial monarch,
And quaff'd his last life's glow,
Then hurled the hallow'd goblet
Into the flood below.

He saw it splashing, drinking,
And plunging in the sea;
His eyes meanwhile were sinking,
And never again drank he.

(She opens the press to put away her clothes,
and perceives the casket.)

How comes this lovely casket here? The press
I locked, of that I'm confident.
'Tis very wonderful! What's in it I can't guess;
Perhaps 'twas brought by some one in distress,
And left in pledge for loan my mother lent.
Here by a ribbon hangs a little key!
I have a mind to open it and see!
Heavens! only look! what have we here!
In all my days ne'er saw I such a sight!
Jewels! which any noble dame might wear,
For some high pageant richly dight!
This chain—how would it look on me!
These splendid gems, whose may they be?

(She puts them on and steps before the glass.)

Were but the ear-rings only mine!
Thus one has quite another air.
What boots it to be young and fair?
It doubtless may be very fine;
But then, alas, none cares for you,
And praise sounds half like pity too.
Gold all doth lure,
Gold doth secure
All things. Alas, we poor!

PROMENADE

FAUST *walking thoughtfully up and down.* To him MEPHIS-
TOPHELES

MEPHISTOPHELES

By all rejected love! By hellish fire I curse,
Would I knew aught to make my imprecation worse!

FAUST

What aileth thee? what chafes thee now so sore?
A face like that I never saw before!

MEPHISTOPHELES

I'd yield me to the devil instantly,
Did it not happen that myself am he!

FAUST

There must be some disorder in thy wit!
To rave thus like a madman, is it fit?

MEPHISTOPHELES

Think! only think! The gems for Gretchen brought,
Them hath a priest now made his own!—
A glimpse of them the mother caught,
And 'gan with secret fear to groan.
The woman's scent is keen enough;
Doth ever in the prayer-book snuff;
Smells every article to ascertain
Whether the thing is holy or profane,
And scented in the jewels rare,
That there was not much blessing there.
"My child," she cries, "ill-gotten good
Ensnares the soul, consumes the blood;
With them we'll deck our Lady's shrine,
She'll cheer our souls with bread divine!"
At this poor Gretchen 'gan to pout;
'Tis a gift-horse, at least, she thought,

And sure, he godless cannot be,
Who brought them here so cleverly.
Straight for a priest the mother sent,
Who, when he understood the jest,
With what he saw was well content.
" This shows a pious mind! " Quoth he:
" Self-conquest is true victory.
The Church hath a good stomach, she, with zest,
Whole countries hath swallow'd down,
And never yet a surfeit known.
The Church alone, be it confessed,
Daughters, can ill-got wealth digest."

FAUST

It is a general custom, too.
Practised alike by king and jew.

MEPHISTOPHELES

With that, clasp, chain, and ring, he swept
As they were mushrooms; and the casket,
Without one word of thanks, he kept,
As if of nuts it were a basket.
Promised reward in heaven, then forth he hied—
And greatly they were edified.

FAUST

And Gretchen!

MEPHISTOPHELES

In unquiet mood
Knows neither what she would or should;
The trinkets night and day thinks o'er,
On him who brought them, dwells still more.

FAUST

The darling's sorrow grieves me, bring
Another set without delay!
The first, methinks, was no great thing.

MEPHISTOPHELES

All's to my gentleman child's play!

FAUST

Plan all things to achieve my end!
Engage the attention of her friend!
No milk-and-water devil be,
And bring fresh jewels instantly!

MEPHISTOPHELES

Ay, sir! Most gladly I'll obey.

(FAUST *exit.*)

MEPHISTOPHELES

Your doting love-sick fool, with ease,
Merely his lady-love to please,
Sun, moon, and stars in sport would puff away. (*Exit.*)

THE NEIGHBOUR'S HOUSE

MARTHA (*alone*)

God pardon my dear husband, he
Doth not in truth act well by me!
Forth in the world abroad to roam,
And leave me on the straw at home.
And yet his will I ne'er did thwart,
God knows, I lov'd him from my heart.

(*She weeps.*)

Perchance he's dead!—oh wretched state!—
Had I but a certificate!

(MARGARET *comes*)

MARGARET

Dame Martha!

MARTHA

Gretchen?

Margaret

Only think!
My knees beneath me well-nigh sink!
Within my press I've found to-day,
Another case, of ebony.
And things—magnificent they are,
More costly than the first, by far.

Martha

You must not name it to your mother!
It would to shrift, just like the other.

Margaret

Nay look at them! now only see!

Martha (*dresses her up*)

Thou happy creature!

Margaret

Woe is me!
Them in the street I cannot wear,
Or in the church, or any where.

Martha

Come often over here to me,
The gems put on quite privately;
And then before the mirror walk an hour or so,
Thus we shall have our pleasure too.
Then suitable occasions we must seize,
As at a feast, to show them by degrees:
A chain at first, pearl ear-drops then,—your mother
Won't see them, or we'll coin some tale or other.

Margaret

But, who, I wonder, could the caskets bring?
I fear there's something wrong about the thing!

(*a knock.*)

Good heavens! can that my mother be?

MARTHA (*peering through the blind*)
'Tis a strange gentleman, I see.
Come in!
(MEPHISTOPHELES *enters*)

MEPHISTOPHELES
I've ventur'd to intrude to-day.
Ladies, excuse the liberty, I pray.
(*He steps back respectfully before* MARGARET.)
After dame Martha Schwerdtlein I inquire!

MARTHA
'Tis I. Pray what have you to say to me?

MEPHISTOPHELES (*aside to her*)
I know you now,—and therefore will retire;
At present you've distinguished company.
Pardon the freedom, Madam, with your leave,
I will make free to call again at eve.

MARTHA (*aloud*)
Why, child, of all strange notions, he
For some grand lady taketh thee!

MARGARET
I am, in truth, of humble blood—
The gentleman is far too good—
Nor gems nor trinkets are my own.

MEPHISTOPHELES
Oh 'tis not the mere ornaments alone;
Her glance and mien far more betray.
Rejoiced I am that I may stay.

MARTHA
Your business, Sir? I long to know—

MEPHISTOPHELES

Would I could happier tidings show!
I trust mine errand you'll not let me rue;
Your husband's dead, and greeteth you.

MARTHA

Is dead? True heart! Oh misery!
My husband dead! Oh, I shall die!

MARGARET

Alas! good Martha! don't despair!

MEPHISTOPHELES

Now listen to the sad affair!

MARGARET

I for this cause should fear to love.
The loss my certain death would prove.

MEPHISTOPHELES

Joy still must sorrow, sorrow joy attend.

MARTHA

Proceed, and tell the story of his end!

MEPHISTOPHELES

At Padua, in St. Anthony's,
In holy ground his body lies;
Quiet and cool his place of rest,
With pious ceremonials blest.

MARTHA

And had you naught besides to bring?

MEPHISTOPHELES

Oh yes! one grave and solemn prayer;
Let them for him three hundred masses sing!
But in my pockets, I have nothing there.

MARTHA

No trinket! no love-token did he send!
What every journeyman safe in his pouch will hoard
There for remembrance fondly stored,
And rather hungers, rather begs than spend!

MEPHISTOPHELES

Madam, in truth, it grieves me sore,
But he his gold not lavishly hath spent.
His failings too he deeply did repent,
Ay! and his evil plight bewail'd still more.

MARGARET

Alas! That men should thus be doomed to woe!
I for his soul will many a requiem pray.

MEPHISTOPHELES

A husband you deserve this very day;
A child so worthy to be loved.

MARGARET
                              Ah no,
That time hath not yet come for me.

MEPHISTOPHELES

If not a spouse, a gallant let it be.
Among heaven's choicest gifts, I place,
So sweet a darling to embrace.

MARGARET

Our land doth no such usage know.

MEPHISTOPHELES

Usage or not, it happens so.

MARTHA

Go on, I pray!

MEPHISTOPHELES

　　　　I stood by his bedside.
Something less foul it was than dung;
'Twas straw half rotten; yet, he as a Christian died.
And sorely hath remorse his conscience wrung.
" Wretch that I was," quoth he, with parting breath,
" So to forsake my business and my wife!
Ah! the remembrance is my death,
Could I but have her pardon in this life!"—

MARTHA (*weeping*)

Dear soul! I've long forgiven him, indeed!

MEPHISTOPHELES

" Though she, God knows, was more to blame than I."

MARTHA

He lied! What, on the brink of death to lie!

MEPHISTOPHELES

If I am skill'd the countenance to read,
He doubtless fabled as he parted hence.—
"No time had I to gape, or take my ease," he said,
"First to get children, and then get them bread;
And bread, too, in the very widest sense;
Nor could I eat in peace even my proper share."

MARTHA

What, all my truth, my love forgotten quite?
My weary drudgery by day and night!

MEPHISTOPHELES

Not so! He thought of you with tender care.
Quoth he: "Heaven knows how fervently I prayed,
For wife and children when from Malta bound;—
The prayer hath heaven with favour crowned;
We took a Turkish vessel which conveyed
Rich store of treasure for the Sultan's court;
It's own reward our gallant action brought;
The captur'd prize was shared among the crew
And of the treasure I received my due."

MARTHA

How? Where? The treasure hath he buried, pray?

MEPHISTOPHELES

Where the four winds have blown it, who can say?
In Naples as he stroll'd, a stranger there,—
A comely maid took pity on my friend;
And gave such tokens of her love and care,
That he retained them to his blessed end.

MARTHA

Scoundrel! to rob his children of their bread!
And all this misery, this bitter need,
Could not his course of recklessness impede!

MEPHISTOPHELES

Well, he hath paid the forfeit, and is dead.
Now were I in your place, my counsel hear;
My weeds I'd wear for one chaste year,
And for another lover meanwhile would look out.

MARTHA

Alas, I might search far and near,
Not quickly should I find another like my first!
There could not be a fonder fool than mine,
Only he loved too well abroad to roam;

Loved foreign women too, and foreign wine,
And loved besides the dice accurs'd.

MEPHISTOPHELES

'All had gone swimmingly, no doubt,
Had he but given you at home,
On his side, just as wide a range.
Upon such terms, to you I swear,
Myself with you would gladly rings exchange!

MARTHA

The gentleman is surely pleas'd to jest!

MEPHISTOPHELES (*aside*)

Now to be off in time, were best!
She'd make the very devil marry her.

(*To* MARGARET.)

How fares it with your heart?

MARGARET

How mean you, Sir?

MEPHISTOPHELES (*aside*)

The sweet young innocent!

(*aloud*)

Ladies, farewell!

MARGARET

Farewell!

MARTHA

But ere you leave us, quickly tell!
I from a witness fain had heard,
Where, how, and when my husband died and was
    interr'd.
To forms I've always been attached indeed,
His death I fain would in the journals read.

MEPHISTOPHELES

Ay, madam, what two witnesses declare
Is held as valid everywhere;
A gallant friend I have, not far from here,
Who will for you before the judge appear.
I'll bring him straight.

MARTHA

I pray you do!

MEPHISTOPHELES

And this young lady, we shall find her too?
A noble youth, far travelled, he
Shows to the sex all courtesy.

MARGARET

I in his presence needs must blush for shame.

MEPHISTOPHELES

Not in the presence of a crowned king!

MARTHA

The garden, then, behind my house, we'll name,
There we'll await you both this evening.

A STREET

FAUST. MEPHISTOPHELES

FAUST

How is it now? How speeds it? Is't in train?

MEPHISTOPHELES

Bravo! I find you all aflame!
Gretchen full soon your own you'll name.
This eve, at neighbour Martha's, her you'll meet again;

The woman seems expressly made
To drive the pimp and gipsy's trade.

FAUST

Good!

MEPHISTOPHELES

But from us she something would request.

FAUST

A favour claims return as this world goes.

MEPHISTOPHELES

We have on oath but duly to attest,
That her dead husband's limbs, outstretch'd, repose
In holy ground at Padua.

FAUST

Sage indeed!
So I suppose we straight must journey there!

MEPHISTOPHELES

Sancta simplicitas! For that no need!
Without much knowledge we have but to swear.

FAUST

If you have nothing better to suggest,
Against your plan I must at once protest.

MEPHISTOPHELES

Oh, holy man! methinks I have you there!
In all your life say, have you ne'er
False witness borne, until this hour?
Have you of God, the world, and all it doth contain,
Of man, and that which worketh in his heart and brain,
Not definitions given, in words of weight and power,
With front unblushing, and a dauntless breast?
Yet, if into the depth of things you go,

Touching these matters, it must be confess'd,
As much as of Herr Schwerdtlein's death you know!

FAUST

Thou art and dost remain liar and sophist too.

MEPHISTOPHELES

Ay, if one did not take a somewhat deeper view!
To-morrow, in all honour, thou
Poor Gretchen wilt befool, and vow
Thy soul's deep love, in lover's fashion.

FAUST

And from my heart.

MEPHISTOPHELES

All good and fair!
Then deathless constancy thou'lt swear;
Speak of one all o'ermastering passion,—
Will that too issue from the heart?

FAUST

Forbear!
When passion sways me, and I seek to frame
Fit utterance for feeling, deep, intense,
And for my frenzy finding no fit name,
Sweep round the ample world with every sense,
Grasp at the loftiest words to speak my flame,
And call the glow, wherewith I burn,
Quenchless, eternal, yea, eterne--
Is that of sophistry a devilish play?

MEPHISTOPHELES

Yet am I right!

FAUST

Mark this, my friend,
And spare my lungs; who would the right maintain,
And hath a tongue wherewith his point to gain,

Will gain it in the end.
But come, of gossip I am weary quite;
Because I've no resource, thou'rt in the right.

GARDEN

MARGARET *on* FAUST'S *arm*. MARTHA *with* MEPHIS-
TOPHELES *walking up and down*

MARGARET

I feel it, you but spare my ignorance,
The gentleman to shame me stoops thus low.
A traveller from complaisance,
Still makes the best of things; I know
Too well, my humble prattle never can
Have power to entertain so wise a man.

FAUST

One glance, one word from thee doth charm me more,
Than the world's wisdom or the sage's lore.

(*He kisses her hand.*)

MARGARET

Nay! trouble not yourself! A hand so coarse,
So rude as mine, how can you kiss!
What constant work at home must I not do perforce!
My mother too exacting is.

(*They pass on.*)

MARTHA

Thus, sir, unceasing travel is your lot?

MEPHISTOPHELES

Traffic and duty urge us! With what pain
Are we compelled to leave full many a spot,
Where yet we dare not once remain!

MARTHA

In youth's wild years, with vigour crown'd,
'Tis not amiss thus through the world to sweep;

But ah, the evil days come round!
And to a lonely grave as bachelor to creep,
A pleasant thing has no one found.

MEPHISTOPHELES

The prospect fills me with dismay.

MARTHA ·

Therefore in time, dear sir, reflect, I pray.

(*They pass on.*)

MARGARET

Ay, out of sight is out of mind!
Politeness easy is to you;
Friends everywhere, and not a few,
Wiser than I am, you will find.

FAUST

O dearest, trust me, what doth pass for sense
Full oft is self-conceit and blindness!

MARGARET

How?

FAUST

Simplicity and holy innocence,—
When will ye learn your hallow'ed worth to know!
Ah, when will meekness and humility,
Kind and all-bounteous nature's loftiest dower—

MARGARET

Only one little moment think of me!
To think of you I shall have many an hour.

FAUST

You are perhaps much alone?

MARGARET

Yes, small our household is, I own,
Yet must I see to it. No maid we keep,

And I must cook, sew, knit, and sweep,
Still early on my feet and late;
My mother is in all things, great and small,
So accurate!
Not that for thrift there is such pressing need;
Than others we might make more show indeed;
My father left behind a small estate,
A house and garden near the city-wall.
But fairly quiet now my days, I own;
As soldier is my brother gone;
My little sister's dead; the babe to rear
Occasion'd me some care and fond annoy;
But I would go through all again with joy,
The darling was to me so dear.

FAUST

An angel, sweet, if it resembled thee!

MARGARET

I reared it up, and it grew fond of me.
After my father's death it saw the day;
We gave my mother up for lost, she lay
In such a wretched plight, and then at length
So very slowly she regain'd her strength.
Weak as she was, 'twas vain for her to try
Herself to suckle the poor babe, so I
Reared it on milk and water all alone;
And thus the child became as 'twere my own;
Within my arms it stretched itself and grew,
And smiling, nestled in my bosom too.

FAUST

Doubtless the purest happiness was thine.

MARGARET

But many weary hours, in sooth, were also mine.
At night its little cradle stood
Close to my bed; so was I wide awake
If it but stirred;

One while I was obliged to give it food,
Or to my arms the darling take;
From bed full oft must rise, whene'er its cry I heard,
And, dancing it, must pace the chamber to and fro;
Stand at the wash-tub early; forthwith go
To market, and then mind the cooking too—
To-morrow like to-day, the whole year through.
Ah, sir, thus living, it must be confess'd
One's spirits are not always of the best;
Yet it a relish gives to food and rest.   (*They pass on.*)

MARTHA

Poor women! we are badly off, I own;
A bachelor's conversion's hard, indeed!

MEPHISTOPHELES

Madam, with one like you it rests alone,
To tutor me a better course to lead.

MARTHA

Speak frankly, sir, none is there you have met?
Has your heart ne'er attach'd itself as yet?

MEPHISTOPHELES

One's own fire-side and a good wife are gold
And pearls of price, so says the proverb old.

MARTHA

I mean, has passion never stirred your breast?

MEPHISTOPHELES

I've everywhere been well received, I own.

MARTHA

Yet hath your heart no earnest preference known?

MEPHISTOPHELES

With ladies one should ne'er presume to jest.

Martha

Ah! you mistake!

Mephistopheles

I'm sorry I'm so blind!
But this I know—that you are very kind.

(*They pass on.*)

Faust

Me, little angel, didst thou recognise,
When in the garden first I came?

Margaret

Did you not see it? I cast down my eyes.

Faust

Thou dost forgive my boldness, dost not blame
The liberty I took that day,
When thou from church didst lately wend thy way?

Margaret

I was confused. So had it never been;
No one of me could any evil say.
Alas, thought I, he doubtless in thy mien,
Something unmaidenly or bold hath seen?
It seemed as if it struck him suddenly,
Here's just a girl with whom one may make free!
Yet I must own that then I scarcely knew
What in your favour here began at once to plead;
Yet I was angry with myself indeed,
That I more angry could not feel with you.

Faust

Sweet love!

MARGARET

Just wait awhile!
(*She gathers a star-flower and plucks off the leaves
one after another.*)

FAUST

A nosegay may that be?

MARGARET

No! It is but a game.

FAUST
How?

MARGARET

Go, you'll laugh at me!
(*She plucks off the leaves and murmurs to herself.*)

FAUST

What murmurest thou?

MARGARET (*half aloud*)
He loves me—loves me not.

FAUST

Sweet angel, with thy face of heavenly bliss!

MARGARET (*continues*)
He loves me—not—he loves me—not—
(*Plucking off the last leaf with fond joy.*)
. He loves me!
FAUST
Yes!

And this flower-language, darling, let it be,
A heavenly oracle! He loveth thee!
Know'st thou the meaning of, He loveth thee?
(*He seizes both her hands.*)

MARGARET

I tremble so!

FAUST

Nay! Do not tremble, love!
Let this hand-pressure, let this glance reveal
Feelings, all power of speech above;
To give oneself up wholly and to feel
A joy that must eternal prove!
Eternal!—Yes, its end would be despair.
No end!—It cannot end!

> (MARGARET *presses his hand, extricates herself,*
> *and runs away. He stands a moment in*
> *thought, and then follows her.*)

MARTHA (*approaching*)

Night's closing.

MEPHISTOPHELES

Yes, we'll presently away.

MARTHA

I would entreat you longer yet to stay;
But 'tis a wicked place, just here about;
It is as if the folk had nothing else to do,
Nothing to think of too,
But gaping watch their neighbours, who goes in and out;
And scandal's busy still, do whatsoe'er one may.
And our young couple?

MEPHISTOPHELES

They have flown up there.
The wanton butterflies!

MARTHA

He seems to take to her.

Mephistopheles

And she to him. 'Tis of the world the way!

A SUMMER-HOUSE

(Margaret *runs in, hides behind the door, holds the tip of her finger to her lip, and peeps through the crevice.*)

Margaret

He comes!

Faust

Ah, little rogue, so thou
Think'st to provoke me! I have caught thee now!
(*He kisses her.*)

Margaret
(*embracing him, and returning the kiss*)
Dearest of men! I love thee from my heart!
(Mephistopheles *knocks.*)

Faust (*stamping*)
Who's there?

Mephistopheles
A friend!

Faust
A brute!

Mephistopheles
'Tis time to part.

MARTHA (*comes*)

Ay, it is late, good sir.

FAUST

       Mayn't I attend you, then?

MARGARET

Oh no—my mother would—adieu, adieu!

FAUST

And must I really then take leave of you?
Farewell!

MARTHA

    Good-bye!

MARGARET

       Ere long to meet again!
   (*Exeunt* FAUST *and* MEPHISTOPHELES.)

MARGARET

Good heavens! how all things far and near
Must fill his mind,—a man like this!
Abash'd before him I appear,
And say to all things only, yes.
Poor simple child, I cannot see,
What 'tis that he can find in me.   (*Exit.*)

FOREST AND CAVERN

FAUST (*alone*)

Spirit sublime! Thou gav'st me, gav'st me all
For which I prayed! Not vainly hast thou turn'd
To me thy countenance in flaming fire:
Gavest me glorious nature for my realm,

And also power to feel her and enjoy;
Not merely with a cold and wondering glance,
Thou dost permit me in her depths profound,
As in the bosom of a friend to gaze.
Before me thou dost lead her living tribes,
And dost in silent grove, in air and stream
Teach me to know my kindred. And when roars
The howling storm-blast through the groaning wood,
Wrenching the giant pine, which in its fall
Crashing sweeps down its neighbour trunks and boughs,
While hollow thunder from the hill resounds;
Then thou dost lead me to some shelter'd cave,
Dost there reveal me to myself, and show
Of my own bosom the mysterious depths.
And when with soothing beam, the moon's pale orb
Full in my view climbs up the pathless sky,
From crag and dewy grove, the silvery forms
Of by-gone ages hover, and assuage
The joy austere of contemplative thought.

Oh, that naught perfect is assign'd to man,
I feel, alas! With this exalted joy,
Which lifts me near and nearer to the gods,
Thou gav'st me this companion, unto whom
I needs must cling, though cold and insolent,
He still degrades me to myself, and turns
Thy glorious gifts to nothing, with a breath.
He in my bosom with malicious zeal
For that fair image fans a raging fire;
From craving to enjoyment thus I reel,
And in enjoyment languish for desire.
                    (MEPHISTOPHELES *enters*.)

MEPHISTOPHELES

Of this lone life have you not had your fill?
How for so long can it have charms for you?
'Tis well enough to try it if you will;
But then away again to something new!

FAUST

Would you could better occupy your leisure,
Than in disturbing thus my hours of joy.

MEPHISTOPHELES

Well! Well! I'll leave you to yourself with pleasure,
A serious tone you hardly dare employ.
To part from one so crazy, harsh, and cross,
Were not in truth a grievous loss.
The live-long day, for you I toil and fret;
Ne'er from his worship's face a hint I get,
What pleases him, or what to let alone.

FAUST

Ay truly! that is just the proper tone!
He wearies me, and would with thanks be paid!

MEPHISTOPHELES

Poor Son of Earth, without my aid,
How would thy weary days have flown?
Thee of thy foolish whims I've cured,
Thy vain imaginations banished,
And but for me, be well assured,
Thou from this sphere must soon have vanished.
In rocky hollows and in caverns drear,
Why like an owl sit moping here?
Wherefore from dripping stones and moss with ooze
    embued,
Dost suck, like any toad, thy food?
A rare, sweet pastime. Verily!
The doctor cleaveth still to thee.

FAUST

Dost comprehend what bliss without alloy
From this wild wand'ring in the desert springs?—
Couldst thou but guess the new life-power it brings,
Thou wouldst be fiend enough to envy me my joy.

MEPHISTOPHELES

What super-earthly ecstasy! at night,
To lie in darkness on the dewy height,
Embracing heaven and earth in rapture high,
The soul dilating to a deity;
With prescient yearnings pierce the core of earth,
Feel in your labouring breast the six-days' birth,
Enjoy, in proud delight what no one knows,
While your love-rapture o'er creation flows,—
The earthly lost in beatific vision,
And then the lofty intuition—

(With a gesture.)

I need not tell you how—to close!

FAUST

Fie on you!

MEPHISTOPHELES

This displeases you? "For shame!"
You are forsooth entitled to exclaim;
We to chaste ears it seems must not pronounce
What, nathless, the chaste heart cannot renounce.
Well, to be brief, the joy as fit occasions rise,
I grudge you not, of specious lies.
But long this mood thou'lt not retain.
Already thou'rt again outworn,
And should this last, thou wilt be torn
By frenzy or remorse and pain.
Enough of this! Thy true love dwells apart,
And all to her seems flat and tame;
Alone thine image fills her heart,
She loves thee with an all-devouring flame.
First came thy passion with o'erpowering rush,
Like mountain torrent, swollen by the melted snow;
Full in her heart didst pour the sudden gush,
Now has thy brooklet ceased to flow.
Instead of sitting throned midst forests wild,
It would become so great a lord

To comfort the enamour'd child,
And the young monkey for her love reward.
To her the hours seem miserably long;
She from the window sees the clouds float by
As o'er the lofty city-walls they fly,
" If I a birdie were ! " so runs her song,
Half through the night and all day long.
Cheerful sometimes, more oft at heart full sore;
Fairly outwept seem now her tears,
Anon she tranquil is, or so appears,
And love-sick evermore.

FAUST

Snake ! Serpent vile !

MEPHISTOPHELES (*aside*)

Good ! If I catch thee with my guile !

FAUST

Vile reprobate ! go get thee hence ;
Forbear the lovely girl to name !
Nor in my half-distracted sense,
Kindle anew the smouldering flame !

MEPHISTOPHELES

What wouldest thou ! She thinks you've taken flight ;
It seems, she's partly in the right.

FAUST

I'm near her still—and should I distant rove,
Her I can ne'er forget, ne'er lose her love ;
And all things touch'd by those sweet lips of hers,
Even the very Host, my envy stirs.

MEPHISTOPHELES

'Tis well ! I oft have envied you indeed,
The twin-pair that among the roses feed.

FAUST

Pander, avaunt!

MEPHISTOPHELES

Go to! I laugh, the while you rail,
The power which fashion'd youth and maid,
Well understood the noble trade;
So neither shall occasion fail.
But hence!—A mighty grief I trow!
Unto thy lov'd one's chamber thou
And not to death shouldst go.

FAUST

What is to me heaven's joy within her arms?
What though my life her bosom warms!—
Do I not ever feel her woe?
The outcast am I not, unhoused, unblest,
Inhuman monster, without aim or rest,
Who, like the greedy surge, from rock to rock,
Sweeps down the dread abyss with desperate shock?
While she, within her lowly cot, which graced
The Alpine slope, beside the waters wild,
Her homely cares in that small world embraced,
Secluded lived, a simple, artless child.
Was't not enough, in thy delirious whirl
To blast the stedfast rocks;
Her, and her peace as well,
Must I, God-hated one, to ruin hurl!
Dost claim this holocaust, remorseless Hell!
Fiend, help me to cut short the hours of dread!
Let what must happen, happen speedily!
Her direful doom fall crushing on my head,
And into ruin let her plunge with me!

MEPHISTOPHELES

Why how again it seethes and glows!
Away, thou fool! Her torment ease!
When such a head no issue sees,

It pictures straight the final close.
Long life to him who boldly dares!
A devil's pluck thou'rt wont to show;
As for a devil who despairs,
Nothing I find so mawkish here below.

MARGARET'S ROOM

MARGARET (*alone at her spinning wheel*)
 My peace is gone,
  My heart is sore,
 I find it never,
  And nevermore!

 Where him I have not,
  Is the grave; and all
 The world to me
  Is turned to gall

 My wilder'd brain
  Is overwrought;
 My feeble senses
  Are distraught.

 My peace is gone,
  My heart is sore,
 I find it never,
  And nevermore!

 For him from the window
  I gaze, at home;
 For him and him only
  Abroad I roam.

 His lofty step,
  His bearing high,
 The smile of his lip,
  The power of his eye,

His witching words,
Their tones of bliss,
His hand's fond pressure,
And ah—his kiss!

My peace is gone,
My heart is sore,
I find it never,
And nevermore.

My bosom aches
To feel him near;
Ah, could I clasp
And fold him here!

Kiss him and kiss him
Again would I,
And on his kisses
I fain would die.

MARTHA'S GARDEN

Margaret *and* Faust

Margaret

Promise me, Henry!

Faust
What I can!

Margaret

How thy religion fares, I fain would hear.
Thou art a good kind-hearted man,
Only that way not well-disposed, I fear.

Faust

Forbear, my child! Thou feelest thee I love;
My heart, my blood I'd give, my love to prove,
And none would of their faith or church bereave.

MARGARET

That's not enough, we must ourselves believe!

FAUST

Must we?

MARGARET

Ah, could I but thy soul inspire!
Thou honourest not the sacraments, alas!

FAUST

I honour them.

MARGARET

But yet without desire;
'Tis long since thou hast been either to shrift or mass.
Dost thou believe in God?

FAUST

My darling, who dares say,
Yes, I in God believe?
Question or priest or sage, and they
Seem, in the answer you receive,
To mock the questioner.

MARGARET

Then thou dost not believe?

FAUST

Sweet one! my meaning do not misconceive!
Him who dare name?
And who proclaim,
Him I believe?
Who that can feel,
His heart can steel,
To say: I believe him not?
The All-embracer,
All-sustainer,

Holds and sustains he not
Thee, me, himself?
Lifts not the Heaven its dome above?
Doth not the firm-set earth beneath us lie?
And beaming tenderly with looks of love,
Climb not the everlasting stars on high?
Do we not gaze into each other's eyes?
Nature's impenetrable agencies,
Are they not thronging on thy heart and brain,
Viewless, or visible to mortal ken,
Around thee weaving their mysterious chain?
Fill thence thy heart, how large soe'er it be;
And in the feeling when thou utterly art blest,
Then call it, what thou wilt,—
Call it Bliss! Heart! Love! God!
I have no name for it!
'Tis feeling all;
Name is but sound and smoke
Shrouding the glow of heaven.

MARGARET

All this is doubtless good and fair;
Almost the same the parson says,
Only in slightly different phrase.

FAUST

Beneath Heaven's sunshine, everywhere,
This is the utterance of the human heart;
Each in his language doth the like impart;
Then why not I in mine?

MARGARET
                    What thus I hear
Sounds plausible, yet I'm not reconciled;
There's something wrong about it; much I fear
That thou art not a Christian.

FAUST
                    My sweet child!

Margaret

Alas! it long hath sorely troubled me,
To see thee in such odious company.

Faust

How so?

Margaret

　　　　The man who comes with thee, I hate,
Yea, in my spirit's inmost depths abhor;
As his loath'd visage, in my life before,
Naught to my heart e'er gave a pang so great.

Faust

Him fear not, my sweet love!

Margaret

　　　　　　His presence chills my blood.
Towards all beside I have a kindly mood;
Yet, though I yearn to gaze on thee, I feel
At sight of him strange horror o'er me steal;
That he's a villain my conviction's strong.
May Heaven forgive me, if I do him wrong!

Faust

Yet such strange fellows in the world must be!

Margaret

I would not live with such an one as he.
If for a moment he but enter here,
He looks around him with a mocking sneer,
And malice ill-conceal'd;
That he with naught on earth can sympathize is clear:
Upon his brow 'tis legibly revealed,
That to his heart no living soul is dear.
So blest I feel, within thine arms,
So warm and happy,—free from all alarms;
And still my heart doth close when he comes near.

FAUST

Foreboding angel! check thy fear!

MARGARET

It so o'ermasters me, that when,
Or wheresoe'er, his step I hear,
I almost think, no more I love thee then.
Besides, when he is near, I ne'er could pray.
This eats into my heart; with thee
The same, my Henry, it must be.

FAUST

This is antipathy!

MARGARET

I must away.

FAUST

For one brief hour then may I never rest,
And heart to heart, and soul to soul be pressed?

MARGARET

Ah, if I slept alone! To-night
The bolt I fain would leave undrawn for thee;
But then my mother's sleep is light,
Were we surprised by her, ah me!
Upon the spot I should be dead.

FAUST

Dear angel! there's no cause for dread.
Here is a little phial,—if she take
Mixed in her drink three drops, 'twill steep
Her nature in a deep and soothing sleep.

MARGARET

What do I not for thy dear sake!
To her it will not harmful prove?

FAUST

Should I advise it else, sweet love?

MARGARET

I know not, dearest, when thy face I see,
What doth my spirit to thy will constrain;
Already I have done so much for thee,
That scarcely more to do doth now remain.

(Exit.)

MEPHISTOPHELES *(enters)*

MEPHISTOPHELES

The monkey! Is she gone?

FAUST

Again hast played the spy?

MEPHISTOPHELES

Of all that pass'd I'm well apprized,
I heard the doctor catechised,
And trust he'll profit much thereby!
Fain would the girls inquire indeed
Touching their lover's faith and creed,
And whether pious in the good old way;
They think, if pliant there, us too he will obey.

FAUST

Thou monster, does not see that this
Pure soul, possessed by ardent love,
Full of the living faith,
To her of bliss
The only pledge, must holy anguish prove,
Holding the man she loves, fore-doomed to endless
death!

MEPHISTOPHELES

Most sensual, supersensualist? The while
A damsel leads thee by the nose!

FAUST

Of filth and fire abortion vile!

MEPHISTOPHELES

In physiognomy strange skill she shows;
She in my presence feels she knows not how;
My mask it seems a hidden sense reveals;
That I'm a genius she must needs allow,
That I'm the very devil perhaps she feels.
So then to-night—

FAUST

What's that to you?

MEPHISTOPHELES

I've my amusement in it too!

AT THE WELL

MARGARET *and* BESSY, *with pitchers*

BESSY

Of Barbara hast nothing heard?

MARGARET

I rarely go from home,—no, not a word

BESSY

'Tis true: Sybilla told me so to-day!
That comes of being proud, methinks;
She played the fool at last.

MARGARET

How so?

BESSY

They say
That two she feedeth when she eats and drinks.

MARGARET

Alas!

BESSY

She's rightly served, in sooth,
How long she hung upon the youth!
What promenades, what jaunts there were,
To dancing booth and village fair!
The first she everywhere must shine,
He always treating her to pastry and to wine.
Of her good looks she was so vain,
So shameless too, that to retain
His presents, she did not disdain;
Sweet words and kisses came anon—
And then the virgin flower was gone.

MARGARET

Poor thing!

BESSY

Forsooth dost pity her?
At night, when at our wheels we sat,
Abroad our mothers ne'er would let us stir.
Then with her lover she must chat,
Or on the bench or in the dusky walk,
Thinking the hours too brief for their sweet talk;
Her proud head she will have to bow,
And in white sheet do penance now!

MARGARET

But he will surely marry her?

BESSY

Not he!

He won't be such a fool! a gallant lad
Like him, can roam o'er land and sea,
Besides, he's off.

MARGARET

That is not fair!

BESSY

If she should get him, 'twere almost as bad!
Her myrtle wreath the boys would tear;
And then we girls would plague her too,
For we chopp'd straw before her door would strew!

(*Exit.*)

MARGARET (*walking towards home*)

How stoutly once I could inveigh,
If a poor maiden went astray;
Not words enough my tongue could find,
'Gainst others' sin to speak my mind!
Black as it seemed, I blacken'd it still more,
And strove to make it blacker than before.
And did myself securely bless—
Now my own trespass doth appear!
Yet ah!—what urg'd me to transgress,
God knows, it was so sweet. so dear!

ZWINGER

Enclosure between the City-wall and the Gate.
(*In the niche of the wall a devotional image of the Mater dolorosa, with flower-pots before it.*)

MARGARET (*putting fresh flowers in the pots*)

Ah, rich in sorrow, thou,
Stoop thy maternal brow,
And mark with pitying eye my misery!

The sword in thy pierced heart,
Thou dost with bitter smart,
Gaze upwards on thy Son's death agony.
To the dear God on high,
Ascends thy piteous sigh,
Pleading for his and thy sore misery.
Ah, who can know
The torturing woe,
The pangs that rack me to the bone?
How my poor heart, without relief,
Trembles and throbs, its yearning grief
Thou knowest, thou alone!
Ah, wheresoe'er I go,
With woe, with woe, with woe,
My anguish'd breast is aching!
When all alone I creep,
I weep, I weep, I weep,
Alas! my heart is breaking!
The flower-pots at my window
Were wet with tears of mine,
The while I pluck'd these blossoms,
At dawn to deck thy shrine!
When early in my chamber
Shone bright the rising morn,
I sat there on my pallet,
My heart with anguish torn.
Help! from disgrace and death deliver me!
Ah! rich in sorrow, thou,
Stoop thy maternal brow,
And mark with pitying eye my misery!

NIGHT.   STREET BEFORE MARGARET'S DOOR

VALENTINE (*a soldier*, MARGARET's *brother*)
When seated 'mong the jovial crowd,
Where merry comrades boasting loud
Each named with pride his favourite lass,

'And in ner honour drain'd his glass;
Upon my elbows I would lean,
With easy quiet view the scene,
Nor give my tongue the rein until
Each swaggering blade had talked his fill.
Then smiling I my beard would stroke,
The while, with brimming glass, I spoke;
"Each to his taste!—but to my mind,
Where in the country will you find,
A maid, as my dear Gretchen fair,
Who with my sister can compare?"
Cling! Clang! so rang the jovial sound!
Shouts of assent went circling round;
Pride of her sex is she!—cried some;
Then were the noisy boasters dumb.

And now!—I could tear out my hair,
Or dash my brains out in despair!—
Me every scurvy knave may twit,
With stinging jest and taunting sneer!
Like skulking debtor I must sit,
And sweat each casual word to hear!
And though I smash'd them one and all,—
Yet them I could not liars call.

Who comes this way? who's sneaking here?
If I mistake not, two draw near.
If he be one, have at him;—well I wot
Alive he shall not leave this spot!

FAUST. MEPHISTOPHELES

FAUST

How from yon sacristy, athwart the night,
Its beams the ever-burning taper throws,
While ever waning, fades the glimmering light,
As gathering darkness doth around it close!
So night-like gloom doth in my bosom reign.

Mephistopheles

I'm like a tom-cat in a thievish vein,
That up fire-ladders tall and steep,
And round the walls doth slyly creep;
Virtuous withal, I feel, with, I confess,
A touch of thievish joy and wantonness.
Thus through my limbs already burns
The glorious Walpurgis night!
After to-morrow it returns,
Then why one wakes, one knows aright!

Faust

Meanwhile, the treasure I see glimmering there,
Will it ascend into the open air?

Mephistopheles

Ere long thou wilt proceed with pleasure,
To raise the casket with its treasure;
I took a peep, therein are stored,
Of lion-dollars a rich hoard.

Faust

And not a trinket? not a ring?
Wherewith my lovely girl to deck?

Mephistopheles

I saw among them some such thing,
A string of pearls to grace her neck.

Faust

'Tis well! I'm always loath to go,
Without some gift my love to show.

Mephistopheles

Some pleasures gratis to enjoy,
Should surely cause you no annoy.
While bright with stars the heavens appear,
I'll sing a masterpiece of art:

A moral song shall charm her ear,
More surely to beguile her heart.

     (*Sings to the guitar.*)
   Kathrina say,
   Why lingering stay
   At dawn of day
   Before your lover's door?
   Maiden, beware,
   Nor enter there,
   Lest forth you fare,
   A maiden never more.

   Maiden take heed!
   Reck well my rede!
   Is't done, the deed?
   Good night, you poor, poor thing!
   The spoiler's lies,
   His arts despise,
   Nor yield your prize,
   Without the marriage ring!

  VALENTINE (*steps forward*)

Whom are you luring here? I'll give it you!
Accursed rat-catchers, your strains I'll end!
First, to the devil the guitar I'll send!
Then to the devil with the singer too!

   MEPHISTOPHELES

The poor guitar! 'tis done for now.

   VALENTINE

Your skull shall follow next, I trow!

  MEPHISTOPHELES (*to* FAUST)

Doctor, stand fast! your strength collect!
Be prompt, and do as I direct.
Out with your whisk, keep close, I pray,
I'll parry! do you thrust away!

VALENTINE
Then parry that!

MEPHISTOPHELES
Why not?

VALENTINE
That too!

MEPHISTOPHELES
With ease!

VALENTINE
The devil fights for you!
Why how is this? my hand's already lamed!

MEPHISTOPHELES (*to* FAUST)
Thrust home!

VALENTINE (*falls*)
Alas!

MEPHISTOPHELES
There! Now the lubber's tamed!
But quick, away! We must at once take wing;
A cry of murder strikes upon the ear;
With the police I know my course to steer,
But with the blood-ban 'tis another thing.

MARTHA (*at the window*)
Without! without!

MARGARET (*at the window*)
Quick, bring a light!

MARTHA (*as above*)
They rail and scuffle, scream and fight!

PEOPLE

One lieth here already dead!

MARTHA (*coming out*)

Where are the murderers? are they fled?

MARGARET (*coming out*)

Who lieth here?

PEOPLE

Thy mother's son.

MARGARET

Almighty God! I am undone!

VALENTINE

I'm dying—'tis a soon-told tale,
And sooner done the deed.
Why, women, do ye howl and wail?
To my last words give heed! (*All gather round him.*)
My Gretchen, see! still young art thou,
Art not discreet enough, I trow,
Thou dost thy matters ill;
Let this in confidence be said:
Since thou the path of shame dost **tread**,
Tread it with right good will!

MARGARET

My brother! God! what can this mean?

VALENTINE

                       Abstain,

Nor dare God's holy name profane!
What's done, alas, is done and past!
Matters will take their course at last;
By stealth thou dost begin with **one**,
Others will follow him anon;

And when a dozen thee have known,
Thou'lt common be to all the town.
When infamy is newly born,
In secret she is brought to light,
And the mysterious veil of night
O'er head and ears is drawn;
The loathsome birth men fain would slay;
But soon, full grown, she waxes bold,
And though not fairer to behold,
With brazen front insults the day:
The more abhorrent to the sight,
The more she courts the day's pure light.

The time already I discern,
When thee all honest folk will spurn,
And shun thy hated form to meet,
As when a corpse infects the street.
Thy heart will sink in blank despair,
When they shall look thee in the face!
A golden chain no more thou'lt wear!
Nor near the altar take in church thy place!
In fair lace collar simply dight
Thou'lt dance no more with spirits light!
In darksome corners thou wilt bide,
Where beggars vile and cripples hide,
And e'en though God thy crime forgive,
On earth, a thing accursed, thou'lt live!

MARTHA

Your parting soul to God commend!
Your dying breath in slander will you spend?

VALENTINE

Could I but reach thy wither'd frame,
Thou wretched beldame, void of shame!
Full measure I might hope to win
Of pardon then for every sin.

MARGARET

Brother! what agonizing pain!

VALENTINE

I tell thee, from vain tears abstain!
'Twas thy dishonour pierced my heart,
Thy fall the fatal death-stab gave.
Through the death-sleep I now depart
To God, a soldier true and brave.   *(dies.)*

CATHEDRAL

Service, Organ, and Anthem

MARGARET *amongst a number of people*

EVIL-SPIRIT *behind* MARGARET

EVIL-SPIRIT

How different, Gretchen, was it once with thee,
When thou, still full of innocence,
Here to the altar camest,
And from the small and well-conn'd book
Didst lisp thy prayer,
Half childish sport,
Half God in thy young heart!
Gretchen!
What thoughts are thine?
What deed of shame
Lurks in thy sinful heart?
Is thy prayer utter'd for thy mother's soul,
Who into long, long torment slept through thee?
Whose blood is on thy threshold?
—And stirs there not already 'neath thy heart ,
Another quick'ning pulse, that even now
Tortures itself and thee
With its foreboding presence?

MARGARET

Woe! Woe!
Oh could I free me from the thoughts

That hither, thither, crowd upon my brain,
Against my will!

CHORUS

Dies iræ, dies illa,
Solvet sæclum in favilla.

(The organ sounds.)

EVIL-SPIRIT

Grim horror seizes thee!
The trumpet sounds!
The graves are shaken!
And thy heart
From ashy rest
For torturing flames
Anew created,
Trembles into life!

MARGARET

Would I were hence!
It is as if the organ
Choked my breath,
As if the choir
Melted my inmost heart!

CHORUS

Judex ergo cum sedebit,
Quidquid latet adparebit,
Nil inultum remanebit.

MARGARET

I feel oppressed!
The pillars of the wall
Imprison me!
The vaulted roof
Weighs down upon me!—air!

EVIL-SPIRIT

Wouldst hide thee? sin and shame
Remain not hidden!
Air! light!
Woe's thee!

CHORUS

Quid sum miser tunc dicturus?
Quem patronum rogaturus!
Cum vix justus sit securus.

EVIL-SPIRIT

The glorified their faces turn
Away from thee!
Shudder the pure to reach
Their hands to thee!
Woe!

CHORUS

Quid sum miser tunc, dicturus—

MARGARET

Neighbour! your smelling bottle!

(*She swoons away.*)

WALPURGIS-NIGHT

THE HARTZ MOUNTAINS. DISTRICT OF SCHIERKE
AND ELEND

FAUST *and* MEPHISTOPHELES

MEPHISTOPHELES

A broomstick dost thou not at least desire?
The roughest he-goat fain would I bestride,
By this road from our goal we're still far wide.

FAUST

While fresh upon my legs, so long I naught require,
Except this knotty staff. Beside,
What boots it to abridge a pleasant way?
Along the labyrinth of these vales to creep,
Then scale these rocks, whence, in eternal spray,

Adown the cliffs the silvery fountains leap:
Such is the joy that seasons paths like these!
Spring weaves already in the birchen trees;
E'en the late pine-grove feels her quickening powers;
Should she not work within these limbs of ours?

MEPHISTOPHELES

Naught of this genial influence do I know!
Within me all is wintry. Frost and snow
I should prefer my dismal path to bound.
How sadly, yonder, with belated glow
Rises the ruddy moon's imperfect round,
Shedding so faint a light, at every tread
One's sure to stumble 'gainst a rock or tree!
An Ignis Fatuus I must call instead.
Yonder one burning merrily, I see.
Holla! my friend! may I request your light?
Why should you flare away so uselessly?
Be kind enough to show us up the height!

IGNIS FATUUS

Through reverence, I hope I may subdue
The lightness of my nature; true,
Our course is but a zigzag one.

MEPHISTOPHELES

      Ho! ho!
So men, forsooth, he thinks to imitate!
Now, in the devil's name, for once go straight!
Or out at once your flickering life I'll blow.

IGNIS FATUUS

That you are master here is obvious quite;
To do your will, I'll cordially essay;
Only reflect! The hill is magic-mad to-night;
And if to show the path you choose a meteor's light,
You must not wonder should we go astray.

FAUST, MEPHISTOPHELES, IGNIS FATUUS
(*in alternate song*)
Through the dream and magic-sphere,
As it seems, we now are speeding;
Honour win, us rightly leading,
That betimes we may appear
In yon wide and desert region!

Trees on trees, a stalwart legion,
Swiftly past us are retreating,
And the cliffs with lowly greeting;
Rocks long-snouted, row on row,
How they snort, and how they blow!

Through the stones and heather springing,
Brook and brooklet haste below;
Hark the rustling!   Hark the singing!
Hearken to love's plaintive lays;
Voices of those heavenly days—
What we hope, and what we love!
Like a tale of olden time,
Echo's voice prolongs the chime.

To-whit!   To-whoo!   It sounds more **near;**
Plover, owl, and jay appear,
All awake, around, above?
Paunchy salamanders too
Peer, long-limbed, the bushes through!
And, like snakes, the roots of trees
Coil themselves from rock and sand,
Stretching many a wondrous band,
Us to frighten, us to seize;
From rude knots with life embued,
Polyp-fangs abroad they spread,
To snare the wanderer!   'Neath our tread,
Mice, in myriads, thousand-hued,
Through the heath and through the moss!
And the fire-flies' glittering throng,
Wildering escort, whirls along,
Here and there, our path across.

Tell me, stand we motionless,
Or still forward do we press?
All things round us whirl and fly;
Rocks and trees make strange grimaces,
Dazzling meteors change their places,
How they puff and multiply!

MEPHISTOPHELES

Now grasp my doublet—we at last
A central peak have reached, which shows,
If round a wondering glance we cast,
How in the mountain Mammon glows.

FAUST

How through the chasms strangely gleams,
A lurid light, like dawn's red glow,
Pervading with its quivering beams,
The gorges of the gulf below!
Here vapours rise, there clouds float by,
Here through the mist the light doth shine;
Now, like a fount, it bursts on high,
Meanders now, a slender line;
Far reaching, with a hundred veins,
Here through the valley see it glide;
Here, where its force the gorge restrains,
At once it scatters, far and wide;
Anear, like showers of golden sand
Strewn broadcast, sputter sparks of light:
And mark yon rocky walls that stand
Ablaze, in all their towering height!

MEPHISTOPHELES

Doth not Sir Mammon for this fête
Grandly illume his palace! Thou
Art lucky to have seen it; now,
The boisterous guests, I feel, are coming straight.

Faust

How through the air the storm doth whirl!
Upon my neck it strikes with sudden shock.

Mephistopheles

Cling to these ancient ribs of granite rock,
Else to yon depths profound it you will hurl.
A murky vapour thickens night.
Hark! Through the woods the tempests roar!
The owlets flit in wild affright.
Hark! Splinter'd are the columns that upbore
The leafy palace, green for aye:
The shivered branches whirr and sigh,
Yawn the huge trunks with mighty groan.
The roots upriven, creak and moan!
In fearful and entangled fall,
One crashing ruin whelms them all,
While through the desolate abyss,
Sweeping the wreck-strewn precipice,
The raging storm-blasts howl and hiss!
Aloft strange voices dost thou hear?
Distant now and now more near?
Hark! the mountain ridge along,
Streameth a raving magic-song!

Witches (*in chorus*)

Now to the Brocken the witches hie,
The stubble is yellow, the corn is green;
Thither the gathering legions fly,
And sitting aloft is Sir Urian seen:
O'er stick and o'er stone they go whirling along,
Witches and he-goats, a motley throng.

Voices

Alone old Baubo's coming now;
She rides upon a farrow sow.

Chorus

Honour to her, to whom honour is due!
Forward, Dame Baubo! Honour to you!
A goodly sow and mother thereon,
The whole witch chorus follows anon.

Voice

Which way didst come?

Voice

O'er Ilsenstein!
There I peep'd in an owlet's nest.
With her broad eye she gazed in mine!

Voice

Drive to the devil, thou hellish pest!
Why ride so hard?

Voice

She has graz'd my side,
Look at the wounds, how deep and how wide!

Witches (*in chorus*)

The way is broad, the way is long;
What mad pursuit! What tumult wild!
Scratches the besom and sticks the prong;
Crush'd is the mother, and stifled the child.

Wizards (*half chorus*)

Like house-encumber'd snail we creep;
While far ahead the women keep,
For when to the devil's house we speed,
By a thousand steps they take the lead.

The Other Half

Not so, precisely do we view it;—
They with a thousand steps may do it;

But let them hasten as they can,
With one long bound 'tis clear'd by man.

VOICES (*above*)

Come with us, come with us from Felsensee.

VOICES (*from below*)

Aloft to you we would mount with glee!
We wash, and free from all stain are we,
Yet barren evermore must be!

BOTH CHORUSES

The wind is hushed, the stars grow pale,
The pensive moon her light doth veil;
And whirling on, the magic choir
Sputters forth sparks of drizzling fire.

VOICE (*from below*)

Stay! stay!

VOICE (*from above*)

What voice of woe
Calls from the cavern'd depths below?

VOICE (*from below*)

Take me with you! Oh take me too!
Three centuries I climb in vain,
And yet can ne'er the summit gain!
To be with my kindred I am fain.

BOTH CHORUSES

Broom and pitch-fork, goat and prong,
Mounted on these we whirl along;
Who vainly strives to climb to-night,
Is evermore a luckless wight!

DEMI-WITCH (*below*)

I hobble after, many a day;
Already the others are far away!

No rest at home can I obtain—
Here too my efforts are in vain!

Chorus of Witches

Salve gives the witches strength to rise;
A rag for a sail does well enough;
A goodly ship is every trough;
To-night who flies not, never flies.

Both Choruses

And when the topmost peak we round,
Then alight ye on the ground;
The heath's wide regions cover ye
With your mad swarms of witchery!
              (*They let themselves down.*)

Mephistopheles

They crowd and jostle, whirl and flutter!
They whisper, babble, twirl, and splutter!
They glimmer, sparkle, stink and flare—
A true witch-element! Beware!
Stick close! else we shall severed be.
Where art thou?

Faust (*in the distance*)
Here!

Mephistopheles

            Already, whirl'd so far away!
The master then indeed I needs must play.
Give ground! Squire Voland comes! Sweet folk, give
        ground!
Here, doctor, grasp me! With a single bound
Let us escape this ceaseless jar;
Even for me too mad these people are.
Hard by there shineth something with peculiar glare,
Yon brake allureth me; it is not far;
Come, come along with me! we'll slip in there.

FAUST

Spirit of contradiction! Lead! I'll follow straight!
'Twas wisely done, however, to repair
On May-night to the Brocken, and when there
By our own choice ourselves to isolate!

MEPHISTOPHELES

Mark, of those flames the motley glare!
A merry club assembles there.
In a small circle one is not alone.

FAUST

I'd rather be above, though, I must own!
Already fire and eddying smoke I view;
The impetuous millions to the devil ride;
Full many a riddle will be there untied.

MEPHISTOPHELES

Ay! and full many a riddle tied anew.
But let the great world rave and riot!
Here will we house ourselves in quiet.
A custom 'tis of ancient date,
Our lesser worlds within the great world to create!
Young witches there I see, naked and bare,
And old ones, veil'd more prudently.
For my sake only courteous be!
The trouble's small, the sport is rare.
Of instruments I hear the cursed din—
One must get used to it. Come in! come in!
There's now no help for it. I'll step before
And introducing you as my good friend,
Confer on you one obligation more.
How say you now? 'Tis no such paltry room;
Why only look, you scarce can see the end.
A hundred fires in rows disperse the gloom;
They dance, they talk, they cook, make love, and drink:
Where could we find aught better, do you think?

FAUST

To introduce us, do you purpose here
As devil or as wizard to appear?

MEPHISTOPHELES

Though I am wont indeed to strict incognito,
Yet upon gala-days one must one's orders show.
No garter have I to distinguish me,
Nathless the cloven foot doth here give dignity.
Seest thou yonder snail? Crawling this way she hies:
With searching feelers, she, no doubt,
Hath me already scented out;
Here, even if I would, for me there's no disguise.
From fire to fire, we'll saunter at our leisure,
The gallant you, I'll cater for your pleasure.
        (*To a party seated round some expiring embers.*)
Old gentleman, apart, why sit ye moping here?
Ye in the midst should be of all this jovial cheer,
Girt round with noise and youthful riot;
At home one surely has enough of quiet.

GENERAL

In nations put his trust, who may,
Whate'er for them one may have done;
For with the people, as with women, they
Honour your rising stars alone!

MINISTER

Now all too far they wander from the right;
I praise the good old ways, to them I hold,
Then was the genuine age of gold,
When we ourselves were foremost in men's sight.

PARVENU

Ne'er were we 'mong your dullards found,
And what we ought not, that to·do were fair;

Yet now are all things turning round and round,
When on firm basis we would them maintain.

Author

Who, as a rule, a treatise now would care
To read, of even moderate sense?
As for the rising generation, ne'er
Has youth displayed such arrogant pretence.

Mephistopheles
(suddenly appearing very old)

Since for the last time I the Brocken scale,
That folk are ripe for doomsday, now one sees;
And just because my cask begins to fail,
So the whole world is also on the lees.

Huckster-Witch

Stop, gentlemen, nor pass me by,
Of wares I have a choice collection:
Pray honour them with your inspection.
Lose not this opportunity!
Yet nothing in my booth you'll find
Without its counterpart on earth; there's naught,
Which to the world, and to mankind,
Hath not some direful mischief wrought.
No dagger here, which hath not flow'd with blood,
No chalice, whence, into some healthy frame
Hath not been poured hot poison's wasting flood.
No trinket, but hath wrought some woman's shame,
No weapon but hath cut some sacred tie,
Or from behind hath stabb'd an enemy.

Mephistopheles

Gossip! For wares like these the time's gone by,
What's done is past! what's past is done!
With novelties your booth supply;
Us novelties attract alone.

FAUST

May this wild scene my senses spare!
This, may in truth be called a fair!

MEPHISTOPHELES

Upward the eddying concourse throng;
Thinking to push, thyself art push'd along.

FAUST

Who's that, pray?

MEPHISTOPHELES

Mark her well! That's Lilith.

FAUST

Who?

MEPHISTOPHELES

Adam's first wife. Of her rich locks beware!
That charm in which she's parallel'd by few;
When in its toils a youth she doth ensnare,
He will not soon escape, I promise you.

FAUST

There sit a pair, the old one with the young;
Already they have bravely danced and sprung!

MEPHISTOPHELES

Here there is no repose to-day.
Another dance begins; we'll join it, come away!

FAUST

(*dancing with the young one*)

Once a fair vision came to me;
Therein I saw an apple-tree,
Two beauteous apples charmed mine eyes;
I climb'd forthwith to reach the prize.

THE FAIR ONE.

Apples still fondly ye desire,
From paradise it hath been so.
Feelings of joy my breast inspire
That such too in my garden grow.

MEPHISTOPHELES (*with the old one*)

Once a weird vision came to me;
Therein I saw a rifted tree.
It had a . . . . . . ;
But as it was it pleased me too.

THE OLD ONE

I beg most humbly to salute
The gallant with the cloven foot!
Let him a . . . have ready here,
If he a . . . does not fear.

PROCTOPHANTASMIST

Accursed mob! How dare ye thus to meet?
Have I not shown and demonstrated too,
That ghosts stand not on ordinary feet?
Yet here ye dance, as other mortals do!

THE FAIR ONE (*dancing*)

Then at our ball, what doth he here?

FAUST (*dancing*)

Oh! He must everywhere appear.
He must adjudge, when others dance;
If on each step his say's not said,
So is that step as good as never made.
He's most annoyed, so soon as we advance;
If ye would circle in one narrow round,
As he in his old mill, then doubtless he
Your dancing would approve,—especially
If ye forthwith salute him with respect profound!

Proctophantasmist

Still here! what arrogance! unheard of quite!
Vanish; we now have fill'd the world with light!
Laws are unheeded by the devil's host;
Wise as we are, yet Tegel hath its ghost!
How long at this conceit I've swept with all my might,
Lost is the labour: 'tis unheard of quite!

The Fair One

Cease here to teaze us any more, I pray.

Proctophantasmist

Spirits, I plainly to your face declare:
No spiritual control myself will bear,
Since my own spirit can exert no sway.
                        (*The dancing continues.*)
To-night, I see, I shall in naught succeed;
But I'm prepar'd my travels to pursue,
And hope, before my final step indeed,
To triumph over bards and devils too.

Mephistopheles

Now in some puddle will he take his station,
Such is his mode of seeking consolation;
Where leeches, feasting on his rump, will drain
Spirits alike and spirit from his brain.
        (*To* Faust, *who has left the dance.*)
But why the charming damsel leave, I pray,
Who to you in the dance so sweetly sang?

Faust

Ah, in the very middle of her lay,
Out of her mouth a small red mouse there sprang.

Mephistopheles

Suppose there did! One must not be too nice.
'Twas well it was not grey, let that suffice.
Who 'mid his pleasures for a trifle cares?

FAUST

Then saw I—

MEPHISTOPHELES
What?

FAUST

                    Mephisto, seest thou there
Standing far off, a lone child, pale and fair?
Slow from the spot her drooping form she tears,
And seems with shackled feet to move along;
I own, within me the delusion's strong,
That she the likeness of my Gretchen wears.

MEPHISTOPHELES

Gaze not upon her! 'Tis not good! Forbear!
'Tis lifeless, magical, a shape of air,
An idol. Such to meet with, bodes no good;
That rigid look of hers doth freeze man's blood,
And well-nigh petrifies his heart to stone:—
The story of Medusa thou hast known.

FAUST

Ay, verily! a corpse's eyes are those,
Which there was no fond loving hand to close.
That is the bosom I so fondly press'd,
That my sweet Gretchen's form, so oft caress'd!

MEPHISTOPHELES

Deluded fool! 'Tis magic, I declare!
To each she doth his lov'd one's image wear.

FAUST

What bliss! what torture! vainly I essay
To turn me from that piteous look away.
How strangely doth a single crimson line
Around that lovely neck its coil entwine,
It shows no broader than a knife's blunt edge!

MEPHISTOPHELES

Quite right. I see it also, and allege
That she beneath her arm her head can bear,
Since Perseus cut it off.—But you I swear
Are craving for illusion still!
Come then, ascend yon little hill!
As on the Prater all is gay,
And if my senses are not gone,
I see a theatre,—what's going on?

SERVIBILIS

They are about to recommence;—the play
Will be the last of seven, and spick-span new—
'Tis usual here that number to present.
A dilettante did the piece invent,
And dilettanti will enact it too.
Excuse me, gentlemen; to me's assign'd
As dilettante to uplift the curtain.

MEPHISTOPHELES

You on the Blocksberg I'm rejoiced to find,
That 'tis your most appropriate sphere is certain.

WALPURGIS-NIGHT'S DREAM
OR
OBERON AND TITANIA'S GOLDEN WEDDING-FEAST
Intermezzo

THEATRE

MANAGER

Vales, where mists still shift and play,
  To ancient hills succeeding,—
These our scenes;—so we, to-day,
  May rest, brave sons of Mieding.

HERALD

That the marriage golden be,
  Must fifty years be ended;
More dear this feast of gold to me,
  Contention now suspended.

OBERON

Spirits, if present, grace the scene,
  And if with me united,
Then gratulate the king and queen,
  Their troth thus newly plighted!

PUCK

Puck draws near and wheels about,
  In mazy circles dancing!
Hundreds swell his joyous shout,
  Behind him still advancing.

ARIEL

Ariel wakes his dainty air,
  His lyre celestial stringing.—
Fools he lureth, and the fair,
  With his celestial singing.

OBERON

Wedded ones, would ye agree,
  We court your imitation:
Would ye fondly love as we,
  We counsel separation.

TITANIA

If husband scold and wife retort,
  Then bear them far asunder;
Her to the burning south transport,
  And him the North Pole under.

The Whole Orchestra (*fortissimo*)
Flies and midges all unite
　　With frog and chirping cricket,
Our orchestra throughout the night,
　　Resounding in the thicket!

(*Solo*)
Yonder doth the bagpipe come!
　　Its sack an airy bubble.
Schnick, schnick, schnack, with nasal hum,
　　Its notes it doth redouble.

Embryo Spirit
Spider's foot and midge's wing,
　　A toad in form and feature;
Together verses it can string,
　　Though scarce a living creature.

A Little Pair
Tiny step and lofty bound,
　　Through dew and exhalation;
Ye trip it deftly on the ground,
　　But gain no elevation.

Inquisitive Traveller
Can I indeed believe my eyes?
　　Is't not mere masquerading?
What! Oberon in beauteous guise,
　　Among the groups parading!

Orthodox
No claws, no tail to whisk about,
　　To fright us at our revel;—
Yet like the gods of Greece, no doubt,
　　He too's a genuine devil.

NORTHERN ARTIST

These that I'm hitting off to-day
  Are sketches unpretending;
Towards Italy without delay,
  My steps I think of bending.

PURIST

Alas! ill-fortune leads me here,
  Where riot still grows louder;
And 'mong the witches gather'd here
  But two alone wear powder!

YOUNG WITCH

Your powder and your petticoat,
  Suit hags, there's no gainsaying;
Hence I sit fearless on my goat,
  My naked charms displaying.

MATRON

We're too well-bred to squabble here,
  Or insult back to render;
But may you wither soon, my dear,
  Although so young and tender.

LEADER OF THE BAND

Nose of fly and gnat's proboscis,
  Throng not the naked beauty!
Frogs and crickets in the mosses,
  Keep time and do your duty!

WEATHERCOCK (*towards one side*)

What charming company I view
  Together here collected!
Gay bachelors, a hopeful crew.
  And brides so unaffected!

WEATHERCOCK (*towards the other side*)
Unless indeed the yawning ground
  Should open to receive them,
From this vile crew, with sudden bound,
  To Hell I'd jump and leave them.

XENIEN

With small sharp shears, in insect guise
  Behold us at your revel!
That we may tender, filial-wise,
  Our homage to the devil.

HENNINGS

Look now at yonder eager crew,
  How naïvely they're jesting!
That they have tender hearts and true,
  They stoutly keep protesting!

MUSAGET

Oneself amid this witchery
  How pleasantly one loses;
For witches easier are to me
  To govern than the Muses!

CI-DEVANT GENIUS OF THE AGE

With proper folks when we appear,
  No one can then surpass us!
Keep close, wide is the Blocksberg here
  As Germany's Parnassus.

INQUISITIVE TRAVELLER

How name ye that stiff formal man,
  Who strides with lofty paces?
He tracks the game where'er he can,
  "He scents the Jesuits' traces."

CRANE

Where waters troubled are or clear,
  To fish I am delighted;
Thus pious gentlemen appear
  With devils here united.

WORLDLING

By pious people, it is true,
  No medium is rejected;
Conventicles, and not a few,
  On Blocksberg are erected.

DANCER

Another chorus now succeeds,
  Far off the drums are beating.
Be still! The bitterns 'mong the reeds
  Their one note are repeating.

DANCING MASTER

Each twirls about and never stops,
  And as he can he fareth.
The crooked leaps, the clumsy hops,
  Nor for appearance careth.

FIDDLER

To take each other's life, I trow,
  Would cordially delight them!
As Orpheus' lyre the beasts, so now
  The bagpipe doth unite them.

DOGMATIST

My views, in spite of doubt and sneer,
  I hold with stout persistence,
Inferring from the devils here,
  The evil one's existence.

Idealist

My every sense rules Phantasy
  With sway quite too potential;
Sure I'm demented if the I
  Alone is the essential.

Realist

This entity's a dreadful bore,
  And cannot choose but vex me;
The ground beneath me ne'er before
  Thus totter'd to perplex me.

Supernaturalist

Well pleased assembled here I view,
  Of spirits this profusion;
From devils, touching angels too,
  I gather some conclusion.

Sceptic

The ignis fatuus they track out,
  And think they're near the treasure.
Devil alliterates with doubt,
  Here I abide with pleasure.

Leader of the Band

Frog and cricket in the mosses,—
  Confound your gasconading!
Nose of fly and gnat's proboscis;—
  Most tuneful serenading!

The Knowing Ones

Sans-souci, so this host we greet,
  Their jovial humour showing;
There's now no walking on our feet,
  So on our heads we're going.

The Awkward Ones

In seasons past we snatch'd, 'tis true,
   Some tit-bits by our cunning;
Our shoes, alas, are now danced through,
   On our bare soles we're running.

Will-o'-the-Wisps

From marshy bogs we sprang to light,
   Yet here behold us dancing;
The gayest gallants of the night,
   In glitt'ring rows advancing.

Shooting Star

With rapid motion from on high,
   I shot in starry splendour;
Now prostrate on the grass I lie;—
   Who aid will kindly render?

The Massive Ones

Room! wheel round! They're coming lo!
   Down sink the bending grasses.
Though spirits, yet their limbs, we know,
   Are huge substantial masses.

Puck

Don't stamp so heavily, I pray;
   Like elephants you're treading!
And 'mong the elves be Puck to-day,
   The stoutest at the wedding!

Ariel

If nature boon, or subtle sprite,
   Endow your soul with pinions;—
Then follow to yon rosy height,
   Through ether's calm dominions!

ORCHESTRA (*pianissimo*)
Drifting cloud and misty wreathes
Are fill'd with light elysian;
O'er reed and leaf the zephyr breathes—
So fades the fairy vision!

A GLOOMY DAY. A PLAIN

FAUST *and* MEPHISTOPHELES

FAUST

In misery! despairing! long wandering pitifully on the face of the earth and now imprisoned! This gentle hapless creature, immured in the dungeon as a malefactor and reserved for horrid tortures! That it should come to this! To this!—Perfidious, worthless spirit, and this thou hast concealed from me!—Stand! ay, stand! roll in malicious rage thy fiendish eyes! Stand and brave me with thine insupportable presence! Imprisoned! In hopeless misery! Delivered over to the power of evil spirits and the judgment of unpitying humanity!—And me, the while, thou wert lulling with tasteless dissipations, concealing from me her growing anguish, and leaving her to perish without help!

MEPHISTOPHELES

She is not the first.

FAUST

Hound! Execrable monster!—Back with him, oh thou infinite spirit! back with the reptile into his dog's shape, in which it was his wont to scamper before me at eventide, to roll before the feet of the harmless wanderer, and to fasten on his shoulders when he fell! Change him again into his favourite shape, that he may crouch on his belly before me in the dust, whilst I spurn him with my foot, the reprobate!—Not the first!—Woe! Woe! By no human soul is it conceivable, that more than one human creature has ever sunk into a depth of wretchedness like this, or that the first in her writhing death-agony should not have atoned in the sight of all-pardoning Heaven for the guilt of all the rest! The misery of this one pierces me to the very marrow, and harrows up my soul; thou art grinning calmly over the doom of thousands!

MEPHISTOPHELES

Now we are once again at our wit's end, just where the reason of you mortals snaps! Why dost thou seek our fellowship, if thou canst not go through with it? Wilt fly, and art not proof against dizziness? Did we force ourselves on thee, or thou on us?

FAUST

Cease thus to gnash thy ravenous fangs at me! I loathe thee!—Great and glorious spirit, thou who didst vouchsafe to reveal thyself unto me, thou who dost know my very heart and soul, why hast thou linked me with this base associate, who feeds on mischief and revels in destruction?

MEPHISTOPHELES

Hast done?

FAUST

Save her!—or woe to thee! The direst of curses on thee for thousands of years!

MEPHISTOPHELES

I cannot loose the bands of the avenger, nor withdraw his bolts.—Save her!—Who was it plunged her into perdition? I or thou?

(FAUST *looks wildly around.*)

MEPHISTOPHELES

Would'st grasp the thunder? Well for you, poor mortals, that 'tis not yours to wield! To smite to atoms the being however innocent, who obstructs his path, such is the tyrant's fashion of relieving himself in difficulties!

FAUST

Convey me thither! She shall be free!

MEPHISTOPHELES

And the danger to which thou dost expose thyself? Know, the guilt of blood, shed by thy hand, lies yet upon the town. Over the place where fell the murdered one, avenging spirits hover and watch for the returning murderer.

FAUST

This too from thee? The death and downfall of a world be on thee, monster! Conduct me thither, I say, and set her free!

MEPHISTOPHELES

I will conduct thee. And what I can do,—hear! Have I all power in heaven and upon earth? I'll cloud the senses of the warder,—do thou possess thyself of the keys and lead her forth with human hand! I will keep watch! The magic steeds are waiting, I bear thee off. Thus much is in my power.

FAUST

Up and away!

NIGHT. OPEN COUNTRY

FAUST. MEPHISTOPHELES

(*Rushing along on black horses*)

FAUST

What weave they yonder round the Ravenstone?

MEPHISTOPHELES

I know not what they shape and brew.

FAUST

They're soaring, swooping, bending, stooping.

MEPHISTOPHELES

A witches' pack.

Faust

They charm, they strew.

Mephistopheles

On! On!

DUNGEON

Faust

*(with a bunch of keys and a lamp before a small iron
    door)*
A fear unwonted o'er my spirit falls;
Man's concentrated woe o'erwhelms me here!
She dwells immur'd within these dripping walls;
Her only trespass a delusion dear!
Thou lingerest at the fatal door,
Thou dread'st to see her face once more?
On! While thou dalliest, draws her death-hour near.

(He seizes the lock. Singing within.)

My mother, the harlot,
She took me and slew!
My father, the scoundrel,
Hath eaten me too!
My sweet little sister
Hath all my bones laid,
Where soft breezes whisper
All in the cool shade!

Then became I a wood-bird, and sang on the spray,
Fly away! little bird, fly away! fly away!

Faust *(opening the lock)*

Ah! she forebodes not that her lover's near,
The clanking chains, the rustling straw, to hear.

(He enters.)

MARGARET
(hiding her face in the bed of straw)

Woe! woe! they come! oh bitter 'tis to die!

FAUST *(softly)*

Hush! hush! be still! I come to set thee free!

MARGARET
(throwing herself at his feet)

If thou art human, feel my misery!

FAUST

Thou wilt awake the jailor with thy cry!
    (He grasps the chains to unlock them.)

MARGARET *(on her knees)*
Who, headsman, unto thee this power
O'er me could give?
Thou com'st for me at midnight-hour.
Be merciful, and let me live!
Is morrow's dawn not time enough?
      (She stands up.)
I'm still so young, so young—
And must so early die!
Fair was I too, and that was my undoing.
My love is now afar, he then was nigh;
Torn lies the garland, the fair blossoms strew'd
Nay, seize me not with hand so rude!
Spare me! What harm have I e'er done to thee?
Oh let me not in vain implore!
I ne'er have seen thee in my life before!

FAUST
Can I endure this bitter agony?

MARGARET

I now am at thy mercy quite.
Let me my babe but suckle once again!
I fondled it the live-long night;
They took it from me but to give me pain,
And now, they say that I my child have slain.
Gladness I ne'er again shall know.
Then they sing songs about me,—'tis wicked of the
    throng—
An ancient ballad endeth so;
Who bade them thus apply the song?

FAUST

(throwing himself on the ground)
A lover at thy feet bends low,
To loose the bonds of wretchedness and woe.

MARGARET

(throws herself beside him)

Oh, let us kneel and move the saints by prayer!
Look! look! yon stairs below,
Under the threshold there,
Hell's flames are all aglow!
Beneath the floor,
With hideous noise,
The devils roar!

FAUST *(aloud)*

Gretchen! Gretchen!

MARGARET *(listening)*

That was my lov'd one's voice!
    (She springs up, the chains fall off.)
Where is he? I heard him calling me.
Free am I! There's none shall hinder me.
To his neck will I fly,
On his bosom will lie!

Gretchen, he called!—On yon threshold he stood;
Amidst all the howling of hell's fiery flood,
The scoff and the scorn of its devilish crew,
The tones of his voice, sweet and loving, I knew.

Faust

'Tis I!

Margaret

'Tis thou! O say so once again!

(*embracing him.*)

Tis he! 'Tis he! where's now the torturing pain?
Where are the fetters? where the dungeon's gloom?
'Tis thou! To save me thou art come!
And I am sav'd!—
Already now the street I see
Where the first time I caught a glimpse of thee.
There too the pleasant garden shade,
Where I and Martha for thy coming stay'd.

Faust

(*endeavouring to lead her away*)

Come! come away!

Margaret

Oh do not haste!
I love to linger where thou stayest.　　(*caressing him.*)

Faust

Ah haste! For if thou still delayest,
Our lingering we shall both deplore.

Margaret

How, dearest? canst thou kiss no more!
So short a time away from me, and yet,
To kiss thou couldst so soon forget!
Why on thy neck so anxious do I feel—
When formerly a perfect heaven of bliss
From thy dear looks and words would o'er me steal?

As thou wouldst stifle me thou then didst kiss!—
Kiss me!
Or I'll kiss thee!   (*She embraces him.*)
Woe! woe! Thy lips are cold,—
Are dumb!
Thy love where hast thou left?
Who hath me of thy love bereft?
                         (*She turns away from him.*)

FAUST

Come! Follow me, my dearest love, be bold!
I'll cherish thee with ardour thousand-fold;
I but entreat thee now to follow me!

MARGARET
(turning towards him)

And art thou he? and art thou really he?

FAUST

'Tis I! O come!

MARGARET

Thou wilt strike off my chain,
And thou wilt take me to thine arms again.
How comes it that thou dost not shrink from me?—
And dost thou know, love, whom thou wouldst set free?

FAUST

Come! come! already night begins to wane.

MARGARET

I sent my mother to her grave,
I drown'd my child beneath the wave.
Was it not given to thee and me—thee too?
'Tis thou thyself! I scarce believe it yet.
Give me thy hand! It is no dream! 'Tis true!
Thine own dear hand!—But how is this? 'Tis wet?
Quick, wipe it off! Meseems that yet
There's blood thereon.

Ah God! what hast thou done?
Put up thy sword,
I beg of thee!

FAUST

Oh, dearest, let the past forgotten be!
Death is in every word.

MARGARET

No, thou must linger here in sorrow!
The graves I will describe to thee,
And thou to them must see
To-morrow:
The best place give to my mother,
Close at her side my brother,
Me at some distance lay—
But not too far away!
And the little one place on my right breast.
Nobody else will near me lie!
To nestle beside thee so lovingly,
That was a rapture, gracious and sweet!
A rapture I never again shall prove;
Methinks I would force myself on thee, love,
And thou dost spurn me, and back retreat—
Yet 'tis thyself, thy fond kind looks I see.

FAUST

If thou dost feel 'tis I, then come with me!

MARGARET

What, there? without?

FAUST

Yes, forth in the free air.

MARGARET

Ay, if the grave's without,—If death lurk there!
Hence to the everlasting resting-place,
And not one step beyond!—Thou'rt leaving me?
Oh Henry! would that I could go with thee!

FAUST

Thou canst! But will it! Open stands the door.

MARGARET

I dare not go! I've naught to hope for more.
What boots it to escape? They lurk for me!
'Tis wretched to beg, as I must do,
And with an evil conscience thereto!
'Tis wretched, in foreign lands to stray;
And me they will catch, do what I may!

FAUST

.With thee will I abide.

MARGARET

Quick! Quick!
Save thy poor child!
Keep to the path
The brook along,
Over the bridge
To the wood beyond,
To the left, where the plank **is,**
In the pond.
Seize it at once!
It fain would rise,
It struggles still!
Save it. Oh save!

FAUST

Dear Gretchen, more collected be!
One little step, and thou art free!

MARGARET

Were we but only past the hill!
There sits my mother upon a stone—
My brain, alas, is cold with dread!—
There sits my mother upon a stone,
And to and fro she shakes her head;

She winks not, she nods not, her head it droops sore;
She slept so long, she waked no more;
She slept, that we might taste of bliss:
Ah! those were happy times, I wis!

FAUST

Since here avails nor argument nor prayer,
Thee hence by force I needs must bear.

MARGARET

Loose me! I will not suffer violence!
With murderous hand hold not so fast!
I have done all to please thee in the past!

FAUST

Day dawns! My love! My love!

MARGARET

                Yes! day draws near.
The day of judgment too will soon appear!
It should have been my bridal! No one tell,
That thy poor Gretchen thou hast known too well.
Woe to my garland!
Its bloom is o'er!
Though not at the dance—
We shall meeet once more.
The crowd doth gather, in silence it rolls;
The squares, the streets,
Scarce hold the throng.
The staff is broken,—the death-bell tolls,—
They bind and seize me! I'm hurried along,
To the seat of blood already I'm bound!
Quivers each neck as the naked steel
Quivers on mine the blow to deal—
The silence of the grave now broods around!

FAUST

Would I had ne'er been born!

MEPHISTOPHELES (*appears without*)
Up! or you're lost.
Vain hesitation! Babbling, quaking!
My steeds are shivering,
Morn is breaking.

MARGARET

What from the floor ascendeth like a ghost?
'Tis he! 'Tis he! Him from my presence chase!
What would he in this holy place?
It is for me he cometh!

FAUST
Thou shalt live!

MARGARET

Judgment of God! To thee my soul I give!

MEPHISTOPHELES (*to* FAUST)
Come, come! With her I'll else abandon thee!

MARGARET

Father, I'm thine! Do thou deliver me!
Ye angels! Ye angelic hosts! descend,
Encamp around to guard me and defend!—
Henry! I shudder now to look on thee!

MEPHISTOPHELES
She now is judged!

VOICES (*from above*)
Is saved!

MEPHISTOPHELES (*to* FAUST)
Come thou with me!
(*Vanishes with* FAUST.)
VOICE (*from within, dying away*)
Henry! Henry!

THE TRAGICAL HISTORY OF DR. FAUSTUS

BY

CHRISTOPHER MARLOWE

INTRODUCTORY NOTE

CHRISTOPHER MARLOWE, *the author of the earliest dramatic version of the Faust legend, was the son of a shoemaker in Canterbury, where he was born in February, 1564, some two months before Shakespeare. After graduating as M.A. from the University of Cambridge in 1587, he seems to have settled in London; and that same year is generally accepted as the latest date for the production of his tragedy of "Tamburlaine," the play which is regarded as having established blank verse as the standard meter of the English Drama. "Doctor Faustus" probably came next in 1588, followed by "The Jew of Malta" and "Edward II." Marlowe had a share in the production of several other plays, wrote the first two sestiads of "Hero and Leander," and made translations from Ovid and Lucan. He met his death in a tavern brawl, June 1, 1593.*

Of Marlowe personally little is known. The common accounts of his atheistical beliefs and dissipated life are probably exaggerated, recent researches having given ground for believing that his heterodoxy may have amounted to little more than a form of Unitarianism. Some of the attacks on his character are based on the evidence of witnesses whose reputation will not bear investigation, while the character of some of his friends and their manner of speaking of him are of weight on the other side.

The most striking feature of Marlowe's dramas is the concentration of interest on an impressive central figure dominated by a single passion, the thirst for the unattainable. In "Tamburlaine" this takes the form of universal power; in "The Jew of Malta," infinite riches; in "Doctor Faustus" universal knowledge. The aspirations of these dominant personalities are uttered in sonorous blank verse, and in a rhetoric which at times rises to the sublime, at times descends to rant. "Doctor Faustus," though disfigured by poor comic scenes for which Marlowe is probably not responsible, and though lacking unity of structure, yet presents the career and fate of the hero with great power, and contains in the speech to Helen of Troy and in the dying utterance of Faustus two of the most superb passages of poetry in the English language.

198

THE TRAGICAL HISTORY OF DR. FAUSTUS

DRAMATIS PERSONÆ

[THE POPE. CARDINAL OF LORRAIN. EMPEROR OF GERMANY.
DUKE OF VANHOLT. FAUSTUS.
VALDES and CORNELIUS, Friends to Faustus.
WAGNER, Servant to FAUSTUS.
Clown. ROBIN. RALPH.
Vintner, Horse-Courser, Knight, Old Man,
Scholars, Friars, and Attendants.

DUCHESS OF VANHOLT.
LUCIFER. BELZEBUB. MEPHISTOPHILIS.
Good Angel, Evil Angel, The Seven Deadly Sins, Devils,
Spirits in the shape of ALEXANDER THE GREAT,
of his Paramour, and of HELEN of TROY.

Chorus.]

Enter CHORUS

Chorus

NOT marching now in fields of Thrasimene,
Where Mars did mate[1] the Carthaginians;
Nor sporting in the dalliance of love,
In courts of kings where state is overturn'd;
Nor in the pomp of proud audacious deeds,
Intends our Muse to vaunt his heavenly verse:
Only this, gentlemen,—we must perform
The form of Faustus' fortunes, good or bad.
To patient judgments we appeal our plaud,[2]
And speak for Faustus in his infancy.
Now is he born, his parents base of stock,

[1] Confound. But Hannibal was victorious at Lake Trasumennus, B. C. 217.
[2] For applause.

199

In Germany, within a town call'd Rhodes;[3]
Of riper years to Wittenberg he went,
Whereas his kinsmen chiefly brought him up.
So soon he profits in divinity,
The fruitful plot of scholarism grac'd,[4]
That shortly he was grac'd with doctor's name,
Excelling all those sweet delight disputes
In heavenly matters of theology;
Till swollen with cunning,[5] of a self-conceit,
His waxen wings[6] did mount above his reach,
And, melting, Heavens conspir'd his overthrow;
For, falling to a devilish exercise,
And glutted [now] with learning's golden gifts,
He surfeits upon cursed necromancy.
Nothing so sweet as magic is to him,
Which he prefers before his chiefest bliss.
And this the man that in his study sits!   [Exit.

[SCENE I.]

FAUSTUS [discovered] in his Study

FAUST. Settle my studies, Faustus, and begin
To sound the depth of that thou wilt profess[7];
Having commenc'd, be a divine in show,
Yet level[8] and at the end of every art,
And live and die in Aristotle's works.
Sweet Analytics,[9] 'tis thou hast ravish'd me,
Bene disserere est finis logices.[10]
Is to dispute well logic's chiefest end?
Affords this art no greater miracle?
Then read no more, thou hast attain'd the end;
A greater subject fitteth Faustus' wit.
Bid ὃν καὶ μὴ ὄν[11] farewell; Galen come,

---

[3] Roda, in the Duchy of Saxe-Altenburg, near Jena.
[4] The garden of scholarship being adorned by him.
[5] Knowledge.
[6] An allusion to the myth of Icarus, who flew too near the sun.
[7] Teach publicly.   [8] Aim.   [9] Logic.
[10] "To argue well is the end of logic."
[11] This is Mr. Bullen's emendation of Q1., Oncaymæon, a corruption of the Aristotelian phrase for "being and not being."

Seeing *Ubi desinit Philosophus ibi incipit Medicus;*[12]
Be a physician, Faustus, heap up gold,
And be eternis'd for some wondrous cure.
Summum bonum medicinæ sanitas,[13]
" The end of physic is our body's health."
Why, Faustus, hast thou not attain'd that end!
Is not thy common talk sound Aphorisms?[14]
Are not thy bills[15] hung up as monuments,
Whereby whole cities have escap'd the plague,
And thousand desperate maladies been eas'd?
Yet art thou still but Faustus and a man.
Couldst thou make men to live eternally,
Or, being dead, raise them to life again,
Then this profession were to be esteem'd.
Physic, farewell.—Where is Justinian?   [*Reads.*]
*Si una eademque res legatur duobus, alter rem, alter valorem
    rei, &c.*[16]
A pretty case of paltry legacies!   [*Reads.*]
Ex hæreditare filium non potest pater nisi, &c.[17]
Such is the subject of the Institute[18]
And universal Body of the Law.[19]
His[20] study fits a mercenary drudge,
Who aims at nothing but external trash;
Too servile and illiberal for me.
When all is done, divinity is best;
Jerome's Bible,[21] Faustus, view it well.   [*Reads.*]
Stipendium peccati mors est. Ha! *Stipendium, &c.*
" The reward of sin is death." That's hard.   [*Reads.*]
Si peccasse negamus fallimur et nulla est in nobis veritas.
" If we say that we have no sin we deceive ourselves, and
there's no truth in us." Why then, belike we must sin and
so consequently die.
'Ay, we must die an everlasting death.
What doctrine call you this, *Che sera sera,*

---

[12] " Where the philosopher leaves off, there the physician begins."
[13] This and the previous quotation are from Aristotle.
[14] Medical maxims.   [15] Announcements.
[16] " If one and the same thing is bequeathed to two persons, one gets
the thing and the other the value of the thing."
[17] " A father cannot disinherit the son except," etc.
[18] Of Justinian, under whom the Roman law was codified.   [19] Q1 ., Church
[20] Its.   [21] The Vulgate.

"What will be shall be?" Divinity, adieu
These metaphysics of magicians
And necromantic books are heavenly;
Lines, circles, scenes, letters, and characters,
Ay, these are those that Faustus most desires.
O what a world of profit and delight,
Of power, of honour, of omnipotence
Is promised to the studious artisan!
All things that move between the quiet poles
Shall be at my command. Emperors and kings
Are but obeyed in their several provinces,
Nor can they raise the wind or rend the clouds;
But his dominion that exceeds[22] in this
Stretcheth as far as doth the mind of man.
A sound magician is a mighty god:
Here, Faustus, try thy[23] brains to gain a deity.
Wagner!

Enter WAGNER

　　　　Commend me to my dearest friends,
The German Valdes and Cornelius;
Request them earnestly to visit me.
　WAG. I will, sir.　　　　　　　　　　　　　*Exit.*
　FAUST. Their conference will be a greater help to me
Than all my labours, plod I ne'er so fast.

Enter GOOD ANGEL *and* EVIL ANGEL

　G. ANG. O Faustus! lay that damned book aside,
And gaze not upon it lest it tempt thy soul,
And heap God's heavy wrath upon thy head.
Read, read the Scriptures: that is blasphemy.
　E. ANG. Go forward, Faustus, in that famous art,
Wherein all Nature's treasure is contain'd:
Be thou on earth as Jove is in the sky,
Lord and commander of these elements. [*Exeunt* Angels.]
　FAUST. How am I glutted with conceit[24] of this!
Shall I make spirits fetch me what I please,
Resolve me of all ambiguities,

[22] Excels.　　[23] Qs., tire my.　　[24] Idea.

Perform what desperate enterprise I will?
I'll have them fly to India for gold,
Ransack the ocean for orient pearl,
And search all corners of the new-found world
For pleasant fruits and princely delicates;
I'll have them read me strange philosophy
And tell the secrets of all foreign kings;
I'll have them wall all Germany with brass,
And make swift Rhine circle fair Wittenberg;
I'll have them fill the public schools with silk,[25]
Wherewith the students shall be bravely clad;
I'll levy soldiers with the coin they bring,
And chase the Prince of Parma from our land,[26]
And reign sole king of all the provinces;
Yea, stranger engines for the brunt of war
Than was the fiery keel[27] at Antwerp's bridge,
I'll make my servile spirits to invent.

Enter VALDES *and* CORNELIUS[28]

Come, German Valdes and Cornelius,
And make me blest with your sage conference.
Valdes, sweet Valdes, and Cornelius,
Know that your words have won me at the last
To practise magic and concealed arts:
Yet not your words only, but mine own fantasy
That will receive no object, for my head
But ruminates on necromantic skill.
Philosophy is odious and obscure,
Both law and physic are for petty wits;
Divinity is basest of the three,
Unpleasant, harsh, contemptible, and vile:
'Tis magic, magic, that hath ravish'd me.
Then, gentle friends, aid me in this attempt;
And I that have with concise syllogisms
Gravell'd the pastors of the German church,
And made the flowering pride of Wittenberg

[25] Qq., skill.
[26] The Netherlands, over which Parma re-established the Spanish dominions.
[27] A ship filled with explosives used to blow up a bridge built by Parma in 1585 at the siege of Antwerp.
[28] The famous Cornelius Agrippa. German Valdes is not known.

Swarm to my problems, as the infernal spirits
On sweet Musæus,[29] when he came to hell,
Will be as cunning as Agrippa was,
Whose shadows made all Europe honour him.

VALD. Faustus, these books, thy wit, and our experience
Shall make all nations to canònise us.
As Indian Moors[30] obey their Spanish lords,
So shall the subjects[31] of every element
Be always serviceable to us three;
Like lions shall they guard us when we please;
Like Almain rutters[32] with their horsemen's staves
Or Lapland giants, trotting by our sides;
Sometimes like women or unwedded maids,
Shadowing more beauty in their airy brows
Than have the white breasts of the queen of love:
From Venice shall they drag huge argosies,
And from America the golden fleece
That yearly stuffs old Philip's treasury;
If learned Faustus will be resolute.

FAUST. Valdes, as resolute am I in this
As thou to live; therefore object it not.

CORN. The miracles that magic will perform
Will make thee vow to study nothing else.
He that is grounded in astrology,
Enrich'd with tongues, as well seen[33] in minerals,
Hath all the principles magic doth require.
Then doubt not, Faustus, but to be renowm'd,
And more frequented for this mystery
Than heretofore the Delphian Oracle.
The spirits tell me they can dry the sea,
And fetch the treasure of all foreign wracks,
Ay, all the wealth that our forefathers hid
Within the massy entrails of the earth;
Then tell me, Faustus, what shall we three want?

FAUST. Nothing, Cornelius! O this cheers my soul!
Come show me some demonstrations magical,
That I may conjure in some lusty grove,
And have these joys in full possession.

[29] Cf. Virgil, Æn. vi. 667; Dryden's trans. vi. 905 ff.
[30] American Indians.   [31] Qs., spirits.   [32] Troopers. Germ. *Reiters.*
[33] Versed.

VALD. Then haste thee to some solitary grove,
And bear wise Bacon's[34] and Albanus'[35] works,
The Hebrew Psalter and New Testament;
And whatsoever else is requisite
We will inform thee ere our conference cease.

CORN. Valdes, first let him know the words of art;
And then, all other ceremonies learn'd,
Faustus may try his cunning by himself.

VALD. First I'll instruct thee in the rudiments,
And then wilt thou be perfecter than I.

FAUST. Then come and dine with me, and after meat,
We'll canvass every quiddity thereof;
For ere I sleep I'll try what I can do:
This night I'll conjure though I die therefore.   [*Exeunt.*

[SCENE II.—*Before* FAUSTUS'S *House*]

Enter two SCHOLARS

IST SCHOL. I wonder what's become of Faustus that was
wont to make our schools ring with *sic probo?*[1]

2ND SCHOL. That shall we know, for see here comes his
boy.

Enter WAGNER

IST SCHOL. How now, sirrah! Where's thy master?

WAG. God in heaven knows!

2ND SCHOL. Why, dost not thou know?

WAG. Yes, I know. But that follows not.

IST SCHOL. Go to, sirrah! Leave your jesting, and tell us
where he is.

WAG. That follows not necessary by force of argument,
that you, being licentiate, should stand upon't: therefore,
acknowledge your error and be attentive.

2ND SCHOL. Why, didst thou not say thou knew'st?

WAG. Have you any witness on't?

IST SCHOL. Yes, sirrah, I heard you.

WAG. Ask my fellow if I be a thief.

2ND SCHOL. Well, you will not tell us?

---

[34] Roger Bacon.
[35] Perhaps Pietro d'Abano, a medieval alchemist; perhaps a misprint for
Albertus (Magnus), the great schoolman.
[1] "Thus I prove"—a common formula in scholastic discussions.

WAG. Yes, sir, I will tell you; yet if you were not dunces, you would never ask me such a question; for is not he *corpus naturale?*[2] and is not that *mobile?* Then wherefore should you ask me such a question? But that I am by nature phlegmatic, slow to wrath, and prone to lechery (to love, I would say), it were not for you to come within forty feet of the place of execution, although I do not doubt to see you both hang'd the next sessions. Thus having triumph'd over you, I will set my countenance like a precisian,[3] and begin to speak thus:—Truly, my dear brethren, my master is within at dinner, with Valdes and Cornelius, as this wine, if it could speak, would inform your worships; and so the Lord bless you, preserve you, and keep you, my dear brethren, my dear brethren.

1ST SCHOL. Nay, then, I fear he has fallen into that damned Art, for which they two are infamous through the world.

2ND SCHOL. Were he a stranger, and not allied to me, yet should I grieve for him. But come, let us go and inform the Rector, and see if he by his grave counsel can reclaim him.

1ST SCHOL. O, but I fear me nothing can reclaim him.

2ND SCHOL. Yet let us try what we can do. [*Exeunt.*

[SCENE III.—*A Grove.*]

Enter FAUSTUS *to conjure*

FAUST. Now that the gloomy shadow of the earth
Longing to view Orion's drizzling look,
Leaps from the antarctic world unto the sky,
And dims the welkin with her pitchy breath,
Faustus, begin thine incantations,
And try if devils will obey thy hest,
Seeing thou hast pray'd and sacrific'd to them.
Within this circle is Jehovah's name,
Forward and backward anagrammatis'd,
The breviated names of holy saints,
Figures of every adjunct to the Heavens,

[2] "'*Corpus naturale seu mobile*' is the current scholastic expression for the subject-matter of Physics."—*Ward.* [3] Puritan.

And characters of signs and erring[1] stars,
By which the spirits are enforc'd to rise:
Then fear not, Faustus, but be resolute,
And try the uttermost magic can perform.

Sint mihi Dei Acherontis propitii! Valeat numen triplex Jehovæ! Ignei, aerii, aquatani spiritus, salvete! Orientis princeps Belzebub, inferni ardentis monarcha, et Demogorgon, propitiamus vos, ut appareat et surgat Mephistophilis. Quid tu moraris? per Jehovam, Gehennam, et consecratum aquam quam nunc spargo, signumque crucis quod nunc facio, et per vota nostra, ipse nunc surgat nobis dicatus Mephistophilis![2]

Enter [MEPHISTOPHILIS] *a* DEVIL

I charge thee to return and change thy shape;
Thou art too ugly to attend on me.
Go, and return an old Franciscan friar;
That holy shape becomes a devil best.   [*Exit* DEVIL
I see there's virtue in my heavenly words;
Who would not be proficient in this art?
How pliant is this Mephistophilis,
Full of obedience and humility!
Such is the force of magic and my spells.
[Now,] Faustus, thou art conjuror laureat,
Thou canst command great Mephistophilis:
Quin regis Mephistophilis fratris imagine.[3]

Re-enter MEPHISTOPHILIS [*like a Franciscan* Friar]

MEPH. Now, Faustus, what would'st thou have me to do?
FAUST. I charge thee wait upon me whilst I live,
To do whatever Faustus shall command,
Be it to make the moon drop from her sphere,
Or the ocean to overwhelm the world.

---

[1] Wandering.
[2] "Be propitious to me, gods of Acheron! May the triple deity of Jehovah prevail! Spirits of fire, air, water, hail! Belzebub, Prince of the East, monarch of burning hell, and Demogorgon, we propitiate ye, that Mephistophilis may appear and rise. Why dost thou delay? By Jehovah, Gehenna, and the holy water which now I sprinkle, and the sign of the cross which now I make, and by our prayer, may Mephistophilis now summoned by us arise!"
[3] "For indeed thou hast power in the image of thy brother Mephistophilis."

MEPH. I am a servant to great Lucifer,
And may not follow thee without his leave
No more than he commands must we perform.
    FAUST. Did not he charge thee to appear to me?
    MEPH. No, I came hither of mine own accord.
    FAUST. Did not my conjuring speeches raise thee?   Speak.
    MEPH. That was the cause, but yet *per accidens;*
For when we hear one rack[4] the name of God,
Abjure the Scriptures and his Saviour Christ,
We fly in hope to get his glorious soul:
Nor will we come, unless he use such means
Whereby he is in danger to be damn'd:
Therefore the shortest cut for conjuring
Is stoutly to abjure the Trinity,
And pray devoutly to the Prince of Hell.
    FAUST. So Faustus hath
Already done; and holds this principle,
There is no chief but only Belzebub,
To whom Faustus doth dedicate himself.
This word " damnation " terrifies not him,
For he confounds hell in Elysium;[5]
His ghost be with the old philosophers!
But, leaving these vain trifles of men's souls,
Tell me what is that Lucifer thy lord?
    MEPH. Arch-regent and commander of all spirits.
    FAUST. Was not that Lucifer an angel once?
    MEPH. Yes, Faustus, and most dearly lov'd of God.
    FAUST. How comes it then that he is Prince of devils?
    MEPH. O, by aspiring pride and insolence;
For which God threw him from the face of Heaven.
    FAUST. And what are you that you live with Lucifer?
    MEPH. Unhappy spirits that fell with Lucifer,
Conspir'd against our God with Lucifer,
And are for ever damn'd with Lucifer.
    FAUST. Where are you damn'd?
    MEPH. In hell.
    FAUST. How comes it then that thou art out of hell?
    MEPH. Why this is hell, nor am I out of it.
Think'st thou that I who saw the face of God,

---

[4] Twist in anagrams.   [5] Heaven and hell are indifferent to him.

And tasted the eternal joys of Heaven,
Am not tormented with ten thousand hells,
In being depriv'd of everlasting bliss?
O Faustus! leave these frivolous demands,
Which strike a terror to my fainting soul.

FAUST. What, is great Mephistophilis so passionate
For being depriv'd of the joys of Heaven?
Learn thou of Faustus manly fortitude,
And scorn those joys thou never shalt possess.
Go bear these tidings to great Lucifer:
Seeing Faustus hath incurr'd eternal death
By desperate thoughts against Jove's deïty,
Say he surrenders up to him his soul,
So he will spare him four and twenty years,
Letting him live in all voluptuousness;
Having thee ever to attend on me;
To give me whatsoever I shall ask,
To tell me whatsoever I demand,
To slay mine enemies, and aid my friends,
And always be obedient to my will.
Go and return to mighty Lucifer,
And meet me in my study at midnight,
And then resolve[6] me of thy master's mind.

MEPH. I will, Faustus.   *Exit.*

FAUST. Had I as many souls as there be stars,
I'd give them all for Mephistophilis.
By him I'll be great Emperor of the world,
And make a bridge through the moving air,
To pass the ocean with a band of men:
I'll join the hills that bind the Afric shore,
And make that [country] continent to Spain,
And both contributory to my crown.
The Emperor shall not live but by my leave,
Nor any potentate of Germany.
Now that I have obtain'd what I desire,
I'll live in speculation[7] of this art
Till Mephistophilis return again.   *Exit.*

[6] Inform.   [7] Study.

[SCENE IV.—*A Street*.]

Enter WAGNER *and* CLOWN

WAG. Sirrah, boy, come hither.

CLOWN. How, boy! Swowns,[1] boy! I hope you have seen many boys with such pickadevaunts[2] as I have. Boy, quotha!

WAG. Tell me, sirrah, hast thou any comings in?

CLOWN. Ay, and goings out too. You may see else.

WAG. Alas, poor slave! See how poverty jesteth in his nakedness! The villain is bare and out of service, and so hungry that I know he would give his soul to the devil for a shoulder of mutton, though it were blood-raw.

CLOWN. How? My soul to the Devil for a shoulder of mutton, though 'twere blood-raw! Not so, good friend. By'r Lady, I had need have it well roasted and good sauce to it, if I pay so dear.

WAG. Well, wilt thou serve me, and I'll make thee go like *Qui mihi discipulus?*[3]

CLOWN. How, in verse?

WAG. No, sirrah; in beaten silk and stavesacre.[4]

CLOWN. How, how, Knave's acre![5] Ay, I thought that was all the land his father left him. Do you hear? I would be sorry to rob you of your living.

WAG. Sirrah, I say in stavesacre.

CLOWN. Oho! Oho! Stavesacre! Why, then, belike if I were your man I should be full of vermin.

WAG. So thou shalt, whether thou beest with me or no. But, sirrah, leave your jesting, and bind yourself presently unto me for seven years, or I'll turn all the lice about thee into familiars, and they shall tear thee in pieces.

CLOWN. Do you hear, sir? You may save that labour; they are too familiar with me already. Swowns! they are as bold with my flesh as if they had paid for [their] meat and drink.

---

[1] Zounds, *i. e.*, God's wounds.
[2] Beards cut to a sharp point (Fr. *pic-à-devant*).
[3] Dyce points out that these are the first words of W. Lily's "*Ad discipulos carmen de moribus.*"
[4] A kind of larkspur, used for destroying lice.
[5] A mean street in London.

WAG. Well, do you hear, sirrah? Hold, take these
guilders. [*Gives money.*]

CLOWN. Gridirons! what be they?

WAG. Why, French crowns.

CLOWN. Mass, but for the name of French crowns, a man
were as good have as many English counters. And what
should I do with these?

WAG. Why, now, sirrah, thou art at an hour's warning,
whensoever and wheresoever the Devil shall fetch thee.

CLOWN. No, no. Here, take your gridirons again.

WAG. Truly I'll none of them.

CLOWN. Truly but you shall.

WAG. Bear witness I gave them him.

CLOWN. Bear witness I gave them you again.

WAG. Well, I will cause two devils presently to fetch
thee away—Baliol and Belcher.

CLOWN. Let your Baliol and your Belcher come here, and
I'll knock them, they were never so knock'd since they were
devils. Say I should kill one of them, what would folks say?
"Do you see yonder tall fellow in the round slop⁶—he has
kill'd the devil." So I should be called Kill-devil all the
parish over.

Enter two Devils: *the* Clown *runs up and down crying*

WAG. Baliol and Belcher! Spirits, away! *Exeunt* Devils.

CLOWN. What, are they gone? A vengeance on them,
they have vile long nails! There was a he-devil, and a she-
devil! I'll tell you how you shall know them: all he-devils
has horns, and all she-devils has clifts and cloven feet.

WAG. Well, sirrah, follow me.

CLOWN. But, do you hear—if I should serve you, would you
teach me to raise up Banios and Belcheos?

WAG. I will teach thee to turn thyself to anything; to a
dog, or a cat, or a mouse, or a rat, or anything.

CLOWN. How! a Christian fellow to a dog or a cat, a
mouse or a rat! No, no, sir. If you turn me into anything,
let it be in the likeness of a little pretty frisky flea, that I may
be here and there and everywhere. Oh, I'll tickle the pretty
wenches' plackets; I'll be amongst them, i' faith.

⁶ Short wide breeches.

WAG. Well, sirrah, come.

CLOWN. But, do you hear, Wagner?

WAG. How! Baliol and Belcher!

CLOWN. O Lord! I pray, sir, let Banio and Belcher go
    sleep.

WAG. Villain—call me Master Wagner, and let thy left
eye be diametarily[7] fixed upon my right heel, with *quasi ves-
tigias nostras insistere.*[8]   *Exit.*

CLOWN. God forgive me, he speaks Dutch fustian. Well,
I'll follow him, I'll serve him, that's flat.   *Exit.*

[SCENE V.]

FAUSTUS [*discovered*] *in his Study*

FAUST. Now, Faustus, must

Thou needs be damn'd, and canst thou not be sav'd:

What boots it then to think of God or Heaven?

Away with such vain fancies, and despair:

Despair in God, and trust in Belzebub.

Now go not backward: no, Faustus, be resolute.

Why waverest thou? O, something soundeth in mine ears

"Abjure this magic, turn to God again!"

Ay, and Faustus will turn to God again.

To God?—He loves thee not—

The God thou serv'st is thine own appetite,

Wherein is fix'd the love of Belzebub;

To him I'll build an altar and a church,

And offer lukewarm blood of new-born babes.

Enter GOOD ANGEL *and* EVIL ANGEL

G. ANG. Sweet Faustus, leave that execrable art.

FAUST. Contrition, prayer, repentance! What of them?

G. ANG. O, they are means to bring thee unto Heaven.

E. ANG. Rather, illusions, fruits of lunacy,

That makes men foolish that do trust them most.

G. ANG. Sweet Faustus, think of Heaven, and heavenly
    things.

[7] For diametrically.   [8] "As if to tread in my tracks."

E. ANG. No, Faustus, think of honour and of wealth.

[*Exeunt* ANGELS.

FAUST. Of wealth!
What the signiory of Embden[1] shall be mine.
When Mephistophilis shall stand by me,
What God can hurt thee, Faustus? Thou art safe;
Cast no more doubts. Come, Mephistophilis,
And bring glad tidings from great Lucifer;—
Is't not midnight? Come, Mephistophilis;
Veni, veni, Mephistophile!

Enter MEPHISTOPHILIS

Now tell me, what says Lucifer thy lord?
MEPH. That I shall wait on Faustus whilst he lives,
So he will buy my service with his soul.
FAUST. Already Faustus hath hazarded that for thee.
MEPH. But, Faustus, thou must bequeath it solemnly,
And write a deed of gift with thine own blood,
For that security craves great Lucifer.
If thou deny it, I will back to hell.
FAUST. Stay, Mephistophilis! and tell me what good
Will my soul do thy lord.
MEPH. Enlarge his kingdom.
FAUST. Is that the reason why he tempts us thus?
MEPH. *Solamen miseris socios habuisse doloris.*[2]
FAUST. Why, have you any pain that torture others?
MEPH. As great as have the human souls of men.
But tell me, Faustus, shall I have thy soul?
And I will be thy slave, and wait on thee,
And give thee more than thou hast wit to ask.
FAUST. Ay, Mephistophilis, I give it thee.
MEPH. Then, Faustus, stab thine arm courageously.
And bind thy soul that at some certain day
Great Lucifer may claim it as his own;
And then be thou as great as Lucifer.
FAUST. [*stabbing his arm.*] Lo, Mephistophilis, for love
of thee,
I cut mine arm, and with my proper blood

---

[1] Emden, near the mouth of the river Ems, was an important commercial town in Elizabethan times. [2] "Misery loves company."

Assure my soul to be great Lucifer's,
Chief lord and regent of perpetual night!
View here the blood that trickles from mine arm.
And let it be propitious for my wish.
    MEPH. But, Faustus, thou must
Write it in manner of a deed of gift.
    FAUST. Ay, so I will. [*Writes.*]   But, Mephistophilis,
My blood congeals, and I can write no more.
    MEPH. I'll fetch thee fire to dissolve it straight.   *Exit.*
    FAUST. What might the staying of my blood portend?
Is it unwilling I should write this bill?
Why streams it not that I may write afresh?
Faustus gives to thee his soul. Ah, there it stay'd.
Why should'st thou not? Is not thy soul thine own?
Then write again, *Faustus gives to thee his soul.*

    Re-enter MEPHISTOPHILIS *with a chafer of coals*
    MEPH. Here's fire. Come, Faustus, set it on.
    FAUST. So now the blood begins to clear again;
Now will I make an end immediately.   [*Writes.*]
    MEPH. O what will not I do to obtain his soul. [*Aside.*]
    FAUST. *Consummatum est:*[3] this bill is ended,
And Faustus hath bequeath'd his soul to Lucifer—
But what is this inscription on mine arm?
Homo, fuge![4] Whither should I fly?
If unto God, he'll throw me down to hell.
My senses are deceiv'd; here's nothing writ:—
I see it plain; here in this place is writ
Homo, fuge! Yet shall not Faustus fly.
    MEPH. I'll fetch him somewhat to delight his mind. [*Exit.*

    Re-enter [MEPHISTOPHILIS] *with* Devils, *giving crowns*
        and rich apparel to FAUSTUS, *dance, and depart*
    FAUST. Speak, Mephistophilis, what means this show?
    MEPH. Nothing, Faustus, but to delight thy mind withal,
And to show thee what magic can perform.
    FAUST. But may I raise up spirits when I please?

            [3] " It is finished."   [4] " Man, fly! "

MEPH. Ay, Faustus, and do greater things than these.

FAUST. Then there's enough for a thousand souls.
Here, Mephistophilis, receive this scroll,
A deed of gift of body and of soul:
But yet conditionally that thou perform
All articles prescrib'd between us both.

MEPH. Faustus, I swear by hell and Lucifer
To effect all promises between us made.

FAUST. Then hear me read them: *On these conditions
following. First, that Faustus may be a spirit in form
and substance. Secondly, that Mephistophilis shall be his
servant, and at his command. Thirdly, that Mephistophilis
shall do for him and bring him whatsoever [he desires].
Fourthly, that he shall be in his chamber or house invisible.
Lastly, that he shall appear to the said John Faustus, at all
times, and in what form or shape soever he pleases. I, John
Faustus, of Wittenberg, Doctor, by these presents do give
both body and soul to Lucifer, Prince of the East, and his
minister, Mephistophilis; and furthermore grant unto them,
that twenty-four years being expired, the articles above
written inviolate, full power to fetch or carry the said John
Faustus, body and soul, flesh, blood, or goods, into their
habitation wheresoever. By me,* John Faustus.

MEPH. Speak, Faustus, do you deliver this as your deed?

FAUST. Ay, take it, and the Devil give thee good on't.

MEPH. Now, Faustus, ask what thou wilt.

FAUST. First will I question with thee about hell.
Tell me where is the place that men call hell?

MEPH. Under the Heaven.

FAUST. Ay, but whereabout?

MEPH. Within the bowels of these elements,
Where we are tortur'd and remain for ever;
Hell hath no limits, nor is circumscrib'd
In one self place; for where we are is hell,
And where hell is there must we ever be:
And, to conclude, when all the world dissolves,
And every creature shall be purified,
All places shall be hell that is not Heaven.

FAUST. Come, I think hell's a fable.

MEPH. Ay, think so still, till experience change thy mind.

FAUST. Why, think'st thou then that Faustus shall be
    damn'd?
MEPH. Ay, of necessity, for here's the scroll
Wherein thou hast given thy soul to Lucifer.
    FAUST. Ay, and body too; but what of that?
Think'st thou that Faustus is so fond[5] to imagine
That, after this life, there is any pain?
Tush; these are trifles, and mere old wives' tales.
    MEPH. But, Faustus, I am an instance to prove the con-
    trary,
For I am damned, and am now in hell.
    FAUST. How! now in hell!
Nay, an this be hell, I'll willingly be damn'd here;
What? walking, disputing, &c.?
But, leaving off this, let me have a wife,
The fairest maid in Germany;
For I am wanton and lascivious,
And cannot live without a wife.
    MEPH. How—a wife?
I prithee, Faustus, talk not of a wife.
    FAUST. Nay, sweet Mephistophilis, fetch me one, for I
    will have one.
    MEPH. Well—thou wilt have one. Sit there till I come:
I'll fetch thee a wife in the Devil's name.   [*Exit.*]

Re-enter MEPHISTOPHILIS *with a* Devil *dressed like a woman,
                with fireworks*
    MEPH. Tell me, Faustus, how dost thou like thy wife?
    FAUST. A plague on her for a hot whore!
    MEPH. Tut, Faustus,
Marriage is but a ceremonial toy;
And if thou lovest me, think no more of it.
I'll cull thee out the fairest courtesans,
And bring them every morning to thy bed;
She whom thine eye shall like, thy heart shall have,
Be she as chaste as was Penelope,
As wise as Saba,[6] or as beautiful
As was bright Lucifer before his fall.

        [5] Foolish.   [6] The Queen of Sheba.

Here, take this book, peruse it thoroughly: [*Gives a book.*]
The iterating⁷ of these lines brings gold;
The framing of this circle on the ground
Brings whirlwinds, tempests, thunder and lightning;
Pronounce this thrice devoutly to thyself,
And men in armour shall appear to thee,
Ready to execute what thou desir'st.

FAUST. Thanks, Mephistophilis; yet fain would I have
a book wherein I might behold all spells and incantations,
that I might raise up spirits when I please.

MEPH. Here they are, in this book.   '*Turns to them.*

FAUST. Now would I have a book where I might see
all characters and planets of the heavens, that I might know
their motions and dispositions.

MEPH. Here they are too.   *Turns to them.*

FAUST. Nay, let me have one book more,—and then I
have done,—wherein I might see all plants, herbs, and trees
that grow upon the earth.

MEPH. Here they be.

FAUST. O, thou art deceived.

MEPH. Tut, I warrant thee.   *Turns to them. Exeunt.*

[SCENE VI.—*The Same.*]

Enter FAUSTUS *and* MEPHISTOPHILIS

FAUST. When I behold the heavens, then I repent,
And curse thee, wicked Mephistophilis,
Because thou hast depriv'd me of those joys.

MEPH. Why, Faustus,
Thinkest thou Heaven is such a glorious thing?
I tell thee 'tis not half so fair as thou,
Or any man that breathes on earth.

FAUST. How provest thou that?

MEPH. 'Twas made for man, therefore is man more excellent.

FAUST. If it were made for man, 'twas made for me:
I will renounce this magic and repent.

Enter GOOD ANGEL *and* EVIL ANGEL

G. ANG. Faustus, repent; yet God will pity thee.

⁷ Repeating.

E. Ang. Thou art a spirit; God can not pity thee.

Faust. Who buzzeth in mine ears I am a spirit?
Be I a devil, yet God may pity me;
Ay, God will pity me if I repent.

E. Ang. Ay, but Faustus never shall repent.

Exeunt Angels.

Faust. My heart's so hard'ned I cannot repent.
Scarce can I name salvation, faith, or heaven,
But fearful echoes thunder in mine ears
"Faustus, thou art damn'd!" Then swords and knives,
Poison, gun, halters, and envenom'd steel
Are laid before me to despatch myself,
And long ere this I should have slain myself,
Had not sweet pleasure conquer'd deep despair.
Have I not made blind Homer sing to me
Of Alexander's love and Œnon's death?
And hath not he that built the walls of Thebes
With ravishing sound of his melodious harp,
Made music with my Mephistophilis?
Why should I die then, or basely despair?
I am resolv'd: Faustus shall ne'er repent.
Come, Mephistophilis, let us dispute again,
And argue of divine astrology.
Tell me, are there many heavens above the moon?
Are all celestial bodies but one globe,
As is the substance of this centric earth?

Meph. As are the elements, such are the spheres
Mutually folded in each other's orb,
And, Faustus,
All jointly move upon one axletree
Whose terminine is termed the world's wide pole;
Nor are the names of Saturn, Mars, or Jupiter
Feign'd, but are erring stars.

Faust. But tell me, have they all one motion, both *situ
et tempore?*[1]

Meph. All jointly move from east to west in twenty-four
hours upon the poles of the world; but differ in their motion
upon the poles of the zodiac.

Faust. Tush!

[1] "In direction and in time?"

These slender trifles Wagner can decide;
Hath Mephistophilis no greater skill?
Who knows not the double motion of the planets?
The first is finish'd in a natural day;
The second thus: as Saturn in thirty years; Jupiter in
twelve; Mars in four; the Sun, Venus, and Mercury in a
year; the moon in twenty-eight days. Tush, these are fresh-
men's suppositions. But tell me, hath every sphere a dominion or *intelligentia?*

MEPH. Ay.

FAUST. How many heavens, or spheres, are there?

MEPH. Nine: the seven planets, the firmament, and the
empyreal heaven.

FAUST. Well, resolve me in this question: Why have we not
conjunctions, oppositions, aspects, eclipses, all at one time,
but in some years we have more, in some less?

MEPH. *Per inæqualem motum respectu totius.*[2]

FAUST. Well, I am answered. Tell me who made the
    world.

MEPH. I will not.

FAUST. Sweet Mephistophilis, tell me.

MEPH. Move me not, for I will not tell thee.

FAUST. Villain, have I not bound thee to tell me anything?

MEPH. Ay, that is not against our kingdom; but this is.
Think thou on hell, Faustus, for thou art damn'd.

FAUST. Think, Faustus, upon God that made the world.

MEPH. Remember this.

FAUST. Ay, go, accursed spirit, to ugly hell.
'Tis thou hast damn'd distressed Faustus' soul.
Is't not too late?

> *Re-enter* GOOD ANGEL *and* EVIL ANGEL.

E. ANG. Too late.

G. ANG. Never too late, if Faustus can repent.

E. ANG. If thou repent, devils shall tear thee in pieces.

G. ANG. Repent, and they shall never raze thy skin.

> [*Exeunt* ANGELS.]

FAUST. Ah, Christ, my Saviour,
Seek to save distressed Faustus' soul.

---

[2] "On account of their unequal motion in relation to the whole."

Enter LUCIFER, BELZEBUB, *and* MEPHISTOPHILIS.

LUC. Christ cannot save thy soul, for he is just;
There's none but I have interest in the same.

FAUST. O, who art thou that look'st so terrible?

LUC. I am Lucifer,
And this is my companion-prince in hell.

FAUST. O Faustus! they are come to fetch away thy soul!

LUC. We come to tell thee thou dost injure us;
Thou talk'st of Christ contrary to thy promise;
Thou should'st not think of God: think of the Devil,
And of his dam, too.

FAUST. Nor will I henceforth: pardon me in this,
And Faustus vows never to look to Heaven,
Never to name God, or to pray to him,
To burn his Scriptures, slay his ministers,
And make my spirits pull his churches down.

LUC. Do so, and we will highly gratify thee. Faustus,
we are come from hell to show thee some pastime. Sit down,
and thou shalt see all the Seven Deadly Sins appear in their
proper shapes.

FAUST. That sight will be as pleasing unto me,
As Paradise was to Adam the first day
Of his creation.

LUC. Talk not of Paradise nor creation, but mark this
show: talk of the Devil, and nothing else.—Come away!

Enter the SEVEN DEADLY SINS.

Now, Faustus, examine them of their several names and
dispositions.

FAUST. What art thou—the first?

PRIDE. I am Pride. I disdain to have any parents. I am
like to Ovid's flea: I can creep into every corner of a wench;
sometimes, like a periwig, I sit upon her brow; or like a fan
of feathers, I kiss her lips; indeed I do—what do I not?
But, fie, what a scent is here! I'll not speak another word,
except the ground were perfum'd, and covered with cloth
of arras.

FAUST. What art thou—the second?

COVET. I am Covetousness, begotten of an old churl in

an old leathern bag; and might I have my wish I would desire that this house and all the people in it were turn'd to gold, that I might lock you up in my good chest. O, my sweet gold!

FAUST. What art thou—the third?

WRATH. I am Wrath. I had neither father nor mother: I leapt out of a lion's mouth when I was scarce half an hour old; and ever since I have run up and down the world with this case[8] of rapiers, wounding myself when I had nobody to fight withal. I was born in hell; and look to it, for some of you shall be my father.

FAUST. What art thou—the fourth?

ENVY. I am Envy, begotten of a chimney sweeper and an oyster-wife. I cannot read, and therefore wish all books were burnt. I am lean with seeing others eat. O that there would come a famine through all the world, that all might die, and I live alone! then thou should'st see how fat I would be. But must thou sit and I stand! Come down with a vengeance!

FAUST. Away, envious rascal! What art thou—the fifth?

GLUT. Who, I, sir? I am Gluttony. My parents are all dead, and the devil a penny they have left me, but a bare pension, and that is thirty meals a day and ten bevers[4]—a small trifle to suffice nature. O, I come of a royal parentage! My grandfather was a Gammon of Bacon, my grandmother a Hogshead of Claret-wine; my godfathers were these, Peter Pickleherring, and Martin Martlemas-beef.[5] O, but my god-mother, she was a jolly gentlewoman, and well beloved in every good town and city; her name was Mistress Margery March-beer. Now, Faustus, thou hast heard all my progeny, wilt thou bid me to supper?

FAUST. No, I'll see thee hanged: thou wilt eat up all my victuals.

GLUT. Then the Devil choke thee!

FAUST. Choke thyself, glutton! Who art thou—the sixth?

SLOTH. I am Sloth. I was begotten on a sunny bank, where I have lain ever since; and you have done me great injury to bring me from thence: let me be carried thither

[8] Pair. [4] Refreshments between meals.
[5] Martlemas or Martinmas was "the customary time for hanging up provisions to dry which had been salted for the winter."—*Nares.*

again by Gluttony and Lechery. I'll not speak another word
for a king's ransom.

FAUST. What are you, Mistress Minx, the seventh and
  last?

LECH. Who, I, sir? I am one that loves an inch of raw
mutton better than an ell of fried stockfish; and the first
letter of my name begins with Lechery.

LUC. Away to hell, to hell!—Now, Faustus, how dost thou
  like this? [*Exeunt the* SINS.

FAUST. O, this feeds my soul!

LUC. Tut, Faustus, in hell is all manner of delight.

FAUST. O might I see hell, and return again,
How happy were I then!

LUC. Thou shalt; I will send for thee at midnight.
In meantime take this book; peruse it throughly,
And thou shalt turn thyself into what shape thou wilt.

FAUST. Great thanks, mighty Lucifer!
This will I keep as chary as my life.

LUC. Farewell, Faustus, and think on the Devil.

FAUST. Farewell, great Lucifer! Come, Mephistophilis.
                                         [*Exeunt.*

Enter CHORUS

CHORUS. Learned Faustus,
To know the secrets of astronomy,
Graven in the book of Jove's high firmament,
Did mount himself to scale Olympus' top,
Being seated in a chariot burning bright,
Drawn by the strength of yoky dragons' necks.
He now is gone to prove cosmography,
And, as I guess, will first arrive at Rome,
To see the Pope and manner of his court,
And take some part of holy Peter's feast,
That to this day is highly solemnis'd. [*Exit*

[SCENE VII.—*The Pope's Privy-chamber.*]

Enter FAUSTUS *and* MEPHISTOPHILIS

FAUST. Having now, my good Mephistophilis,
Passed with delight the stately town of Trier,[1]

---

[1] Treves.

Environ'd round with airy mountain-tops,
With walls of flint, and deep entrenched lakes,
Not to be won by any conquering prince;
From Paris next, coasting the realm of France,
We saw the river Maine fall into Rhine,
Whose banks are set with groves of fruitful vines;
Then up to Naples, rich Campania,
Whose buildings fair and gorgeous to the eye,
The streets straight forth, and pav'd with finest brick,
Quarter the town in four equivalents.
There saw we learned Maro's[2] golden tomb,
The way he cut, an English mile in length,
Thorough a rock of stone in one night's space;
From thence to Venice, Padua, and the rest,
In one of which a sumptuous temple stands,
That threats the stars with her aspiring top.
Thus hitherto has Faustus spent his time:
But tell me, now, what resting-place is this?
Hast thou, as erst I did command,
Conducted me within the walls of Rome?

MEPH. Faustus, I have; and because we will not be un-
provided, I have taken up his Holiness' privy-chamber for
our use.

FAUST. I hope his Holiness will bid us welcome.

MEPH. Tut, 'tis no matter, man, we'll be bold with his
good cheer.
And now, my Faustus, that thou may'st perceive
What Rome containeth to delight thee with,
Know that this city stands upon seven hills
That underprop the groundwork of the same.
[Just through the midst runs flowing Tiber's stream,
With winding banks that cut it in two parts:]
Over the which four stately bridges lean,
That make safe passage to each part of Rome:
Upon the bridge called Ponto Angelo
Erected is a castle passing strong,
Within whose walls such store of ordnance are,
And double cannons fram'd of carved brass,

---

[2] Virgil, who was reputed a magician in the Middle Ages, was buried
at Naples.

As match the days within one còmplete year;
Besides the gates and high pyramides,
Which Julius Cæsar brought from Africa.

FAUST. Now by the kingdoms of infernal rule,
Of Styx, of Acheron, and the fiery lake
Of ever-burning Phlegethon, I swear
That I do long to see the monuments
And situation of bright-splendent Rome:
Come therefore, let's away.

MEPH. Nay, Faustus, stay; I know. you'd see the Pope,
And take some part of holy Peter's feast,
Where thou shalt see a troop of bald-pate friars,
Whose *summum bonum* is in belly-cheer.

FAUST. Well, I'm content to compass then some sport,
And by their folly make us merriment.
Then charm me, [Mephistophilis,] that I
May be invisible, to do what I please
Unseen of any whilst I stay in Rome.

                        [MEPHISTOPHILIS *charms him.*]

MEPH. So. Faustus, now
Do what thou wilt, thou shalt not be discern'd.

Sound a sennet.[3] *Enter the* POPE *and the* CARDINAL *of*
    LORRAIN *to the banquet, with* FRIARS *attending*

POPE. My Lord of Lorrain, wilt please you draw near?
FAUST. Fall to, and the devil choke you an[4] you spare!
POPE. How now! Who's that which spake?—Friars, look
    about.
FIRST FRIAR. Here's nobody, if it like your Holiness.
POPE. My lord, here is a dainty dish was sent me from the
Bishop of Milan.
FAUST. I thank you, sir.   [*Snatches the dish.*]
POPE. How now! Who's that which snatched the meat
from me? Will no man look? My Lord, this dish was sent
me from the Cardinal of Florence.
FAUST. You say true; I'll ha't.   [*Snatches the dish.*]
POPE. What, again! My lord, I'll drink to your Grace.
FAUST. I'll pledge your Grace.   [*Snatches the cup.*]

---

[3] A particular set of notes on the trumpet or cornet, different from a
flourish."—*Nares.*
[4] If.

C. OF LOR. My lord, it may be some ghost newly crept out of purgatory, come to beg a pardon of your Holiness.

POPE. It may be so. Friars, prepare a dirge to lay the fury of this ghost. Once again, my lord, fall to.

The POPE *crosses himself.*

FAUST. What, are you crossing of yourself? Well, use that trick no more I would advise you.

The POPE *crosses himself again.*

Well, there's the second time. Aware the third, I give you fair warning.

The POPE *crosses himself again, and* FAUSTUS *hits him a box 'f the ear; and they all run away.*

Come on, Mephistophilis, what shall we do?

MEPH. Nay, I know not. We shall be curs'd with bell, book, and candle.

FAUST. How! bell, book, and candle,—candle, book, and bell, Forward and backward to curse Faustus to hell! Anon you shall hear a hog grunt, a calf bleat, and an ass bray, Because it is Saint Peter's holiday.

Re-enter all the FRIARS *to sing the Dirge*

1ST. FRIAR. Come, brethren, let's about our business with good devotion.

They sing:

Cursed be he that stole away his Holiness' meat from the table! *Maledicat Dominus!*[5]

Cursed be he that struck his Holiness a blow on the face! *Maledicat Dominus!*

Cursed be he that took Friar Sandelo a blow on the pate! *Maledicat Dominus!*

Cursed be he that disturbeth our holy dirge! *Maledicat Dominus!*

Cursed be he that took away his Holiness' wine! *Maledicat Dominus! Et omnes sancti!*[6] *Amen!*

[MEPHISTOPHILIS *and* FAUSTUS *beat the* FRIARS, *and fling fireworks among them: and so exeunt.*

[5] "May the Lord curse him."   [6] And all the saints."

Enter CHORUS

CHORUS. When Faustus had with pleasure ta'en the view
Of rarest things, and royal courts of kings,
He stay'd his course, and so returned home;
Where such as bear his absence but with grief,
I mean his friends, and near'st companions,
Did gratulate his safety with kind words,
And in their conference of what befell,
Touching his journey through the world and air,
They put forth questions of Astrology,
Which Faustus answer'd with such learned skill,
As they admir'd and wond'red at his wit.
Now is his fame spread forth in every land;
Amongst the rest the Emperor is one,
Carolus the Fifth, at whose palace now
Faustus is feasted 'mongst his noblemen.
What there he did in trial of his art,
I leave untold—your eyes shall see perform'd.   [*Exit.*]

[SCENE VIII.—*An Inn-yard.*]

Enter ROBIN *the Ostler with a book in his hand*

ROBIN. O, this is admirable! here I ha' stolen one of Dr. Faustus's conjuring books, and i' faith I mean to search some circles for my own use. Now will I make all the maidens in our parish dance at my pleasure, stark naked before me; and so by that means I shall see more than e'er I felt or saw yet.

Enter RALPH *calling* ROBIN

RALPH. Robin, prithee come away; there's a gentleman tarries to have his horse, and he would have his things rubb'd and made clean. He keeps such a chafing with my mistress about it; and she has sent me to look thee out; prithee come away.

ROBIN. Keep out, keep out, or else you are blown up; you

are dismemb'red, Ralph: keep out, for I am about a roaring piece of work.

RALPH. Come, what dost thou with that same book? Thou canst not read.

ROBIN. Yes, my master and mistress shall find that I can read, he for his forehead, she for her private study; she's born to bear with me, or else my art fails.

RALPH. Why, Robin, what book is that?

ROBIN. What book! Why, the most intolerable book for conjuring that e'er was invented by any brimstone devil.

RALPH. Canst thou conjure with it?

ROBIN. I can do all these things easily with it: first, I can make thee drunk with ippocras[1] at any tabern[2] in Europe for nothing; that's one of my conjuring works.

RALPH. Our Master Parson says that's nothing.

ROBIN. True, Ralph; and more, Ralph, if thou hast any mind to Nan Spit, our kitchenmaid, then turn her and wind her to thy own use as often as thou wilt, and at midnight.

RALPH. O brave Robin, shall I have Nan Spit, and to mine own use? On that condition I'll feed thy devil with horsebread as long as he lives, of free cost.

ROBIN. No more, sweet Ralph: let's go and make clean our boots, which lie foul upon our hands, and then to our conjuring in the Devil's name. *Exeunt.*

[SCENE IX.—*An Inn.*]

Enter ROBIN *and* RALPH *with a silver goblet.*

ROBIN. Come, Ralph, did not I tell thee we were for ever made by this Doctor Faustus' book? *Ecce signum,*[1] here's a simple purchase[2] for horsekeepers; our horses shall eat no hay as long as this lasts.

Enter the VINTNER

RALPH. But, Robin, here come the vintner.

ROBIN. Hush! I'll gull him supernaturally.

---

[1] Wine mixed with sugar and spices.   [2] Tavern.
[1] " Behold a sign.   [2] Gain.

Drawer, I hope all is paid: God be with you. Come, Ralph.

VINT. Soft, sir; a word with you. I must yet have a goblet paid from you, ere you go.

ROBIN. I, a goblet, Ralph; I, a goblet! I scorn you, and you are but a,[3] &c. I, a goblet! search me.

VINT. I mean so, sir, with your favour.   [*Searches him.*]

ROBIN. How say you now?

VINT. I must say somewhat to your fellow. You, sir!

RALPH. Me, sir! me, sir! search your fill. [VINTNER *searches him.*] Now, sir, you may be ashamed to burden honest men with a matter of truth.

VINT. Well, t'one of you hath this goblet about you.

ROBIN. You lie, drawer, 'tis afore me. [*Aside.*]   Sirrah you, I'll teach ye to impeach honest men;—stand by;—I'll scour you for a goblet!—stand aside you had best, I charge you in the name of Belzebub. Look to the goblet, Ralph.

[*Aside to* RALPH.]

VINT. What mean you, sirrah?

ROBIN. I'll tell you what I mean.   *Reads* [*from a book.*] *Sanctobulorum. Periphrasticon*—Nay, I'll tickle you, vintner. Look to the goblet, Ralph.   [*Aside to* RALPH.]
Polypragmos Belseborams framanto pacostiphos tostu, Mephistophilis, &c.   [*Reads.*

Enter MEPHISTOPHILIS, *sets squibs at their backs,* [*and then exit*]. *They run about*

VINT. *O nomine Domini!*[4] what meanest thou, Robin? Thou hast no goblet.

RALPH. *Peccatum peccatorum!*[5] Here's thy goblet, good vintner.   [*Gives the goblet to* VINTNER, *who exit.*]

ROBIN. *Misericordia pro nobis!*[6] What shall I do? Good Devil, forgive me now, and I'll never rob thy library more.

Re-enter MEPHISTOPHILIS

MEPH. Monarch of hell, under whose black survey
Great potentates do kneel with awful fear,

[3] The abuse was left to the actor's inventiveness.
[4] "In the name of the Lord."   [5] "Sin of sins."   [6] "Mercy on us."

Upon whose altars thousand souls do lie,
How am I vexed with these villains' charms?
From Constantinople am I hither come
Only for pleasure of these damned slaves.

ROBIN. How from Constantinople? You have had a great journey. Will you take sixpence in your purse to pay for your supper, and begone?

MEPH. Well, villains, for your presumption, I transform thee into an ape, and thee into a dog; and so begone. [*Exit.*

ROBIN. How, into an ape? That's brave! I'll have fine sport with the boys. I'll get nuts and apples enow.

RALPH. And I must be a dog.

ROBIN. I'faith thy head will never be out of the pottage pot. *Exeunt.*

[SCENE X.—*The Court of the Emperor.*]

Enter EMPEROR, FAUSTUS, *and a* KNIGHT *with attendants*

EMP. Master Doctor Faustus, I have heard strange report of thy knowledge in the black art, how that none in my empire nor in the whole world can compare with thee for the rare effects of magic; they say thou hast a familiar spirit, by whom thou canst accomplish what thou list. This therefore is my request, that thou let me see some proof of thy skill, that mine eyes may be witnesses to confirm what mine ears have heard reported; and here I swear to thee by the honour of mine imperial crown, that, whatever thou doest, thou shalt be no ways prejudiced or endamaged.

KNIGHT. I'faith he looks much like a conjuror. *Aside.*

FAUST. My gracious sovereign, though I must confess myself far inferior to the report men have published, and nothing answerable[1] to the honour of your imperial majesty, yet for that love and duty binds me thereunto, I am content to do whatsoever your majesty shall command me.

EMP. Then, Doctor Faustus, mark what I shall say.
As I was sometime solitary set
Within my closet, sundry thoughts arose
About the honour of mine ancestors,

---

[1] Proportionate.

How they had won by prowess such exploits,
Got such riches, subdued so many kingdoms
As we that do succeed, or they that shall
Hereafter possess our throne, shall
(I fear me) ne'er attain to that degree
Of high renown and great authority;
Amongst which kings is Alexander the Great,
Chief spectacle of the world's pre-eminence,
The bright shining of whose glorious acts
Lightens the world with his[2] reflecting beams,
As when I heard but motion[3] made of him
It grieves my soul I never saw the man.
If therefore thou by cunning of thine art
Canst raise this man from hollow vaults below,
Where lies entomb'd this famous conqueror,
And bring with him his beauteous paramour,
Both in their right shapes, gesture, and attire
They us'd to wear during their time of life,
Thou shalt both satisfy my just desire,
And give me cause to praise thee whilst I live.

FAUST. My gracious lord, I am ready to accomplish your request so far forth as by art, and power of my Spirit, I am able to perform.

KNIGHT. I'faith that's just nothing at all. *Aside.*

FAUST. But, if it like your Grace, it is not in my ability to present before your eyes the true substantial bodies of those two deceased princes, which long since are consumed to dust.

KNIGHT. Ay, marry, Master Doctor, now there's a sign of grace in you, when you will confess the truth. *Aside.*

FAUST. But such spirits as can lively resemble Alexander and his paramour shall appear before your Grace in that manner that they [best] lived in, in their most flourishing estate; which I doubt not shall sufficiently content your imperial majesty.

EMP. Go to, Master Doctor, let me see them presently.

KNIGHT. Do you hear, Master Doctor? You bring Alexander and his paramour before the Emperor!

FAUST. How then, sir?

[2] Its.   [3] Mention.

KNIGHT. I'faith that's as true as Diana turn'd me to a stag!

FAUST. No, sir, but when Actæon died, he left the horns for you. Mephistophilis, begone.   *Exit* MEPHISTO.

KNIGHT. Nay, an you go to conjuring, I'll begone.   *Exit.*

FAUST. I'll meet with you anon for interrupting me so. Here they are, my gracious lord.

Re-enter MEPHISTOPHILIS *with* [SPIRITS *in the shape of*] ALEXANDER *and his* PARAMOUR

EMP. Master Doctor, I heard this lady while she liv'd had a wart or mole in her neck: how shall I know whether it be so or no?

FAUST. Your Highness may boldly go and see.

EMP. Sure these are no spirits, but the true substantial bodies of those two deceased princes.   [*Exeunt* Spirits.]

FAUST. Will't please your Highness now to send for the knight that was so pleasant with me here of late?

EMP. One of you call him forth.   [*Exit* Attendant.]

Re-enter the KNIGHT *with a pair of horns on his head*

How now, sir knight! why I had thought thou had'st been a bachelor, but now I see thou hast a wife, that not only gives thee horns, but makes thee wear them. Feel on thy head.

KNIGHT. Thou damned wretch and execrable dog,
Bred in the concave of some monstrous rock,
How darest thou thus abuse a gentleman?
Villain, I say, undo what thou hast done!

FAUST. O, not so fast, sir; there's no haste; but, good, are you rememb'red how you crossed me in my conference with the Emperor? I think I have met with you for it.

EMP. Good Master Doctor, at my entreaty release him; he hath done penance sufficient.

FAUST. My gracious lord, not so much for the injury he off'red me here in your presence, as to delight you with some mirth, hath Faustus worthily requited this injurious knight; which, being all I desire, I am content to release him of his horns: and, sir knight, hereafter speak well of scholars. Mephistophilis, transform him straight.   [MEPHISTOPHILIS *removes the horns.*] Now, my good lord, having done my duty I humbly take my leave.

EMP. Farewell, Master Doctor; yet, ere you go, Expect from me a bounteous reward.   [*Exeunt.*

[SCENE XI.—*A Green; afterwards the House of Faustus.*]

[*Enter* FAUSTUS *and* MEPHISTOPHILIS]

FAUST. Now, Mephistophilis, the restless course
That Time doth run with calm and silent foot,
Short'ning my days and thread of vital life,
Calls for the payment of my latest years;
Therefore, sweet Mephistophilis, let us
Make haste to Wittenberg.

MEPH. What, will you go on horseback or on foot?

FAUST. Nay, till I'm past this fair and pleasant green,
I'll walk on foot.

Enter a HORSE-COURSER

HORSE-C. I have been all this day seeking one Master Fustian: mass, see where he is! God save you, Master Doctor!

FAUST. What, horse-courser! You are well met.

HORSE-C. Do you hear, sir? I have brought you forty dollars for your horse.

FAUST. I cannot sell him so: if thou likest him for fifty take him.

HORSE-C. Alas, sir, I have no more.—I pray you speak for me.

MEPH. I pray you let him have him: he is an honest fellow, and he has a great charge, neither wife nor child.

FAUST. Well, come, give me your money. [HORSE-COURSER *gives* FAUSTUS *the money.*] My boy will deliver him to you. But I must tell you one thing before you have him; ride him not into the water at any hand.

HORSE-C. Why, sir, will he not drink of all waters?

FAUST. O yes, he will drink of all waters, but ride him not into the water: ride him over hedge or ditch, or where thou wilt, but not into the water.

HORSE-C. Well, sir.—Now I am made man for ever. I'll not leave my horse for forty. If he had but the quality of hey-ding-ding, hey-ding-ding, I'd made a brave living on him: he has a buttock as slick as an eel. [*Aside.*] Well, God b' wi' ye, sir, your boy will deliver him me: but hark you, sir; if my horse be sick or ill at ease, if I bring his water to you, you'll tell me what it is.

FAUST. Away, you villain; what, dost think I am a horse-doctor? *Exit* HORSE-COURSER.
What art thou, Faustus, but a man condemn'd to die?
Thy fatal time doth draw to final end;
Despair doth drive distrust unto my thoughts:
Confound these passions with a quiet sleep:
Tush, Christ did call the thief upon the cross;
Then rest thee, Faustus, quiet in conceit.

Sleeps in his chair.

Re-enter HORSE-COURSER, *all wet, crying*

HORSE-C. Alas, alas! Doctor Fustian quotha? Mass, Doctor Lopus[1] was never such a doctor. Has given me a purgation has purg'd me of forty dollars; I shall never see them more. But yet, like an ass as I was, I would not be ruled by him, for he bade me I should ride him into no water. Now I, thinking my horse had had some rare quality that he would not have had me known of, I, like a venturous youth, rid him into the deep pond at the town's end. I was no sooner in the middle of the pond, but my horse vanished away, and I sat upon a bottle of hay, never so near drowning in my life. But I'll seek out my Doctor, and have my forty dollars again, or I'll make it the dearest horse!—O, yonder is his snipper-snapper.—Do you hear? You hey-pass,[2] where's your master?

MEPH. Why, sir, what would you? You cannot speak with him.

HORSE-C. But I will speak with him.

MEPH. Why, he's fast asleep. Come some other time.

---

[1] Dr. Lopez, physician to Queen Elizabeth, was hanged in 1594 on the charge of conspiring to poison the Queen.
[2] A juggler's term, like " presto, fly! " Hence applied to the juggler himself.—*Bullen.*

Horse-C. I'll speak with him now, or I'll break his glass windows about his ears.

Meph. I tell thee he has not slept this eight nights.

Horse-C. An he have not slept this eight weeks, I'll speak with him.

Meph. See where he is, fast asleep.

Horse-C. Ay, this is he. God save you, Master Doctor! Master Doctor, Master Doctor Fustian!—Forty dollars, forty dollars for a bottle of hay!

Meph. Why, thou seest he hears thee not.

Horse-C. So ho, ho!—so ho, ho! (*Hollas in his ear.*) No, will you not wake? I'll make you wake ere I go. (*Pulls* Faustus *by the leg, and pulls it away.*) Alas, I am undone! What shall I do?

Faust. O my leg, my leg! Help, Mephistophilis! call the officers. My leg, my leg!

Meph. Come, villain, to the constable.

Horse-C. O lord, sir, let me go, and I'll give you forty dollars more.

Meph. Where be they?

Horse-C. I have none about me. Come to my ostry* and I'll give them you.

Meph. Begone quickly.   Horse-Courser *runs away.*

Faust. What, is he gone? Farewell he! Faustus has his leg again, and the horse-courser, I take it, a bottle of hay for his labour. Well, this trick shall cost him forty dollars more.

Enter Wagner

How now, Wagner, what's the news with thee?

Wag. Sir, the Duke of Vanholt doth earnestly entreat your company.

Faust. The Duke of Vanholt! an honourable gentleman, to whom I must be no niggard of my cunning. Come, Mephistophilis, let's away to him.   *Exeunt.*

* Inn.

[SCENE XII—*The Court of the Duke of Vanholt.*]

Enter the DUKE [*of* VANHOLT], *the* DUCHESS, FAUSTUS,
and MEPHISTOPHILIS

DUKE. Believe me, Master Doctor, this merriment hath much pleased me.

FAUST. My gracious lord, I am glad it contents you so well.—But it may be, madam, you take no delight in this. I have heard that great-bellied women do long for some dainties or other. What is it, madam? Tell me, and you shall have it.

DUCHESS. Thanks, good Master Doctor; and for I see your courteous intent to pleasure me, I will not hide from you the thing my heart desires; and were it now summer, as it is January and the dead time of the winter, I would desire no better meat than a dish of ripe grapes.

FAUST. Alas, madam, that's nothing! Mephistophilis, begone. (*Exit* MEPHISTOPHILIS.) Were it a greater thing than this, so it would content you, you should have it.

Re-enter MEPHISTOPHILIS *with the grapes*

Here they be, madam; wilt please you taste on them?

DUKE. Believe me, Master Doctor, this makes me wonder above the rest, that being in the dead time of winter, and in the month of January, how you should come by these grapes.

FAUST. If it like your Grace, the year is divided into two circles over the whole world, that, when it is here winter with us, in the contrary circle it is summer with them, as in India, Saba, and farther countries in the East; and by means of a swift spirit that I have I had them brought hither, as ye see.—How do you like them, madam; be they good?

DUCHESS. Believe me, Master Doctor, they be the best grapes that I e'er tasted in my life before.

FAUST. I am glad they content you so, madam.

DUKE. Come, madam, let us in, where you must well reward this learned man for the great kindness he hath show'd to you.

DUCHESS. And so I will, my lord; and, whilst I live, rest beholding for this courtesy.

FAUST. I humbly thank your Grace.

DUKE. Come, Master Doctor, follow us and receive your reward. [*Exeunt.*

[SCENE XIII.—*A room in Faustus's House.*]

Enter WAGNER

WAG. I think my master shortly means to die,
For he hath given to me all his goods;
And yet, methinks, if that death were so near,
He would not banquet and carouse and swill
Amongst the students, as even now he doth,
Who are at supper with such belly-cheer
As Wagner ne'er beheld in all his life.
See where they come! Belike the feast is ended.

Enter FAUSTUS, *with two or three* SCHOLARS [*and*
MEPHISTOPHILIS]

1ST SCHOL. Master Doctor Faustus, since our conference
about fair ladies, which was the beautifullest in all the world,
we have determined with ourselves that Helen of Greece
was the admirablest lady that ever lived: therefore, Master
Doctor, if you will do us that favour, as to let us see that
peerless dame of Greece, whom all the world admires for
majesty, we should think ourselves much beholding unto
you.

FAUST. Gentlemen,
For that I know your friendship is unfeigned,
And Faustus' custom is not to deny
The just requests of those that wish him well,
You shall behold that peerless dame of Greece,
No otherways for pomp and majesty
Than when Sir Paris cross'd the seas with her,
And brought the spoils to rich Dardania.
Be silent, then, for danger is in words.

Music sounds, and HELEN *passeth over the stage.*

2ND SCHOL. Too simple is my wit to tell her praise,
Whom all the world admires for majesty.

3RD SCHOL. No marvel though the angry Greeks pursued

With ten years' war the rape of such a queen,
Whose heavenly beauty passeth all compare.
   ıst SCHOL. Since we have seen the pride of Nature's
      works,
And only paragon of excellence,
Let us depart; and for this glorious deed
Happy and blest be Faustus evermore.
   FAUSTUS. Gentlemen, farewell—the same I wish to you.
                     Exeunt SCHOLARS [*and* WAGNER]

              Enter an OLD MAN
   OLD MAN. Ah, Doctor Faustus, that I might prevail
To guide thy steps unto the way of life,
By which sweet path thou may'st attain the goal
That shall conduct thee to celestial rest!
Break heart, drop blood, and mingle it with tears,
Tears falling from repentant heaviness
Of thy most vile and loathsome filthiness,
The stench whereof corrupts the inward soul
With such flagitious crimes of heinous sins
As no commiseration may expel,
But mercy, Faustus, of thy Saviour sweet,
Whose blood alone must wash away thy guilt.
   FAUST. Where art thou, Faustus?   Wretch, what hast
      thou done?
Damn'd art thou, Faustus, damn'd; despair and die!
Hell calls for right, and with a roaring voice
Says "Faustus! come! thine hour is [almost] come!"
And Faustus [now] will come to do the right.
           MEPHISTOPHILIS *gives him a dagger.*
   OLD MAN. Ah stay, good Faustus, stay thy desperate steps!
I see an angel hovers o'er thy head,
And, with a vial full of precious grace,
Offers to pour the same into thy soul:
Then call for mercy, and avoid despair.
   FAUST. Ah, my sweet friend, I feel
Thy words do comfort my distressed soul.
Leave me a while to ponder on my sins.

OLD MAN. I go, sweet Faustus, but with heavy cheer,
Fearing the ruin of thy hopeless soul.   [*Exit.*]

FAUST. Accursed Faustus, where is mercy now?
I do repent; and yet I do despair;
Hell strives with grace for conquest in my breast:
What shall I do to shun the snares of death?

MEPH. Thou traitor, Faustus, I arrest thy soul
For disobedience to my sovereign lord;
Revolt, or I'll in piecemeal tear thy flesh.

FAUST. Sweet Mephistophilis, entreat thy lord
To pardon my unjust presumption.
And with my blood again I will confirm
My former vow I made to Lucifer.

MEPH. Do it then quickly, with unfeigned heart,
Lest greater danger do attend thy drift.

   [FAUSTUS *stabs his arm and writes on a paper with his
      blood.*]

FAUST. Torment, sweet friend, that base and crooked age,[1]
That durst dissuade me from my Lucifer,
With greatest torments that our hell affords.

MEPH. His faith is great, I cannot touch his soul;
But what I may afflict his body with
I will attempt, which is but little worth.

FAUST. One thing, good servant, let me crave of thee,
To glut the longing of my heart's desire,—
That I might have unto my paramour
That heavenly Helen, which I saw of late,
Whose sweet embracings may extinguish clean
These thoughts that do dissuade me from my vow,
And keep mine oath I made to Lucifer.

MEPH. Faustus, this or what else thou shalt desire
Shall be perform'd in twinkling of an eye.

Re-enter HELEN

FAUST. Was this the face that launched a thousand ships
And burnt the topless[2] towers of Ilium?
Sweet Helen, make me immortal with a kiss.   [*Kisses her.*]
Her lips suck forth my soul; see where it flies!—

---

[1] Old man   [2] Unsurpassed in height.

Come, Helen, come, give me my soul again.
Here will I dwell, for Heaven is in these lips,
And all is dross that is not Helena.   *Enter* OLD MAN.
I will be Paris, and for love of thee,
Instead of Troy, shall Wittenberg be sack'd;
And I will combat with weak Menelaus,
And wear thy colours on my plumed crest;
Yea, I will wound Achilles in the heel,
And then return to Helen for a kiss.
Oh, thou art fairer than the evening air
Clad in the beauty of a thousand stars;
Brighter art thou than flaming Jupiter
When he appear'd to hapless Semele:
More lovely than the monarch of the sky
In wanton Arethusa's azured arms:
And none but thou shalt be my paramour.   *Exeunt.*
  OLD MAN. Accursed Faustus, miserable man,
That from thy soul exclud'st the grace of Heaven,
And fly'st the throne of his tribunal seat!

Enter DEVILS

Satan begins to sift me with his pride:
As in this furnace God shall try my faith,
My faith, vile hell, shall triumph over thee.
Ambitious fiends! see how the heavens smiles
At your repulse, and laughs your state to scorn!
Hence, hell! for hence I fly unto my God.
  Exeunt [on one side DEVILS, *on the other,* OLD MAN.]

[SCENE XIV.—*The Same.*]

Enter FAUSTUS *with* SCHOLARS

FAUST. Ah, gentlemen!
  IST SCHOL. What ails Faustus?
  FAUST. Ah, my sweet chamber-fellow, had I lived with
thee, then had I lived still! but now I die eternally. Look,
comes he not, comes he not?

2ND SCHOL. What means Faustus?

3RD SCHOL. Belike he is grown into some sickness by being over solitary.

1ST SCHOL. If it be so, we'll have physicians to cure him. 'Tis but a surfeit. Never fear, man.

FAUST. A surfeit of deadly sin that hath damn'd both body and soul.

2ND SCHOL. Yet, Faustus, look up to Heaven; remember God's mercies are infinite.

FAUST. But Faustus' offences can never be pardoned: the serpent that tempted Eve may be sav'd, but not Faustus. Ah, gentlemen, hear me with patience, and tremble not at my speeches! Though my heart pants and quivers to remember that I have been a student here these thirty years, oh, would I had never seen Wittenberg, never read book! And what wonders I have done, all Germany can witness, yea, the world; for which Faustus hath lost both Germany and the world, yea Heaven itself, Heaven, the seat of God, the throne of the blessed, the kingdom of joy; and must remain in hell for ever, hell, ah, hell, for ever! Sweet friends! what shall become of Faustus being in hell for ever?

3RD SCHOL. Yet, Faustus, call on God.

FAUST. On God, whom Faustus hath abjur'd! on God, whom Faustus hath blasphemed! Ah, my God, I would weep, but the Devil draws in my tears. Gush forth blood instead of tears! Yea, life and soul! Oh, he stays my tongue! I would lift up my hands, but see, they hold them, they hold them!

ALL. Who, Faustus?

FAUST. Lucifer and Mephistophilis. Ah, gentlemen, I gave them my soul for my cunning!

ALL. God forbid!

FAUST. God forbade it indeed; but Faustus hath done it. For vain pleasure of twenty-four years hath Faustus lost eternal joy and felicity. I writ them a bill with mine own blood: the date is expired; the time will come, and he will fetch me.

1ST SCHOL. Why did not Faustus tell us of this before, that divines might have pray'd for thee?

FAUST. Oft have I thought to have done so; but the

Devil threat'ned to tear me in pieces if I nam'd God; to
fetch both body and soul if I once gave ear to divinity:
and now 'tis too late. Gentlemen, away! lest you perish
with me.

2ND SCHOL. Oh, what shall we do to save Faustus?

FAUST. Talk not of me, but save yourselves, and depart.

3RD SCHOL. God will strengthen me. I will stay with
Faustus.

IST SCHOL. Tempt not God, sweet friend; but let us into
the next room, and there pray for him.

FAUST. Ay, pray for me, pray for me! and what noise
soever ye hear, come not unto me, for nothing can rescue me.

2ND SCHOL. Pray thou, and we will pray that God may
have mercy upon thee.

FAUST. Gentlemen, farewell! If I live till morning I'll
visit you: if not—Faustus is gone to hell.

ALL. Faustus, farewell!

> *Exeunt* SCHOLARS. *The clock strikes eleven.*

FAUST. Ah, Faustus,
Now hast thou but one bare hour to live,
And then thou must be damn'd perpetually!
Stand still, you ever-moving spheres of Heaven,
That time may cease, and midnight never come;
Fair Nature's eye, rise, rise again and make
Perpetual day; or let this hour be but
A year, a month, a week, a natural day,
That Faustus may repent and save his soul!
O lente, lente, curite noctis equi![1]
The stars move still,[2] time runs, the clock will strike,
The Devil will come, and Faustus must be damn'd.
O, I'll leap up to my God! Who pulls me down?
See, see where Christ's blood streams in the firmament!
One drop would save my soul—half a drop: ah, my Christ!
Ah, rend not my heart for naming of my Christ!
Yet will I call on him: O spare me, Lucifer!—
Where is it now? 'Tis gone; and see where God
Stretcheth out his arm, and bends his ireful brows!
Mountain and hills come, come and fall on me,

---

[1] " Run softly, softly, horses of the night."—Ovid's *Amores,* i. 13.
[2] Without ceasing.

And hide me from the heavy wrath of God!
No! no!
Then will I headlong run into the earth;
Earth gape! O no, it will not harbour me!
You stars that reign'd at my nativity,
Whose influence hath alloted death and hell,
Now draw up Faustus like a foggy mist
Into the entrails of yon labouring clouds,
That when they vomit forth into the air,
My limbs may issue from their smoky mouths,
So that my soul may but ascend to Heaven.

The watch strikes [the half hour].

Ah, half the hour is past! 'Twill all be past anon!
O God!
If thou wilt not have mercy on my soul,
Yet for Christ's sake whose blood hath ransom'd me,
Impose some end to my incessant pain;
Let Faustus live in hell a thousand years—
A hundred thousand, and—at last—be sav'd!
O, no end is limited to damned souls!
Why wert thou not a creature wanting soul?
Or why is this immortal that thou hast?
Ah, Pythagoras' metempsychosis! were that true,
This soul should fly from me, and I be chang'd
Unto some brutish beast! All beasts are happy,
For, when they die,
Their souls are soon dissolv'd in elements;
But mine must live, still to be plagu'd in hell.
Curst be the parents that engend'red me!
No, Faustus: curse thyself: curse Lucifer
That hath depriv'd thee of the joys of Heaven.

The clock striketh twelve.

O, it strikes, it strikes! Now, body, turn to air,
Or Lucifer will bear thee quick to hell.

Thunder and lightning.

O soul, be chang'd into little water-drops,
And fall into the ocean—ne'er be found.
My God! my God! look not so fierce on me! *Enter* DEVILS.
Adders and serpents, let me breathe awhile!

Ugly hell, gape not! come not, Lucifer!
I'll burn my books!—Ah. Mephistophilis!

Exeunt DEVILS *with* FAUSTUS.

Enter CHORUS

CHO. Cut *is* the branch that might have grown full
    straight,
And burned is Apollo's laurel bough,
That sometime grew within this learned man.
Faustus is gone; regard his hellish fall,
Whose fiendful fortune may exhort the wise
Only to wonder at unlawful things,
Whose deepness doth entice such forward wits
To practise more than heavenly power permits.   [*Exit.*]

EGMONT
A TRAGEDY IN FIVE ACTS

BY
GOETHE

TRANSLATED BY
ANNA SWANWICK

INTRODUCTORY NOTE

In 1775, when Goethe was twenty-six, and before he went to Weimar, he began to write "Egmont." After working on it at intervals for twelve years, he finished it at Rome in 1787.

The scene of the drama is laid in the Low Countries at the beginning of the revolt against Spain. In the fifteenth century Philip of Burgundy had usurped dominion over several of the provinces of the Netherlands, and through him they had passed into the power of his descendant, the Emperor Charles V. This powerful ruler abolished the constitutional rights of the provinces, and introduced the Inquisition in order to stamp out Protestantism. Prominent among his officers was the Fleming, Lamoral, Count Egmont, upon whom he lavished honors and opportunities of service—opportunities so well improved that, by his victories over the French at Saint-Quentin (1557) and Gravelines (1558) Egmont made a reputation as one of the most brilliant generals in Europe, and became the idol of his countrymen. When in 1559 a new Regent of the Netherlands was to be created, the people hoped that Philip II, who had succeeded Charles, would choose Egmont; but instead he appointed his half-sister Margaret, Duchess of Parma. Under the new Regent the persecution of the Protestants was rigorously pressed, and in 1565 Egmont, though a Catholic, was sent to Madrid to plead for clemency. He was received by the King with every appearance of cordiality, but shortly after his return home the Duke of Alva was sent to the Netherlands with instructions to put down with an iron hand all resistance to his master's will. How terribly he carried out his orders has been told by Prescott and Motley. Egmont was an early victim, but his martyrdom, with that of Count Horn, and later the assassination of William of Orange, roused the Netherlands to a resistance that ended only with the complete throwing off of the Spanish yoke.

Such in outline is the background chosen by Goethe for his tragedy. With many changes in detail, the dramatist has still preserved a picture of a historical situation of absorbing interest, and has painted a group of admirable portraits. The drama has long been a favorite on the stage, where it enjoys the advantage of Beethoven's musical setting.

EGMONT

DRAMATIS PERSONÆ

MARGARET OF PARMA, *Daughter of Charles V.,*
and Regent of the Netherlands

COUNT EGMONT, *Prince of Gaure*   THE DUKE OF ALVA
WILLIAM OF ORANGE   FERDINAND, *his natural Son*
MACHIAVEL, *in the service of the*   RICHARD, EGMONT'S *Private Secre-*
  Regent   *tary*
SILVA, } *in the service of Alva*   CLARA, *the Beloved of* EGMONT
GOMEZ, }   HER MOTHER

BRACKENBURG, *a Citizen's Son, and* VANSEN, *a Clerk*

SOEST, *a Shopkeeper,* ⎫
JETTER, *a Tailor,*   ⎬ *Citizens of Brussels*
A CARPENTER,   ⎪
A SOAPBOILER,   ⎭

BUYCK, *a Hollander, a Soldier un-*   RUYSUM, *a Frieslander, an invalid*
  der EGMONT   *Soldier, and deaf*

People, Attendants, Guards, &c.

The Scene is laid in Brussels.

ACT I

SCENE I.—*Soldiers and Citizens (with cross-bows)*

JETTER (*steps forward, and bends his cross-bow*).
SOEST, BUYCK, RUYSUM

Soest.

COME, shoot away, and have done with it! You won't beat me! Three black rings, you never made such a shot in all your life. And so I'm master for this year.

JETTER. Master and king to boot; who envies you? You'll have to pay double reckoning; 'tis only fair you should pay for your dexterity.

BUYCK. Jetter, I'll buy your shot, share the prize, and

treat the company. I have already been here so long, and am a debtor for so many civilities. If I miss, then it shall be as if you had shot.

SOEST. I ought to have a voice, for in fact I am the loser. No matter! Come, Buyck, shoot away.

BUYCK (*shoots*). Now, corporal, look out!—One! Two! Three! Four!

SOEST. Four rings! So be it!

ALL. Hurrah! Long live the King! Hurrah! Hurrah!

BUYCK. Thanks, sirs, master even were too much! Thanks for the honour.

JETTER. You have no one to thank but yourself.

RUYSUM. Let me tell you—

SOEST. How now, grey-beard?

RUYSUM. Let me tell you!—He shoots like his master, he shoots like Egmont.

BUYCK. Compared with him I am only a bungler. He aims with the rifle as no one else does. Not only when he's lucky or in the vein; no! he levels, and the bull's-eye is pierced. I have learned from him. He were indeed a block-head, who could serve under him and learn nothing!—But, sirs, let us not forget! A king maintains his followers; and so, wine here, at the king's charge!

JETTER. We have agreed among ourselves that each—

BUYCK. I am a foreigner, and a king, and care not a jot for your laws and customs.

JETTER. Why, you are worse than the Spaniard, who has not yet ventured to meddle with them.

RUYSUM. What does he say?

SOEST (*loud to* RUYSUM). He wants to treat us; he will not hear of our clubbing together, the king paying only a double share.

RUYSUM. Let him! under protest, however! 'Tis his mas-ter's fashion, too, to be munificent, and to let the money flow in a good cause.   (*Wine is brought.*)

ALL. Here's to his Majesty! Hurrah!

JETTER (*to* BUYCK). That means your Majesty, of course.

BUYCK. My hearty thanks, if it be so.

SOEST. Assuredly! A Netherlander does not find it easy to drink the health of his Spanish majesty from his heart.

RUYSUM. Who?

SOEST (*aloud*). Philip the Second, King of Spain.

RUYSUM. Our most gracious king and master! Long life to him.

SOEST. Did you not like his father, Charles the Fifth, better?

RUYSUM. God bless him! He was a king indeed! His hand reached over the whole earth, and he was all in all. Yet, when he met you, he'd greet you just as one neighbour greets another,—and if you were frightened, he knew so well how to put you at your ease—ay, you understand me—he walked out, rode out, just as it came into his head, with very few followers. We all wept when he resigned the government here to his son. You understand me—he is another sort of man, he's more majestic.

JETTER. When he was here, he never appeared in public, except in pomp and royal state. He speaks little, they say.

SOEST. He is no king for us Netherlanders. Our princes must be joyous and free like ourselves, must live and let live. We will neither be despised nor oppressed, good-natured fools though we be.

JETTER. The king, methinks, were a gracious sovereign enough, if he had only better counsellors.

SOEST. No, no! He has no affection for us Netherlanders; he has no heart for the people; he loves us not; how then can we love him? Why is everybody so fond of Count Egmont? Why are we all so devoted to him? Why, because one can read in his face that he loves us; because joyousness, open-heartedness, and good-nature, speak in his eyes; because he possesses nothing that he does not share with him who needs it, ay, and with him who needs it not. Long live Count Egmont! Buyck, it is for you to give the first toast; give us your master's health.

BUYCK. With all my heart; here's to Count Egmont! Hurrah!

RUYSUM. Conqueror of St. Quintin.

BUYCK. The hero of Gravelines.

ALL. Hurrah!

RUYSUM. St. Quintin was my last battle. I was hardly able to crawl along, and could with difficulty carry my heavy rifle. I managed, notwithstanding, to singe the skin of the French once more, and, as a parting gift, received a grazing shot in my right leg.

BUYCK. Gravelines! Ha, my friends, we had sharp work of it there! The victory was all our own. Did not those French dogs carry fire and desolation into the very heart of Flanders? We gave it them, however! The old hard-fisted veterans held out bravely for a while, but we pushed on, fired away, and laid about us, till they made wry faces, and their lines gave way. Then Egmont's horse was shot under him; and for a long time we fought pell-mell, man to man, horse to horse, troop to troop, on the broad, flat, sea-sand. Suddenly, as if from heaven, down came the cannon shot from the mouth of the river, bang, bang, right into the midst of the French. These were English, who, under Admiral Malin, happened to be sailing past from Dunkirk. They did not help us much, 'tis true; they could only approach with their smallest vessels, and that not near enough; —besides, their shot fell sometimes among our troops. It did some good, however! It broke the French lines, and raised our courage. Away it went. Helter-skelter! topsy-turvy! all struck dead, or forced into the water; the fellows were drowned the moment they tasted the water, while we Hollanders dashed in after them. Being amphibious, we were as much in our element as frogs, and hacked away at the enemy, and shot them down as if they had been ducks. The few who struggled through, were struck dead in their flight by the peasant women, armed with hoes and pitchforks. His Gallic majesty was compelled at once to hold out his paw and make peace. And that peace you owe to us, to the great Egmont.

ALL. Hurrah, for the great Egmont! Hurrah! Hurrah!

JETTER. Had they but appointed him Regent, instead of Margaret of Parma!

SOEST. Not so! Truth is truth! I'll not hear Margaret abused. Now it is my turn. Long live our gracious lady!

ALL. Long life to her!

SOEST. Truly, there are excellent women in that family. Long live the Regent!

JETTER. Prudent is she, and moderate in all she does; if

she would only not hold so fast and stiffly with the priests. It is partly her fault, too, that we have the fourteen new mitres in the land. Of what use are they, I should like to know? Why, that foreigners may be shoved into the good benefices, where formerly abbots were chosen out of the chapters! And we're to believe it's for the sake of religion. We know better. Three bishops were enough for us; things went on decently and reputably. Now each must busy himself as if he were needed; and this gives rise every moment, to dissensions and ill-will. And the more you agitate the matter, so much the worse it grows. (*They drink.*)

SOEST. But it was the will of the king; she cannot alter it, one way or another.

JETTER. Then we may not even sing the new psalms; but ribald songs, as many as we please. And why? There is heresy in them, they say, and heaven knows what. I have sung some of them, however; they are new, to be sure, but I see no harm in them.

BUYCK. Ask their leave, forsooth! In our province, we sing just what we please. That's because Count Egmont is our stadtholder, who does not trouble himself about such matters. In Ghent, Ypres, and throughout the whole of Flanders, anybody sings them that chooses. (*Aloud to* RUYSUM.) There is nothing more harmless than a spiritual song—Is there, father?

RUYSUM. What, indeed! It is a godly work, and truly edifying.

JETTER. They say, however, that they are not of the right sort, not of their sort, and, since it is dangerous, we had better leave them alone. The officers of the Inquisition are always lurking and spying about; many an honest fellow has already fallen into their clutches. They had not gone so far as to meddle with conscience! If they will not allow me to do what I like, they might at least let me think and sing as I please.

SOEST. The Inquisition won't do here. We are not made like the Spaniards, to let our consciences be tyrannized over. The nobles must look to it, and clip its wings betimes.

JETTER. It is a great bore. Whenever it comes into their worships' heads to break into my house, and I am sitting there at my work, humming a French psalm, thinking nothing about it, neither good nor bad—singing it just because it is in my throat;—forthwith I'm a heretic, and am clapped into prison. Or if I am passing through the country, and stand near a crowd listening to a new preacher, one of those who have come from Germany; instantly I'm called a rebel, and am in danger of losing my head! Have you ever heard one of these preachers?

SOEST. Brave fellows! Not long ago, I heard one of them preach in a field, before thousands and thousands of people. A different sort of dish he gave us from that of our humdrum preachers, who, from the pulpit, choke their hearers with scraps of Latin. He spoke from his heart; told us how we had till now been led by the nose, how we had been kept in darkness, and how we might procure more light;—ay, and he proved it all out of the Bible.

JETTER. There may be something in it. I always said as much, and have often pondered over the matter. It has long been running in my head.

BUYCK. All the people run after them.

SOEST. No wonder, since they hear both what is good and what is new.

JETTER. And what is it all about? Surely they might let every one preach after his own fashion.

BUYCK. Come, sirs! While you are talking, you forget the wine and the Prince of Orange.

JETTER. We must not forget him. He's a very wall of defence. In thinking of him, one fancies, that if one could only hide behind him, the devil himself could not get at one. Here's to William of Orange! Hurrah!

ALL. Hurrah! Hurrah!

SOEST. Now, grey-beard, let's have your toast.

RUYSUM. Here's to old soldiers! To all soldiers! War for ever!

BUYCK. Bravo, old fellow. Here's to all soldiers. War for ever!

JETTER. War! War! Do ye know what ye are shouting about? That it should slip glibly from your tongue is natural enough; but what wretched work it is for us, I have not words to tell you. To be stunned the whole year round by the beating of the drum; to hear of nothing except how one troop marched here, and another there; how they came over this height, and halted near that mill; how many were left dead on this field, and how many on that; how they press forward, and how one wins, and another loses, without being able to comprehend what they are fighting about; how a town is taken, how the citizens are put to the sword, and how it fares with the poor women and innocent children. This is a grief and a trouble, and then one thinks every moment, "Here they come! It will be our turn next."

SOEST. Therefore every citizen must be practised in the use of arms.

JETTER. Fine talking, indeed, for him who has a wife and children. And yet I would rather hear of soldiers than see them.

BUYCK. I might take offence at that.

JETTER. It was not intended for you, countryman. When we got rid of the Spanish garrison, we breathed freely again.

SOEST. Faith! They pressed on you heavily enough.

JETTER. Mind your own business.

SOEST. They came to sharp quarters with you.

JETTER. Hold your tongue.

SOEST. They drove him out of kitchen, cellar, chamber —and bed. (*They laugh.*)

JETTER. You are a blockhead.

BUYCK. Peace, sirs! Must the soldier cry peace? Since you will not hear anything about us, let us have a toast of your own—a citizen's toast.

JETTER. We're all ready for that! Safety and peace!

SOEST. Order and freedom!

BUYCK. Bravo! That will content us all.

(*They ring their glasses together, and joyously repeat the words, but in such a manner that each utters a different sound, and it becomes a kind of chant. The old man listens, and at length joins in.*)

ALL. Safety and peace! Order and freedom!

SCENE II.—*Palace of the Regent*

MARGARET OF PARMA (*in a hunting dress*). COURTIERS,
PAGES, SERVANTS

REGENT. Put off the hunt, I shall not ride to-day. Bid
Machiavel attend me.　　　　　[*Exeunt all but the* REGENT.

The thought of these terrible events leaves me no repose!
Nothing can amuse, nothing divert my mind. These images,
these cares are always before me. The king will now say
that these are the natural fruits of my kindness, of my
clemency; yet my conscience assures me that I have adopted
the wisest, the most prudent course. Ought I sooner to have
kindled, and spread abroad these flames with the breath of
wrath? My hope was to keep them in, to let them smoulder
in their own ashes. Yes, my inward conviction, and my
knowledge of the circumstances, justify my conduct in my
own eyes; but in what light will it appear to my brother!
For, can it be denied that the insolence of these foreign
teachers waxes daily more audacious? They have desecrated our sanctuaries, unsettled the dull minds of the people,
and conjured up amongst them a spirit of delusion. Impure
spirits have mingled among the insurgents, horrible deeds
have been perpetrated, which to think of makes one shudder,
and of these a circumstantial account must be transmitted
instantly to court. Prompt and minute must be my communication, lest rumour outrun my messenger, and the king
suspect that some particulars have been purposely withheld.
I can see no means, severe or mild, by which to stem the
evil. Oh, what are we great ones on the waves of humanity?
We think to control them, and are ourselves driven to and
fro, hither and thither.

Enter MACHIAVEL

REGENT. Are the despatches to the king prepared?

MACHIAVEL. In an hour they will be ready for your
signature.

REGENT. Have you made the report sufficiently circumstantial?

MACHIAVEL. Full and circumstantial, as the king loves to

have it. I relate how the rage of the iconoclasts first broke out at St. Omer. How a furious multitude, with staves, hatchets, hammers, ladders, and cords, accompanied by a few armed men, first assailed the chapels, churches, and convents, drove out the worshippers, forced the barred gates, threw everything into confusion, tore down the altars, destroyed the statues of the saints, defaced the pictures, and dashed to atoms, and trampled under foot, whatever came in their way that was consecrated and holy. How the crowd increased as it advanced, and how the inhabitants of Ypres opened their gates at its approach. How, with incredible rapidity, they demolished the cathedral, and burned the library of the bishop. How a vast multitude, possessed by the like frenzy, dispersed themselves through Menin, Comines, Verviers, Lille, nowhere encountered opposition; and how, through almost the whole of Flanders, in a single moment, the monstrous conspiracy declared itself, and was accomplished.

REGENT. Alas! Your recital rends my heart anew; and the fear that the evil will wax greater and greater, adds to my grief. Tell me your thoughts, Machiavel!

MACHIAVEL. Pardon me, your Highness, my thoughts will appear to you but as idle fancies; and though you always seem well satisfied with my services, you have seldom felt inclined to follow my advice. How often have you said in jest: "You see too far, Machiavel! You should be an historian; he who acts, must provide for the exigence of the hour." And yet have I not predicted this terrible history? Have I not foreseen it all?

REGENT. I too foresee many things, without being able to avert them.

MACHIAVEL. In one word, then:—you will not be able to suppress the new faith. Let it be recognized, separate its votaries from the true believers, give them churches of their own, include them within the pale of social order, subject them to the restraints of law,—do this, and you will at once tranquillize the insurgents. All other measures will prove abortive, and you will depopulate the country.

REGENT. Have you forgotten with what aversion the mere suggestion of toleration was rejected by my brother? Know you not, how in every letter he urgently recommends to me the maintenance of the true faith? That he will not hear of tranquillity and order being restored at the expense of religion? Even in the provinces, does he not maintain spies, unknown to us, in order to ascertain who inclines to the new doctrines? Has he not, to our astonishment, named to us this or that individual residing in our very neighbourhood, who, without its being known, was obnoxious to the charge of heresy? Does he not enjoin harshness and severity? and am I to be lenient? Am I to recommend for his adoption measures of indulgence and toleration? Should I not thus lose all credit with him, and at once forfeit his confidence?

MACHIAVEL. I know it. The king commands and puts you in full possession of his intentions. You are to restore tranquillity and peace by measures which cannot fail still more to embitter men's minds, and which must inevitably kindle the flames of war from one extremity of the country to the other. Consider well what you are doing. The principal merchants are infected—nobles, citizens, soldiers. What avails persisting in our opinion, when everything is changing around us? Oh, that some good genius would suggest to Philip that it better becomes a monarch to govern burghers of two different creeds, than to excite them to mutual destruction.

REGENT. Never let me hear such words again. Full well I know that the policy of statesmen rarely maintains truth and fidelity; that it excludes from the heart candour, charity, toleration. In secular affairs, this is, alas! only too true; but shall we trifle with God as we do with each other? Shall we be indifferent to our established faith, for the sake of which so many have sacrificed their lives? Shall we abandon it to these far-fetched, uncertain, and self-contradicting heresies?

MACHIAVEL. Think not the worse of me for what I have uttered.

REGENT. I know you and your fidelity. I know too that a man may be both honest and sagacious, and yet miss the best and nearest way to the salvation of his soul. There are others, Machiavel, men whom I esteem, yet whom I needs must blame.

MACHIAVEL. To whom do you refer?

REGENT. I must confess that Egmont caused me to-day deep and heart-felt annoyance.

MACHIAVEL. How so?

REGENT. By his accustomed demeanour, his usual indifference and levity. I received the fatal tidings as I was leaving church, attended by him and several others. I did not restrain my anguish, I broke forth into lamentations, loud and deep, and turning to him, exclaimed, " See what is going on in your province! Do you suffer it, Count, you, in whom the king confided so implicitly? "

MACHIAVEL. And what was his reply?

REGENT. As if it were a mere trifle, an affair of no moment, he answered: " Were the Netherlanders but satisfied as to their constitution! The rest would soon follow."

MACHIAVEL. There was, perhaps, more truth than discretion or piety in his words. How can we hope to acquire and to maintain the confidence of the Netherlander, when he sees that we are more interested in appropriating his possessions, than in promoting his welfare, temporal or spiritual? Does the number of souls saved by the new bishops exceed that of the fat benefices they have swallowed? And are they not for the most part foreigners? As yet, the office of stadtholder has been held by Netherlanders; but do not the Spaniards betray their great and irresistible desire to possess themselves of these places? Will not people prefer being governed by their own countrymen, and according to their ancient customs, rather than by foreigners, who, from their first entrance into the land, endeavour to enrich themselves at the general expense, who measure everything by a foreign standard, and who exercise their authority without cordiality or sympathy?

REGENT. You take part with our opponents?

MACHIAVEL. Assuredly not in my heart. Would that with my understanding I could be wholly on our side!

REGENT. If such your disposition, it were better I should resign the regency to them; for both Egmont and Orange entertained great hopes of occupying this position. Then they were adversaries, now they are leagued against me, and have become friends—inseparable friends.

MACHIAVEL. A dangerous pair.

REGENT. To speak candidly, I fear Orange.—I fear for Egmont.—Orange meditates some dangerous scheme, his thoughts are far-reaching, he is reserved, appears to accede to everything, never contradicts, and while maintaining the show of reverence, with clear foresight accomplishes his own designs.

MACHIAVEL. Egmont, on the contrary, advances with a bold step, as if the world were all his own.

REGENT. He bears his head as proudly as if the hand of majesty were not suspended over him.

MACHIAVEL. The eyes of all the people are fixed upon him, and he is the idol of their hearts.

REGENT. He has never assumed the least disguise, and carries himself as if no one had a right to call him to account. He still bears the name of Egmont. Count Egmont is the title by which he loves to hear himself addressed, as though he would fain be reminded that his ancestors were masters of Guelderland. Why does he not assume his proper title,—Prince of Gaure? What object has he in view? Would he again revive extinguished claims?

MACHIAVEL. I hold him for a faithful servant of the king.

REGENT. Were he so inclined, what important service could he not render to the government? Whereas. now, without benefiting himself, he has caused us unspeakable vexation. His banquets and entertainment have done more to unite the nobles and to knit them together than the most dangerous secret associations. With his toasts, his guests have drunk in a permanent intoxication, a giddy frenzy, that never subsides. How often have his facetious jests stirred up the minds of the populace? and what an excitement was produced among the mob by the new liveries, and the extravagant devices of his followers!

MACHIAVEL. I am convinced he had no design.

REGENT. Be that as it may, it is bad enough. As I said before, he injures us without benefiting himself. He treats as a jest matters of serious import; and, not to appear negligent and remiss, we are forced to treat seriously what he intended as a jest. Thus one urges on the other; and what we are endeavouring to avert is actually brought to pass. He is more dangerous than the acknowledged head of a conspiracy; and I am much mistaken if it is not all remembered against him at court. I cannot deny that scarcely a day passes in which he does not wound me—deeply wound me.

MACHIAVEL. He appears to me to act on all occasions, according to the dictates of his conscience.

REGENT. His conscience has a convenient mirror. His demeanour is often offensive. He carries himself as if he felt he were the master here, and were withheld by courtesy alone from making us feel his supremacy; as if he would not exactly drive us out of the country; there'll be no need for that.

MACHIAVEL. I entreat you, put not too harsh a construction upon his frank and joyous temper, which treats lightly matters of serious moment. You but injure yourself and him.

REGENT. I interpret nothing. I speak only of inevitable consequences, and I know him. His patent of nobility and the Golden Fleece upon his breast strengthen his confidence, his audacity. Both can protect him against any sudden outbreak of royal displeasure. Consider the matter closely, and he is alone responsible for the whole mischief that has broken out in Flanders. From the first, he connived at the proceedings of the foreign teachers, avoided stringent measures, and perhaps rejoiced in secret that they gave us so much to do. Let me alone; on this occasion, I will give utterance to that which weighs upon my heart; I will not shoot my arrow in vain. I know where he is vulnerable. For he is vulnerable.

MACHIAVEL. Have you summoned the council? Will Orange attend?

REGENT. I have sent for him to Antwerp. I will lay upon their shoulders the burden of responsibility; they shall either strenuously co-operate with me in quelling the evil, or at once declare themselves rebels. Let the letters be completed without delay, and bring them for my signature. Then hasten to despatch the trusty Vasca to Madrid, he is faithful and indefatigable; let him use all diligence, that he may not be anticipated by common report, that my brother may receive the intelligence first through him. I will myself speak with him ere he departs.

MACHIAVEL. Your orders shall be promptly and punctually obeyed.

SCENE III.—*Citizen's House*

CLARA, *her* MOTHER, BRACKENBURG

CLARA. Will you not hold the yarn for me, Brackenburg?

BRACKENBURG. I entreat you, excuse me, Clara.

CLARA. What ails you? Why refuse me this trifling service?

BRACKENBURG. When I hold the yarn, I stand as it were spell-bound before you, and cannot escape your eyes.

CLARA. Nonsense! Come and hold!

MOTHER (*knitting in her arm-chair*). Give us a song! Brackenburg sings so good a second. You used to be merry once, and I had always something to laugh at.

BRACKENBURG. Once!

CLARA. Well, let us sing.

BRACKENBURG. As you please.

CLARA. Merrily, then, and sing away! 'Tis a soldier's song, my favourite.

(*She winds yarn, and sings with* BRACKENBURG.)

> The drum is resounding,
> And shrill the fife plays;
> My love, for the battle,
> His brave troop arrays;
> He lifts his lance high,
> And the people he sways.
> My blood it is boiling!
> My heart throbs pit-pat!
> Oh, had I a jacket,
> With hose and with hat!
>
> How boldly I'd follow,
> And march through the gate;
> Through all the wide province
> I'd follow him straight.

The foe yield, we capture
Or shoot them! Ah, me!
What heart-thrilling rapture
A soldier to be!

*(During the song, BRACKENBURG has frequently looked at
CLARA; at length his voice falters, his eyes fill with
tears, he lets the skein fall, and goes to the window.
CLARA finishes the song alone, her mother motions to
her, half displeased, she rises, advances a few steps
towards him, turns back, as if irresolute, and again
sits down.)*

MOTHER. What is going on in the street, Brackenburg?
I hear soldiers marching.

BRACKENBURG. It is the Regent's body-guard.

CLARA. At this hour? What can it mean? *(She rises
and joins BRACKENBURG at the window.)* That is not the
daily guard; it is more numerous! almost all the troops!
Oh, Brackenburg, go! Learn what it means. It must be
something unusual. Go, good Brackenburg, do me this
favour.

BRACKENBURG. I am going! I will return immediately.
(He offers his hand to CLARA, and she gives him hers.)
                                        [*Exit* BRACKENBURG.

MOTHER. Thou sendest him away so soon!

CLARA. I am curious; and, besides—do not be angry,
mother—his presence pains me. I never know how I
ought to behave towards him. I have done him a wrong,
and it goes to my very heart to see how deeply he feels it.
Well, it can't be helped now!

MOTHER. He is such a true-hearted fellow!

CLARA. I cannot help it, I must treat him kindly. Often
without a thought, I return the gentle, loving pressure
of his hand. I reproach myself that I am deceiving him,
that I am nourishing in his heart a vain hope. I am
in a sad plight! God knows, I do not willingly deceive
him. I do not wish him to hope, yet I cannot let him
despair!

MOTHER. That is not as it should be.

CLARA. I liked him once, and in my soul I like him still.

I could have married him; yet I believe I was never really in love with him.

MOTHER. Thou wouldst always have been happy with him.

CLARA. I should have been provided for, and have led a quiet life.

MOTHER. And through thy fault it has all been trifled away.

CLARA. I am in a strange position. When I think how it has come to pass, I know it, indeed, and I know it not. But I have only to look upon Egmont, and I understand it all; ay, and stranger things would seem natural then. Oh, what a man he is! All the provinces worship him. And in his arms, should I not be the happiest creature in the world?

MOTHER. And how will it be in the future?

CLARA. I only ask, does he love me?—does he love me?— as if there were any doubt about it.

MOTHER. One has nothing but anxiety of heart with one's children. Always care and sorrow, whatever may be the end of it! It cannot come to good! Thou hast made thyself wretched! Thou hast made thy mother wretched too.

CLARA (*quietly*). Yet thou didst allow it in the beginning.

MOTHER. Alas! I was too indulgent; I am always too indulgent.

CLARA. When Egmont rode by, and I ran to the window, did you chide me then? Did you not come to the window yourself? When he looked up, smiled, nodded, and greeted me, was it displeasing to you? Did you not feel yourself honoured in your daughter?

MOTHER. Go on with your reproaches.

CLARA (*with emotion*). Then, when he passed more frequently, and we felt sure that it was on my account that he came this way, did you not remark it yourself with secret joy? Did you call me away when I stood behind the window-pane and awaited him?

MOTHER. Could I imagine that it would go so far?

CLARA (*with faltering voice, and repressed tears*). And then, one evening, when, enveloped in his mantle, he surprised us as we sat at our lamp, who busied herself in receiving him, while I remained, lost in astonishment, as if fastened to my chair?

MOTHER. Could I imagine that the prudent Clara would so soon be carried away by this unhappy love? I must now endure that my daughter—

CLARA (*bursting into tears*). Mother! How can you? You take pleasure in tormenting me!

MOTHER (*weeping*). Ay, weep away! Make me yet more wretched by thy grief. Is it not misery enough that my only daughter is a castaway?

CLARA (*rising, and speaking coldly*). A castaway! The beloved of Egmont a castaway!—What princess would not envy the poor Clara a place in his heart? Oh, mother,— my own mother, you were not wont to speak thus! Dear mother, be kind!—Let the people think, let the neighbours whisper what they like—this chamber, this lowly house is a paradise, since Egmont's love dwelt here.

MOTHER. One cannot help liking him, that is true. He is always so kind, frank, and open-hearted.

CLARA. There is not a drop of false blood in his veins. And then, mother, he is indeed the great Egmont; yet, when he comes to me, how tender he is, how kind! How he tries to conceal from me his rank, his bravery! How anxious he is about me! so entirely the man, the friend, the lover.

MOTHER. Do you expect him to-day?

CLARA. Have you not seen how often I go to the window? Have you not noticed how I listen to every noise at the door?—Though I know that he will not come before night, yet, from the time when I rise in the morning, I keep expecting him every moment. Were I but a boy, to follow him always, to the court and everywhere! Could I but carry his colours in the field!—

MOTHER. You were always such a lively, restless creature; even as a little child, now wild, now thoughtful. Will you not dress yourself a little better?

CLARA. Perhaps, mother, if I want something to do.— Yesterday, some of his people went by, singing songs in honour. At least his name was in the songs! The rest I could not understand. My heart leaped up into my throat,—I would fain have called them back if I had not felt ashamed.

MOTHER. Take care! Thy impetuous nature will ruin all. Thou wilt betray thyself before the people; as, not long ago, at thy cousin's, when thou foundest out the woodcut with the description, and didst exclaim, with a cry: "Count Egmont!"—I grew as red as fire.

CLARA. Could I help crying out? It was the battle of Gravelines, and I found in the picture the letter C. and then looked for it in the description below. There it stood, "Count Egmont, with his horse shot under him." I shuddered, and afterwards I could not help laughing at the woodcut figure of Egmont, as tall as the neighbouring tower of Gravelines, and the English ships at the side.—When I remember how I used to conceive of a battle, and what an idea I had, as a girl, of Count Egmont; when I listened to descriptions of him, and of all the other earls and princes; —and think how it is with me now!

Enter BRACKENBURG

CLARA. Well, what is going on?

BRACKENBURG. Nothing certain is known. It is rumoured that an insurrection has lately broken out in Flanders; the Regent is afraid of its spreading here. The castle is strongly garrisoned, the burghers are crowding to the gates, and the streets are thronged with people. I will hasten at once to my old father. (*As if about to go.*)

CLARA. Shall we see you to-morrow? I must change my dress a little. I am expecting my cousin, and I look too untidy. Come, mother, help me a moment. Take the book, Brackenburg, and bring me such another story.

MOTHER. Farewell.

BRACKENBURG (*extending his hand*). Your hand.

CLARA (*refusing hers*). When you come next.

[*Exeunt* MOTHER and DAUGHTER.

BRACKENBURG (*alone*). I had resolved to go away again at once; and yet, when she takes me at my word, and lets me leave her, I feel as if I could go mad.—Wretched man! Does the fate of thy fatherland, does the growing disturbance fail to move thee?—Are countryman and Spaniard the same to thee? and carest thou not who rules, and who is in the right?—I was a different sort of fellow as a schoolboy! —Then, when an exercise in oratory was given; "Brutus' Speech for Liberty," for instance, Fritz was ever the first, and the rector would say: "If it were only spoken more deliberately, the words not all huddled together."—Then my blood boiled, and longed for action.—Now I drag along, bound by the eyes of a maiden. I cannot leave her! yet she, alas, cannot love me!—ah—no—she—she cannot have entirely rejected me—not entirely—yet half love is no love!— I will endure it no longer!—Can it be true what a friend lately whispered in my ear, that she secretly admits a man into the house by night, when she always sends me away modestly before evening? No, it cannot be true! It is a lie! A base, slanderous lie! Clara is as innocent as I am wretched.—She has rejected me, has thrust me from her heart—and shall I live on thus? I cannot, I will not endure it. Already my native land is convulsed by internal strife, and do I perish abjectly amid the tumult? I will not endure it! When the trumpet sounds, when a shot falls, it thrills through my bone and marrow! But, alas, it does not rouse me! It does not summon me to join the onslaught, to rescue, to dare.—Wretched, degrading position! Better end it at once! Not long ago, I threw myself into the water; I sank —but nature in her agony was too strong for me; I felt that I could swim, and saved myself against my will. Could I but forget the time when she loved me, seemed to love me!— Why has this happiness penetrated my very bone and marrow? Why have these hopes, while disclosing to me a distant paradise, consumed all the enjoyment of life?—And that first, that only kiss!—Here (*laying his hand upon the table*), here we were alone,—she had always been kind and friendly towards me,—then she seemed to soften,—she looked at me,—my brain reeled,—I felt her lips on mine,—and —and now?—Die, wretch! Why dost thou hesitate? (*He draws a phial from his pocket.*) Thou healing poison, it shall not have been in vain that I stole thee from my brother's medicine chest! From this anxious fear, this dizziness, this death-agony, thou shalt deliver me at once.

ACT II

Scene I.—*Square in Brussels*

JETTER *and a* MASTER CARPENTER (*meeting*)

CARPENTER. Did I not tell you beforehand? Eight days ago, at the guild, I said there would be serious disturbances?

JETTER. Is it, then, true that they have plundered the churches in Flanders?

CARPENTER. They have utterly destroyed both churches and chapels. They have left nothing standing but the four bare walls. The lowest rabble! And this it is that damages our good cause. We ought rather to have laid our claims before the Regent, formally and decidedly, and then have stood by them. If we speak now, if we assemble now, it will be said that we are joining the insurgents.

JETTER. Ay, so every one thinks at first. Why should you thrust your nose into the mess? The neck is closely connected with it.

CARPENTER. I am always uneasy when tumults arise among the mob—among people who have nothing to lose. They use as a pretext that to which we also must appeal, and plunge the country in misery.

Enter SOEST

SOEST. Good day, sirs! What news? Is it true that the image-breakers are coming straight in this direction?

CARPENTER. Here they shall touch nothing, at any rate.

SOEST. A soldier came into my shop just now to buy tobacco; I questioned him about the matter. The Regent, though so brave and prudent a lady, has for once lost her presence of mind. Things must be bad indeed when she thus takes refuge behind her guards. The castle is strongly garrisoned. It is even rumoured that she means to fly from the town.

CARPENTER. Forth she shall not go! Her presence protects us, and we will ensure her safety better than her mustachioed gentry. If she only maintains our rights and privileges, we will stand faithfully by her.

Enter a SOAPBOILER

SOAPBOILER. An ugly business this! a bad business! Troubles are beginning; all things are going wrong! Mind you keep quiet, or they'll take you also for rioters.

SOEST. Here come the seven wise men of Greece.

SOAPBOILER. I know there are many who in secret hold with the Calvinists, abuse the bishops, and care not for the king. But a loyal subject, a sincere Catholic!—

(*By degrees others join the speakers, and listen.*)

Enter VANSEN

VANSEN. God save you, sirs! What news?

CARPENTER. Have nothing to do with him, he's a dangerous fellow.

JETTER. Is he not secretary to Dr. Wiets?

CARPENTER. He has already had several masters. First he was a clerk, and as one patron after another turned him off, on account of his roguish tricks, he now dabbles in the business of notary and advocate, and is a brandy-drinker to boot. (*More people gather round and stand in groups.*)

VANSEN. So here you are, putting your heads together. Well, it is worth talking about.

SOEST. I think so too.

VANSEN. Now if only one of you had heart and another head enough for the work, we might break the Spanish fetters at once.

SOEST. Sirs! you must not talk thus. We have taken our oath to the king.

VANSEN. And the king to us. Mark that!

JETTER. There's sense in that? Tell us your opinion.

OTHERS. Hearken to him; he's a clever fellow. He's sharp enough.

VANSEN. I had an old master once, who possessed a collection of parchments, among which were charters of ancient constitutions, contracts, and privileges. He set great store, too, by the rarest books. One of these contained our whole constitution; how, at first, we Nether-landers had princes of our own, who governed according to hereditary laws, rights, and usages; how our ancestors paid due honour to their sovereign so long as he governed them equitably; and how they were immediately on their guard the moment he was for overstepping his bounds. The states were down upon him at once; for every province, however small, had its own chamber and representatives.

CARPENTER. Hold your tongue! We knew that long ago! Every honest citizen learns as much about the constitution as he needs.

JETTER. Let him speak; one may always learn something.

SOEST. He is quite right.

SEVERAL CITIZENS. Go on! Go on! One does not hear this every day.

VANSEN. You citizens, forsooth! You live only in the present; and as you tamely follow the trade inherited from your fathers, so you let the government do with you just as it pleases. You make no inquiry into the origin, the history, or the rights of a Regent; and in consequence of this negligence, the Spaniard has drawn the net over your ears.

SOEST. Who cares for that, if one has only daily bread?

JETTER. The devil! Why did not some one come forward and tell us this in time?

VANSEN. I tell it you now. The King of Spain, whose good fortune it is to bear sway over these provinces, has no right to govern them otherwise than the petty princes who formerly possessed them separately. Do you under-stand that?

JETTER. Explain it to us.

VANSEN. Why, it is as clear as the sun. Must you not be governed according to your provincial laws? How comes that?

A CITIZEN. Certainly!

VANSEN. Has not the burgher of Brussels a different law from the burgher of Antwerp? The burgher of Antwerp from the burgher of Ghent? How comes that?

ANOTHER CITIZEN. By heavens!

VANSEN. But if you let matters run on thus, they will

soon tell you a different story. Fie on you! Philip, through a woman, now ventures to do what neither Charles the Bold, Frederick the Warrior, nor Charles the Fifth could accomplish.

SOEST. Yes, yes! The old princes tried it also.

VANSEN. Ay! But our ancestors kept a sharp look-out. If they thought themselves aggrieved by their sovereign, they would perhaps get his son and heir into their hands, detain him as a hostage, and surrender him only on the most favourable conditions. Our fathers were men! They knew their own interests! They knew how to lay hold on what they wanted, and to get it established! They were men of the right sort! and hence it is that our privileges are so clearly defined, our liberties so well secured.

SOEST. What are you saying about our liberties?

ALL. Our liberties! our privileges! Tell us about our privileges.

VANSEN. All the provinces have their peculiar advantages, but we of Brabant are the most splendidly provided for. I have read it all.

SOEST. Say on.

JETTER. Let us hear.

A CITIZEN. Pray do.

VANSEN. First, it stands written:—The Duke of Brabant shall be to us a good and faithful sovereign.

SOEST. Good! Stands it so?

JETTER. Faithful? Is that true?

VANSEN. As I tell you. He is bound to us as we are to him. Secondly: In the exercise of his authority he shall neither exert arbitrary power, nor exhibit caprice, himself, nor shall he, either directly or indirectly, sanction them in others.

JETTER. Bravo! Bravo! Not exert arbitrary power.

SOEST. Nor exhibit caprice.

ANOTHER. And not sanction them in others! That is the main point. Not sanction them, either directly or indirectly.

VANSEN. In express words.

JETTER. Get us the book.

A CITIZEN. Yes, we must see it.

OTHERS. The book! The book!

ANOTHER. We will to the Regent with the book.

ANOTHER. Sir doctor, you shall be spokesman.

SOAPBOILER. Oh, the dolts!

OTHERS. Something more out of the book!

SOAPBOILER. I'll knock his teeth down his throat if he says another word.

PEOPLE. We'll see who dares to lay hands upon him. Tell us about our privileges! Have we any more privileges?

VANSEN. Many, very good and very wholesome ones too. Thus it stands: The sovereign shall neither benefit the clergy, nor increase their number, without the consent of the nobles and of the states. Mark that! Nor shall he alter the constitution of the country.

SOEST. Stands it so?

VANSEN. I'll show it you, as it was written down two or three centuries ago.

A CITIZEN. And we tolerate the new bishops? The nobles must protect us, we will make a row else!

OTHERS. And we suffer ourselves to be intimidated by the Inquisition?

VANSEN. It is your own fault.

PEOPLE. We have Egmont! We have Orange! They will protect our interests.

VANSEN. Your brothers in Flanders are beginning the good work.

SOAPBOILER. Dog! (*Strikes him.*)

OTHERS *oppose the* SOAPBOILER, *and exclaim,* Are you also a Spaniard?

ANOTHER. What! This honourable man?

ANOTHER. This learned man?

(*They attack the* SOAPBOILER.)

CARPENTER. For heaven's sake, peace!

(*Others mingle in the fray.*)

CARPENTER. Citizens, what means this?

(*Boys whistle, throw stones, set on dogs; citizens stand and gape, people come running up, others walk quietly to and fro, others play all sorts of pranks, shout and huzza.*)

OTHERS. Freedom and privilege! Privilege and freedom!

Enter Egmont, *with followers*

Egmont. Peace! Peace! good people. What is the matter? Peace, I say! Separate them.

Carpenter. My good lord, you come like an angel from heaven. Hush! See you nothing? Count Egmont! Honour to Count Egmont!

Egmont. Here, too! What are you about? Burgher against burgher! Does not even the neighbourhood of our royal mistress oppose a barrier to this frenzy? Disperse yourselves, and go about your business. 'Tis a bad sign when you thus keep holiday on working days. How did the disturbance begin?

(*The tumult gradually subsides, and the people gather around* Egmont.)

Carpenter. They are fighting about their privileges.

Egmont. Which they will forfeit through their own folly —and who are you? You seem honest people.

Carpenter. 'Tis our wish to be so.

Egmont. Your calling?

Carpenter. A carpenter, and master of the guild.

Egmont. And you?

Soest. A shopkeeper.

Egmont. And you?

Jetter. A tailor.

Egmont. I remember, you were employed upon the liveries of my people. Your name is Jetter.

Jetter. To think of your grace remembering it!

Egmont. I do not easily forget any one whom I have seen or conversed with. Do what you can, good people, to keep the peace; you stand in bad repute enough already. Provoke not the king still farther. The power, after all, is in his hands. An honest burgher, who maintains himself industriously, has everywhere as much freedom as he wants.

Carpenter. That now is just our misfortune! With all due deference, your grace, 'tis the idle portion of the community, your drunkards and vagabonds, who quarrel for want of something to do, and clamour about privilege because they are hungry; they impose upon the curious and the credulous, and, in order to obtain a pot of beer, excite disturbances that will bring misery upon thousands. That is just what they want. We keep our houses and chests too well guarded; they would fain drive us away from them with fire-brands.

EGMONT. You shall have all needful assistance; measures have been taken to stem the evil by force. Make a firm stand against the new doctrines, and do not imagine that privileges are secured by sedition. Remain at home; suffer no crowds to assemble in the streets. Sensible people can accomplish much.

(*In the meantime the crowd has for the most part dispersed.*)

CARPENTER. Thanks, your excellency—thanks for your good opinion! We will do what in us lies. (*Exit* EGMONT.) A gracious lord! A true Netherlander! Nothing of the Spaniard about him.

JETTER. If we had only him for a regent? 'Tis a pleasure to follow him.

SOEST. The king won't hear of that. He takes care to appoint his own people to the place.

JETTER. Did you notice his dress? It was of the newest fashion—after the Spanish cut.

CARPENTER. A handsome gentleman.

JETTER. His head now were a dainty morsel for a headsman.

SOEST. Are you mad? What are you thinking about?

JETTER. It is stupid enough that such an idea should come into one's head! But so it is. Whenever I see a fine long neck, I cannot help thinking how well it would suit the block. These cursed executions! One cannot get them out of one's head. When the lads are swimming, and I chance to see a naked back, I think forthwith of the dozens I have seen beaten with rods. If I meet a portly gentleman, I fancy I already see him roasting at the stake. At night, in my dreams, I am tortured in every limb; one cannot have a single hour's enjoyment; all merriment and fun have long been forgotten. These terrible images seem burnt in upon my brain.

SCENE II.—EGMONT'S *residence*

His SECRETARY (*at a desk with papers. He rises impatiently*)

SECRETARY. Still he comes not! And I have been waiting already full two hours, pen in hand, the paper before me; and just to-day I was anxious to be out so early. The floor burns under my feet. I can with difficulty restrain my impatience. " Be punctual to the hour." Such was his parting injunction; now he comes not. There is so much business to get through, I shall not have finished before midnight. He overlooks one's faults, it is true; methinks it would be better though, were he more strict, so he dismissed one at the appointed time. One could then arrange one's plans. It is now full two hours since he left the Regent; who knows whom he may have chanced to meet by the way?

Enter EGMONT

EGMONT. Well, how do matters look?

SECRETARY. I am ready, and three couriers are waiting.

EGMONT. I have detained you too long; you look somewhat out of humour.

SECRETARY. In obedience to your command I have already been in attendance for some time. Here are the papers!

EGMONT. Donna Elvira will be angry with me, when she learns that I have detained you.

SECRETARY. You are pleased to jest.

EGMONT. No, no. Be not ashamed. I admire your taste. She is pretty, and I have no objection that you should have a friend at the castle. What say the letters?

SECRETARY. Much, my lord, but withal little that is satisfactory.

EGMONT. 'Tis well that we have pleasures at home, we have the less occasion to seek them from abroad. Is there much that requires attention?

SECRETARY. Enough, my lord; three couriers are in attendance.

EGMONT. Proceed! The most important.

SECRETARY. All is important.

EGMONT. One after the other; only be prompt.

SECRETARY. Captain Breda sends an account of the occurrences that have further taken place in Ghent and the surrounding districts. The tumult is for the most part allayed.

EGMONT. He doubtless reports individual acts of folly and temerity?

SECRETARY. He does, my lord.

EGMONT. Spare me the recital.

SECRETARY. Six of the mob who tore down the image of the Virgin at Verviers have been arrested. He inquires whether they are to be hanged like the others.

EGMONT. I am weary of hanging; let them be flogged and discharged.

SECRETARY. There are two women among them; are they to be flogged also?

EGMONT. He may admonish them and let them go.

SECRETARY. Brink, of Breda's company, wants to marry; the captain hopes you will not allow it. There are so many women among the troops, he writes, that when on the march, they resemble a gang of gypsies rather than regular soldiers.

EGMONT. We must overlook it in his case. He is a fine young fellow, and moreover entreated me so earnestly before I came away. This must be the last time, however; though it grieves me to refuse the poor fellows their best pastime; they have enough without that to torment them.

SECRETARY. Two of your people, Seter and Hart, have ill-treated a damsel, the daughter of an inn-keeper. They got her alone and she could not escape from them.

EGMONT. If she be an honest maiden and they used violence, let them be flogged three days in succession; and if they have any property, let him retain as much of it as will portion the girl.

SECRETARY. One of the foreign preachers has been discovered passing secretly through Comines. He swore that he was on the point of leaving for France. According to orders, he ought to be beheaded.

EGMONT. Let him be conducted quietly to the frontier, and there admonished that, the next time, he will not escape so easily.

SECRETARY. A letter from your steward. He writes that money comes in slowly, he can with difficulty send you the required sum within the week; the late disturbances have thrown everything into the greatest confusion.

EGMONT. Money must be had! It is for him to look to the means.

SECRETARY. He says he will do his utmost, and at length proposes to sue and imprison Raymond, who has been so long in your debt.

EGMONT. But he has promised to pay!

SECRETARY. The last time he fixed a fortnight himself.

EGMONT. Well, grant him another fortnight; after that he may proceed against him.

SECRETARY. You do well. His non-payment of the money proceeds not from inability, but from want of inclination. He will trifle no longer when he sees that you are in earnest. The steward further proposes to withhold, for half a month, the pensions which you allow to the old soldiers, widows, and others. In the meantime some expedient may be devised; they must make their arrangements accordingly.

EGMONT. But what arrangements can be made here? These poor people want the money more than I do. He must not think of it.

SECRETARY. How then, my lord, is he to raise the required sum?

EGMONT. It is his business to think of that. He was told so in a former letter.

SECRETARY. And therefore he makes these proposals.

EGMONT. They will never do;—he must think of something else. Let him suggest expedients that are admissible, and, before all, let him procure the money.

SECRETARY. I have again before me the letter from Count Oliva. Pardon my recalling it to your remembrance. Before all others, the aged count deserves a detailed reply. You proposed writing to him with your own hand. Doubtless, he loves you as a father.

EGMONT. I cannot command the time;—and of all detestable things, writing is to me the most detestable. You imitate my hand so admirably, do you write in my name. I am expecting Orange. I cannot do it;—I wish, however, that something soothing should be written, to allay his fears.

SECRETARY. Just give me a notion of what you wish to communicate; I will at once draw up the answer, and lay it before you. It shall be so written that it might pass for your hand in a court of justice.

EGMONT. Give me the letter. (*After glancing over it.*) Dear, excellent, old man! Wert thou then so cautious in thy youth? Didst thou never mount a breach? Didst thou remain in the rear of battle at the suggestion of prudence?— What affectionate solicitude! He has indeed my safety and happiness at heart, but considers not, that he who lives but to save his life, is already dead.—Charge him not to be anxious on my account; I act as circumstances require, and shall be upon my guard. Let him use his influence at court in my favour, and be assured of my warmest thanks.

SECRETARY. Is that all? He expects still more.

EGMONT. What can I say? If you choose to write more fully, do so. The matter turns upon a single point; he would have me live as I cannot live. That I am joyous, live fast, take matters easily, is my good fortune; nor would I exchange it for the safety of a sepulchre. My blood rebels against the Spanish mode of life, nor have I the least inclination to regulate my movements by the new and cautious measures of the court. Do I live only to think of life? Am I to forego the enjoyment of the present moment in order to secure the next? And must that in its turn be consumed in anxieties and idle fears?

SECRETARY. I entreat you, my lord, be not so harsh towards the venerable man. You are wont to be friendly towards every one. Say a kindly word to allay the anxiety of your noble friend. See how considerate he is, with what delicacy he warns you.

EGMONT. Yet he harps continually on the same string. He knows of old how I detest these admonitions. They serve only to perplex and are of no avail. What if I were a somnambulist, and trod the giddy summit of a lofty house, —were it the part of friendship to call me by my name, to warn me of my danger, to waken, to kill me? Let each choose his own path, and provide for his own safety.

SECRETARY. It may become you to be without a fear, but those who know and love you—

EGMONT (*looking over the letter*). Then he recalls the old story of our sayings and doings, one evening, in the wantonness of conviviality and wine; and what conclusions and inferences were thence drawn and circulated throughout the whole kingdom! Well, we had a cap and bells embroidered on the sleeves of our servants' liveries, and afterwards exchanged this senseless device for a bundle of arrows;—a still more dangerous symbol for those who are bent upon discovering a meaning where nothing is meant. These and similar follies were conceived and brought forth in a moment of merriment. It was at our suggestion that a noble troop, with beggars' wallets, and a self-chosen nickname, with mock humility recalled the King's duty to his remembrance. It was at our suggestion too—well, what does it signify? Is a carnival jest to be construed into high treason? Are we to be grudged the scanty, variegated rags, wherewith a youthful spirit and heated imagination would adorn the poor nakedness of life? Take life too seriously, and what is it worth? If the morning wake us to no new joys, if in the evening we have no pleasures to hope for, is it worth the trouble of dressing and undressing? Does the sun shine on me to-day, that I may reflect on what happened yesterday? That I may endeavour to foresee and control, what can neither be foreseen nor controlled,—the destiny of the morrow? Spare me these reflections, we will leave them to scholars and courtiers. Let them ponder and contrive, creep hither and thither, and surreptitiously achieve their ends.—If you can make use of these suggestions, without swelling your letter into a volume, it is well. Everything appears of exaggerated importance to the good old man. 'Tis thus the friend, who has long held our hand, grasps it more warmly ere he quits his hold.

SECRETARY. Pardon me, the pedestrian grows dizzy when he beholds the charioteer drive past with whirling speed.

EGMONT. Child! Child! Forbear! As if goaded by invisible spirits, the sun-steeds of time bear onward the light car of our destiny; and nothing remains for us but, with calm self-possession, firmly to grasp the reins, and now right.

now left, to steer the wheels here from the precipice and there from the rock. Whither he is hasting, who knows? Does any one consider whence he came?

SECRETARY. My lord! my lord!

EGMONT. I stand high, but I can and must rise yet higher. Courage, strength, and hope possess my soul. Not yet have I attained the height of my ambition; that once achieved, I will stand firmly and without fear. Should I fall, should a thunder-clap, a storm-blast, ay, a false step of my own, precipitate me into the abyss, so be it! I shall lie there with thousands of others. I have never disdained, even for a trifling stake, to throw the bloody die with my gallant comrades; and shall I hesitate now, when all that is most precious in life is set upon the cast?

SECRETARY. Oh, my lord! you know not what you say! May Heaven protect you!

EGMONT. Collect your papers. Orange is coming. Dispatch what is most urgent, that the couriers may set forth before the gates are closed. The rest may wait. Leave the Count's letter till to-morrow. Fail not to visit Elvira, and greet her from me. Inform yourself concerning the Regent's health. She cannot be well, though she would fain conceal it. [*Exit* SECRETARY.

Enter ORANGE

EGMONT. Welcome, Orange; you appear somewhat disturbed.

ORANGE. What say you to our conference with the Regent?

EGMONT. I found nothing extraordinary in her manner of receiving us. I have often seen her thus before. She appeared to me to be somewhat indisposed.

ORANGE. Marked you not that she was more reserved than usual? She began by cautiously approving our conduct during the late insurrection; glanced at the false light in which, nevertheless, it might be viewed: and finally turned the discourse to her favourite topic—that her gracious demeanour, her friendship for us Netherlanders, had never been sufficiently recognized, never appreciated as it deserved; that nothing came to a prosperous issue: that for her part she was beginning to grow weary of it; that

the king must at last resolve upon other measures. Did
you hear that?

EGMONT. Not all; I was thinking at the time of something
else. She is a woman, good Orange, and all women expect
that every one shall submit passively to their gentle yoke;
that every Hercules shall lay aside his lion's skin, assume
the distaff, and swell their train; and, because they are themselves peaceably inclined, imagine forsooth, that the ferment
which seizes a nation, the storm which powerful rivals excite
against one another, may be allayed by one soothing word,
and the most discordant elements be brought to unite in
tranquil harmony at their feet. 'Tis thus with her; and
since she cannot accomplish her object, why she has no
resource left but to lose her temper, to menace us with
direful prospects for the future, and to threaten to take
her departure.

ORANGE. Think you not that this time she will fulfil her
threat?

EGMONT. Never! How often have I seen her actually
prepared for the journey? Whither should she go? Being
here a stadtholder, a queen, think you that she could endure
to spend her days in insignificance at her brother's court, or
to repair to Italy, and there drag on her existence among her
old family connections?

ORANGE. She is held incapable of this determination, because you have already seen her hesitate and draw back;
nevertheless, it lies in her to take this step; new circumstances may impel her to the long-delayed resolve. What
if she were to depart, and the king to send another?

EGMONT. Why, he would come, and he also would have
business enough upon his hands. He would arrive with vast
projects and schemes to reduce all things to order, to subjugate and combine; and to-day he would be occupied with
this trifle, to-morrow with that, and the day following have
to deal with some unexpected hindrance. He would spend
one month in forming plans, another in mortification at their
failure, and half a year would be consumed in cares for a
single province. With him also time would pass, his head
grow dizzy, and things hold on their ordinary course, till
instead of sailing into the open sea, according to the plan

which he had previously marked out, he might thank God, if, amid the tempest, he were able to keep his vessel off the rocks.

ORANGE. What if the king were advised to try an experiment?

EGMONT. Which should be—?

ORANGE. To try how the body would get on without the head.

EGMONT. How?

ORANGE. Egmont, our interests have for years weighed upon my heart; I ever stand as over a chess-board, and regard no move of my adversary as insignificant; and as men of science carefully investigate the secrets of nature, so I hold it to be the duty, ay, the very vocation of a prince, to acquaint himself with the dispositions and intentions of all parties. I have reason to fear an outbreak. The king has long acted according to certain principles; he finds that they do not lead to a prosperous issue; what more probable than that he should seek it some other way?

EGMONT. I do not believe it. When a man grows old, has attempted much, and finds that the world cannot be made to move according to his will, he must needs grow weary of it at last.

ORANGE. One thing has yet to be attempted.

EGMONT. What?

ORANGE. To spare the people, and to put an end to the princes.

EGMONT. How many have long been haunted by this dread? There is no cause for such anxiety.

ORANGE. Once I felt anxious; gradually I became suspicious; suspicion has at length grown into certainty.

EGMONT. Has the king more faithful servants than ourselves?

ORANGE. We serve him after our own fashion; and, between ourselves, it must be confessed that we understand pretty well how to make the interests of the king square with our own.

EGMONT. And who does not? He has our duty and submission, in so far as they are his due.

ORANGE. But what if he should arrogate still more, and

regard as disloyalty what we esteem the maintenance of our just rights?

EGMONT. We shall know in that case how to defend ourselves. Let him assemble the Knights of the Golden Fleece; we will submit ourselves to their decision.

ORANGE. What if the sentence were to precede the trial? punishment, the sentence?

EGMONT. It were an injustice of which Philip is incapable; a folly which I cannot impute either to him or to his counsellors.

ORANGE. And how if they were both unjust and foolish?

EGMONT. No, Orange, it is impossible. Who would venture to lay hands on us? The attempt to capture us were a vain and fruitless enterprize. No, they dare not raise the standard of tyranny so high. The breeze that should waft these tidings over the land would kindle a mighty conflagration. And what object would they have in view? The king alone has no power either to judge or to condemn us and would they attempt our lives by assassination? They cannot intend it. A terrible league would unite the entire people. Direful hate and eternal separation from the crown of Spain would, on the instant, be forcibly declared.

ORANGE. The flames would then rage over our grave, and the blood of our enemies flow, a vain oblation. Let us consider, Egmont.

EGMONT. But how could they effect this purpose?

ORANGE. Alva is on the way.

EGMONT. I do not believe it.

ORANGE. I know it.

EGMONT. The Regent appeared to know nothing of it.

ORANGE. And, therefore, the stronger is my conviction. The Regent will give place to him. I know his blood-thirsty disposition, and he brings an army with him.

EGMONT. To harass the provinces anew? The people will be exasperated to the last degree.

ORANGE. Their leaders will be secured.

EGMONT. No! No!

ORANGE. Let us retire, each to his province. There we can strengthen ourselves; the duke will not begin with open violence

EGMONT. Must we not greet him when he comes?

ORANGE. We will delay.

EGMONT. What if, on his arrival, he should summon us in the king's name?

ORANGE. We will answer evasively.

EGMONT. And if he is urgent?

ORANGE. We will excuse ourselves.

EGMONT. And if he insist?

ORANGE. We shall be the less disposed to come.

EGMONT. Then war is declared; and we are rebels. Do not suffer prudence to mislead you, Orange. I know it is not fear that makes you yield. Consider this step.

ORANGE. I have considered it.

EGMONT. Consider for what you are answerable if you are wrong. For the most fatal war that ever yet desolated a country. Your refusal is the signal that at once summons the provinces to arms, that justifies every cruelty for which Spain has hitherto so anxiously sought a pretext. With a single nod you will excite to the direst confusion what, with patient effort, we have so long kept in abeyance. Think of the towns, the nobles, the people; think of commerce, agriculture, trade! Realize the murder, the desolation! Calmly the soldier beholds his comrade fall beside him in the battlefield. But towards you, carried downwards by the stream, shall float the corpses of citizens, of children, of maidens, till, aghast with horror, you shall no longer know whose cause you are defending, since you shall see those, for whose liberty you drew the sword, perishing around you. And what will be your emotions when conscience whispers, "It was for my own safety that I drew it"?

ORANGE. We are not ordinary men, Egmont. If it becomes us to sacrifice ourselves for thousands, it becomes us no less to spare ourselves for thousands.

EGMONT. He who spares himself becomes an object of suspicion ever to himself.

ORANGE. He who is sure of his own motives can, with confidence, advance or retreat.

EGMONT. Your own act will render certain the evil that you dread.

ORANGE. Wisdom and courage alike prompt us to meet an inevitable evil.

EGMONT. When the danger is imminent the faintest hope should be taken into account.

ORANGE. We have not the smallest footing left; we are on the very brink of the precipice.

EGMONT. Is the king's favour on ground so narrow?

ORANGE. Not narrow, perhaps, but slippery.

EGMONT. By heavens! he is belied. I cannot endure that he should be so meanly thought of! He is Charles's son, and incapable of meanness.

ORANGE. Kings of course do nothing mean.

EGMONT. He should be better known.

ORANGE. Our knowledge counsels us not to await the result of a dangerous experiment.

EGMONT. No experiment is dangerous, the result of which we have the courage to meet.

ORANGE. You are irritated, Egmont.

EGMONT. I must see with my own eyes.

ORANGE. Oh that for once you saw with mine! My friend, because your eyes are open, you imagine that you see. I go! Await Alva's arrival, and God be with you! My refusal to do so may perhaps save you. The dragon may deem the prey not worth seizing, if he cannot swallow us both. Perhaps he may delay, in order more surely to execute his purpose; in the meantime you may see matters in their true light. But then, be prompt! Lose not a moment! Save,—oh, save yourself! Farewell!—Let nothing escape your vigilance:—how many troops he brings with him; how he garrisons the town; what force the Regent retains; how your friends are prepared. Send me tidings—Egmont—

EGMONT. What would you?

ORANGE (*grasping his hand*). Be persuaded! Go with me!

EGMONT. How! Tears, Orange!

ORANGE To weep for a lost friend is not unmanly.

EGMONT. You deem me lost?

ORANGE. You are lost! Consider! Only a brief respite is left you. Farewell. [*Exit.*

EGMONT (*alone*). Strange that the thoughts of other men

should exert such an influence over us. These fears would never have entered my mind; and this man infects me with his solicitude. Away! 'Tis a foreign drop in my blood! Kind nature, cast it forth! And to erase the furrowed lines from my brow there yet remains indeed a friendly means.

ACT III

SCENE I.—*Palace of the Regent*

MARGARET OF PARMA

REGENT. I might have expected it. Ha! when we live immersed in anxiety and toil, we imagine that we achieve the utmost that is possible; while he, who, from a distance, looks on and commands, believes that he requires only the possible. O ye kings! I had not thought it could have galled me thus. It is so sweet to reign!—and to abdicate? I know not how my father could do so; but I will also.

MACHIAVEL *appears in the back-ground*

REGENT. Approach, Machiavel. I am thinking over this letter from my brother.

MACHIAVEL. May I know what it contains?

REGENT. As much tender consideration for me as anxiety for his states. He extols the firmness, the industry, the fidelity, with which I have hitherto watched over the interests of his Majesty in these provinces. He condoles with me that the unbridled people occasion me so much trouble. He is so thoroughly convinced of the depth of my views, so extraordinarily satisfied with the prudence of my conduct, that I must almost say the letter is too politely written for a king—certainly for a brother.

MACHIAVEL. It is not the first time that he has testified to you his just satisfaction.

REGENT. But the first time that it is a mere rhetorical figure.

MACHIAVEL. I do not understand you.

REGENT. You soon will.—For after this preamble he is of opinion that without soldiers, without a small army indeed,— I shall always cut a sorry figure here! We did wrong, he says, to withdraw our troops from the provinces at the remonstrance of the inhabitants; a garrison, he thinks, which shall press upon the neck of the burgher, will prevent him, by its weight, from making any lofty spring.

MACHIAVEL. It would irritate the public mind to the last degree.

REGENT. The king thinks, however, do you hear?—he thinks that a clever general, one who never listens to reason, will be able to deal promptly with all parties;—people and nobles, citizens and peasants; he therefore sends, with a powerful army, the Duke of Alva.

MACHIAVEL. Alva?

REGENT. You are surprised.

MACHIAVEL. You say, he sends, he asks doubtless whether he should send.

REGENT. The king asks not, he sends.

MACHIAVEL. You will then have an experienced warrior in your service.

REGENT. In my service? Speak out, Machiavel.

MACHIAVEL. I would not anticipate you.

REGENT. And I would I could dissimulate. It wounds me —wounds me to the quick. I had rather my brother would speak his mind than attach his signature to formal epistles drawn up by a secretary of state.

MACHIAVEL. Can they not comprehend?—

REGENT. I know them both within and without. They would fain make a clean sweep; and since they cannot set about it themselves, they give their confidence to any one who comes with a besom in his hand. Oh, it seems to me as if I saw the king and his council worked upon this tapestry.

MACHIAVEL. So distinctly!

REGENT. No feature is wanting. There are good men among them. The honest Roderigo, so experienced and so moderate, who does not aim too high, yet lets nothing sink too low; the upright Alonzo, the diligent Freneda, the steadfast Las Vargas, and others who join them when the good party are in power. But there sits the hollow-eyed Toledan, with brazen front and deep fire-glance, muttering between his teeth about womanish softness, ill-timed concession, and that women can ride trained steeds, well enough, but are themselves bad masters of the horse, and the like pleasantries, which, in former times, I have been compelled to hear from political gentlemen.

MACHIAVEL. You have chosen good colours for your picture.

REGENT. Confess, Machiavel, among the tints from which I might select, there is no hue so livid, so jaundice-like, as Alva's complexion, and the colour he is wont to paint with. He regards every one as a blasphemer or traitor, for under this head they can all be racked, impaled, quartered, and burnt at pleasure. The good I have accomplished here appears as nothing seen from a distance, just because it is good. Then he dwells on every outbreak that is past, recalls every disturbance that is quieted, and brings before the king such a picture of mutiny, sedition, and audacity, that we appear to him to be actually devouring one another, when with us the transient explosion of a rude people has long been forgotten. Thus he conceives a cordial hatred for the poor people; he views them with horror, as beasts and monsters; looks around for fire and sword, and imagines that by such means human beings are subdued.

MACHIAVEL. You appear to me too vehement; you take the matter too seriously. Do you not remain Regent?

REGENT. I am aware of that. He will bring his instructions. I am old enough in state affairs to understand how people can be supplanted, without being actually deprived of office. First, he will produce a commission, couched in terms somewhat obscure and equivocal; he will stretch his authority, for the power is in his hands; if I complain, he will hint at secret instructions; if I desire to see them, he will answer evasively; if I insist, he will produce a paper of totally different import; and if this fail to satisfy me, he will go on precisely as if I had never interfered. Meanwhile he will have accomplished what I dread, and have frustrated my most cherished schemes.

MACHIAVEL. I wish I could contradict you.

REGENT. His harshness and cruelty will again arouse the turbulent spirit, which, with unspeakable patience, I have succeeded in quelling; I shall see my work destroyed before my eyes, and have besides to bear the blame of his wrong-doing.

MACHIAVEL. Await it, your Highness.

REGENT. I have sufficient self-command to remain quiet. Let him come; I will make way for him with the best grace ere he pushes me aside.

MACHIAVEL. So important a step thus suddenly?

REGENT. 'Tis harder than you imagine. He who is accustomed to rule, to hold daily in his hand the destiny of thousands, descends from the throne as into the grave. Better thus, however, than linger a spectre among the living, and with hollow aspect endeavour to maintain a place which another has inherited, and already possesses and enjoys.

SCENE II.—CLARA'S *dwelling*

CLARA *and her* MOTHER

MOTHER. Such a love as Brackenburg's I have never seen; I thought it was to be found only in romance books.

CLARA (*walking up and down the room, humming a song*).

> With love's thrilling rapture
> What joy can compare!

MOTHER. He suspects thy attachment to Egmont; and yet, if thou wouldst but treat him a little kindly, I do believe he would marry thee still, if thou wouldst have him.

CLARA (*sings*).

> Blissful
> And tearful,
> With thought-teeming brain;
> Hoping
> And fearing
> In passionate pain;
> Now shouting in triumph,
> Now sunk in despair;—
> With love's thrilling rapture
> What joy can compare!

MOTHER. Have done with such baby-nonsense!

CLARA. Nay, do not abuse it; 'tis a song of marvellous virtue. Many a time have I lulled a grown child to sleep with it.

MOTHER. Ay! Thou canst think of nothing but thy love. If it only did not put everything else out of thy head. Thou shouldst have more regard for Brackenburg, I tell thee. He may make thee happy yet some day.

CLARA. He?

MOTHER. Oh, yes! A time will come! You children live only in the present, and give no ear to our experience. Youth and happy love, all has an end; and there comes a time when one thanks God if one has any corner to creep into.

CLARA (*shudders, and after a pause stands up*). Mother, let that time come—like death. To think of it beforehand is horrible! And if it come! If we must—then—we will bear ourselves as we may. Live without thee, Egmont! (*Weeping.*) No! It is impossible.

Enter EGMONT (*enveloped in a horseman's cloak, his hat drawn over his face*)

EGMONT. Clara!

CLARA (*utters a cry and starts back*). Egmont! (*She hastens towards him.*) Egmont! (*She embraces and leans upon him.*) O thou good, kind, sweet Egmont! Art thou come? Art thou here indeed!

EGMONT. Good evening, mother?

MOTHER. God save you, noble sir! My daughter has wellnigh pined to death, because you have stayed away so long; she talks and sings about you the live-long day.

EGMONT. You will give me some supper?

MOTHER. You do us too much honour. If we only had anything—

CLARA. Certainly! Be quiet, mother; I have provided everything; there is something prepared. Do not betray me, mother.

MOTHER. There's little enough.

CLARA. Never mind! And then I think when he is with me I am never hungry; so he cannot, I should think, have any great appetite when I am with him.

EGMONT. Do you think so? (CLARA *stamps with her foot and turns pettishly away.*) What ails you?

CLARA. How cold you are to-day! You have not yet offered me a kiss. Why do you keep your arms enveloped in your mantle, like a new-born babe? It becomes neither a soldier nor a lover to keep his arms muffled up.

EGMONT. Sometimes, dearest, sometimes. When the soldier stands in ambush and would delude the foe, he collects his thoughts, gathers his mantle around him, and matures his plan and a lover—

MOTHER. Will you not take a seat, and make yourself comfortable? I must to the kitchen, Clara thinks of nothing when you are here. You must put up with what we have.

EGMONT. Your good-will is the best seasoning.

[*Exit* MOTHER.

CLARA. And what then is my love?

EGMONT. Just what thou wilt.

CLARA. Liken it to anything, if you have the heart.

EGMONT. But first. (*He flings aside his mantle, and appears arrayed in a magnificent dress.*)

CLARA. Oh heavens!

EGMONT. Now my arms are free! (*Embraces her.*)

CLARA. Don't! You will spoil your dress. (*She steps back.*) How magnificent! I dare not touch you.

EGMONT. Art thou satisfied? I promised to come once arrayed in Spanish fashion.

CLARA. I had ceased to remind you of it; I thought you did not like it—ah, and the Golden Fleece!

EGMONT. Thou seest it now.

CLARA. And did the emperor really hang it round thy neck!

EGMONT. He did, my child! And this chain and Order invest the wearer with the noblest privileges. On earth I acknowledge no judge over my actions, except the grand master of the Order, with the assembled chapter of knights.

CLARA. Oh, thou mightest let the whole world sit in judgment over thee. The velvet is too splendid! and the braiding! and the embroidery! One knows not where to begin.

EGMONT. There, look thy fill.

CLARA. And the Golden Fleece! You told me its history,

and said it is the symbol of everything great and precious, of everything that can be merited and won by diligence and toil. It is very precious—I may liken it to thy love;—even so I wear it next my heart;—and then—

EGMONT. What wilt thou say?

CLARA. And then again it is not like.

EGMONT. How so?

CLARA. I have not won it by diligence and toil, I have not deserved it.

EGMONT. It is otherwise in love. Thou dost deserve it because thou hast not sought it—and, for the most part, those only obtain love who seek it not.

CLARA. Is it from thine own experience that thou hast learned this? Didst thou make that proud remark in reference to thyself? Thou, whom all the people love?

EGMONT. Would that I had done something for them! That I could do anything for them! It is their own good pleasure to love me.

CLARA. Thou hast doubtless been with the Regent to-day?

EGMONT. I have.

CLARA. Art thou upon good terms with her?

EGMONT. So it would appear. We are kind and serviceable to each other.

CLARA. And in thy heart?

EGMONT. I like her. True, we have each our own views; but that is nothing to the purpose. She is an excellent woman, knows with whom she has to deal, and would be penetrating enough were she not quite so suspicious. I give her plenty of employment, because she is always suspecting some secret motive in my conduct when, in fact, I have none.

CLARA. Really none?

EGMONT. Well, with one little exception, perhaps. All wine deposits lees in the cask in the course of time. Orange furnishes her still better entertainment, and is a perpetual riddle. He has got the credit of harbouring some secret design; and she studies his brow to discover his thoughts, and his steps, to learn in what direction they are bent.

CLARA. Does she dissemble?

EGMONT. She is Regent—and do you ask?

CLARA. Pardon me; I meant to say, is she false?

EGMONT. Neither more nor less than everyone who has his own objects to attain.

CLARA. I should never feel at home in the world. But she has a masculine spirit, and is another sort of woman from us housewives and sempstresses. She is great, steadfast, resolute.

EGMONT. Yes, when matters are not too much involved For once, however, she is a little disconcerted.

CLARA. How so?

EGMONT. She has a moustache, too, on her upper lip, and occasionally an attack of the gout. A regular Amazon.

CLARA. A majestic woman! I should dread to appear before her.

EGMONT. Yet thou art not wont to be timid! It would not be fear, only maidenly bashfulness.

> (CLARA *casts down her eyes, takes his hand, and leans upon him.*)

EGMONT. I understand thee, dearest! Thou mayst raise thine eyes. (*He kisses her eyes.*)

CLARA. Let me be silent! Let me embrace thee! Let me look into thine eyes, and find there everything—hope and comfort, joy and sorrow! (*She embraces and gazes on him.*) Tell me! Oh, tell me! It seems so strange—art thou indeed Egmont! Count Egmont! The great Egmont, who makes so much noise in the world, who figures in the newspapers, who is the support and stay of the provinces?

EGMONT. No, Clara, I am not he.

CLARA. How?

EGMONT. Seest thou, Clara? Let me sit down! (*He seats himself, she kneels on a footstool before him, rests her arms on his knees and looks up in his face.*) That Egmont is a morose, cold, unbending Egmont, obliged to be upon his guard, to assume now this appearance and now that; harassed, misapprehended and perplexed, when the crowd esteem him light-hearted and gay; beloved by a people who do not know their own minds; honoured and extolled by the intractable multitude; surrounded by friends in whom he dares not confide; observed by men who are on the watch to supplant him; toiling and striving, often without an object, generally without a reward. O let me conceal how it fares with him, let me not speak of his feelings! But this Egmont, Clara, is calm, unreserved, happy, beloved and known by the best of hearts, which is also thoroughly known to him, and which he presses to his own with unbounded confidence and love. (*He embraces her.*)   This is thy Egmont.

CLARA. So let me die! The world has no joy after this!

ACT IV

Scene I.—*A Street*

JETTER, CARPENTER

JETTER. Hist! neighbour,—a word!

CARPENTER. Go your way and be quiet.

JETTER. Only one word. Is there nothing new?

CARPENTER. Nothing, except that we are anew forbidden to speak.

JETTER. How?

CARPENTER. Step here, close to this house. Take heed! Immediately on his arrival, the Duke of Alva published a decree, by which two or three, found conversing together in the streets, are without trial, declared guilty of high treason.

JETTER. Alas!

CARPENTER. To speak of state affairs is prohibited on pain of perpetual imprisonment.

JETTER. Alas for our liberty!

CARPENTER. And no one, on pain of death, shall censure the measures of government.

JETTER. Alas, for our heads!

CARPENTER. And fathers, mothers, children, kindred, friends, and servants, are invited, by the promise of large rewards, to disclose what passes in the privacy of our homes, before an expressly appointed tribunal.

JETTER. Let us go home.

CARPENTER. And the obedient are promised that they shall suffer no injury, either in person or estate.

JETTER. How gracious!—I felt ill at ease the moment the

duke entered the town. Since then, it has seemed to me, as though the heavens were covered with black crape, which hangs so low, that one must stoop down to avoid knocking one's head against it.

CARPENTER. And how do you like his soldiers? They are a different sort of crabs from those we have been used to.

JETTER. Faugh! It gives one the cramp at one's heart to see such a troop march down the street. As straight as tapers, with fixed look, only one step, however many there may be; and when they stand sentinel, and you pass one of them, it seems as though he would look you through and through; and he looks so stiff and morose, that you fancy you see a task-master at every corner. They offend my sight. Our militia were merry fellows; they took liberties, stood their legs astride, their hats over their ears, they lived and let live; these fellows are like machines with a devil inside them.

CARPENTER. Were such an one to cry, "Halt!" and to level his musket, think you one would stand?

JETTER. I should fall dead upon the spot.

CARPENTER. Let us go home!

JETTER. No good can come of it. Farewell.

Enter SOEST

SOEST. Friends! Neighbours!

CARPENTER. Hush! Let us go.

SOEST. Have you heard?

JETTER. Only too much!

SOEST. The Regent is gone.

JETTER. Then Heaven help us.

CARPENTER. She was some stay to us.

SOEST. Her departure was sudden and secret. She could not agree with the duke; she has sent word to the nobles that she intends to return. No one believes it, however.

CARPENTER. God pardon the nobles for letting this new yoke be laid upon our necks. They might have prevented it. Our privileges are gone.

JETTER. For Heaven's sake not a word about privileges.

I already scent an execution; the sun will not come forth; the fogs are rank.

SOEST. Orange, too, is gone.

CARPENTER. Then are we quite deserted!

SOEST. Count Egmont is still here.

JETTER. God be thanked! Strengthen him, all ye saints, to do his utmost; he is the only one who can help us.

Enter VANSEN

VANSEN. Have I at length found a few brave citizens who have not crept out of sight?

JETTER. Do us the favour to pass on.

VANSEN. You are not civil.

JETTER. This is no time for compliments. Does your back itch again? are your wounds already healed?

VANSEN. Ask a soldier about his wounds? Had I cared for blows, nothing good would have come of me.

JETTER. Matters may grow more serious.

VANSEN. You feel from the gathering storm a pitiful weakness in your limbs, it seems.

CARPENTER. Your limbs will soon be in motion elsewhere, if you do not keep quiet.

VANSEN. Poor mice! The master of the house procures a new cat, and ye are straight in despair! The difference is very trifling; we shall get on as we did before, only be quiet.

CARPENTER. You are an insolent knave.

VANSEN. Gossip! Let the duke alone. The old cat looks as though he had swallowed devils, instead of mice, and could not now digest them. Let him alone, I say; he must eat, drink, and sleep, like other men. I am not afraid if we only watch our opportunity. At first he makes quick work of it; by-and-by, however, he too will find that it is pleasanter to live in the larder, among flitches of bacon, and to rest by night, than to entrap a few solitary mice in the granary. Go to! I know the stadtholders.

CARPENTER. What such a fellow can say with impunity! Had I said such a thing, I should not hold myself safe a moment.

VANSEN. Do not make yourselves uneasy! God in heaven does not trouble himself about you, poor worms, much less the Regent.

JETTER. Slanderer!

VANSEN. I know some for whom it would be better if, instead of their own high spirits, they had a little tailor's blood in their veins.

CARPENTER. What mean you by that?

VANSEN. Hum! I mean the count.

JETTER. Egmont! What has he to fear?

VANSEN. I'm a poor devil, and could live a whole year round on what he loses in a single night; yet he would do well to give me his revenue for a twelvemonth, to have my head upon his shoulders for one quarter of an hour.

JETTER. You think yourself very clever; yet there is more sense in the hairs of Egmont's head, than in your brains.

VANSEN. Perhaps so! Not more shrewdness, however. These gentry are the most apt to deceive themselves. He should be more chary of his confidence.

JETTER. How his tongue wags! Such a gentleman!

VANSEN. Just because he is not a tailor.

JETTER. You audacious scoundrel!

VANSEN. I only wish he had your courage in his limbs for an hour to make him uneasy, and plague and torment him, till he were compelled to leave the town.

JETTER. What nonsense you talk; why he's as safe as a star in heaven.

VANSEN. Have you ever seen one snuff itself out? Off it went!

CARPENTER. Who would dare to meddle with him?

VANSEN. Will you interfere to prevent it? Will you stir up an insurrection if he is arrested?

JETTER. Ah!

VANSEN. Will you risk your ribs for his sake?

SOEST. Eh!

VANSEN (*mimicking them*). Eh! Oh! Ah! Run through the alphabet in your wonderment. So it is, and so it will remain. Heaven help him!

JETTER. Confound your impudence. Can such a noble, upright man have anything to fear?

VANSEN. In this world the rogue has everywhere the advantage. At the bar, he makes a fool of the judge; on the bench, he takes pleasure in convicting the accused. I have had to copy out a protocol, where the commissary was handsomely rewarded by the court, both with praise and money, because through his cross-examination, an honest devil, against whom they had a grudge, was made out to be a rogue.

CARPENTER. Why, that again is a downright lie. What can they want to get out of a man if he is innocent?

VANSEN. Oh, you blockhead! When nothing can be worked out of a man by cross-examination, they work it into him. Honesty is rash and withal somewhat presumptuous; at first they question quietly enough, and the prisoner, proud of his innocence, as they call it, comes out with much that a sensible man would keep back! then, from these answers the inquisitor proceeds to put new questions, and is on the watch for the slightest contradiction; there he fastens his line; and, let the poor devil lose his self-possession, say too much here, or too little there, or, Heaven knows from what whim or other, let him withhold some trifling circumstance, or at any moment give way to fear—then we're on the right track, and, I assure you, no beggar-woman seeks for rags among the rubbish with more care than such a fabricator of rogues, from trifling, crooked, disjointed, misplaced, misprinted, and concealed facts and information, acknowledged or denied, endeavours at length to patch up a scarecrow, by means of which he may at least hang his victim in effigy; and the poor devil may thank Heaven if he is in a condition to see himself hanged.

JETTER. He has a ready tongue of his own.

CARPENTER. This may serve well enough with flies. Wasps laugh at your cunning web.

VANSEN. According to the kind of spider. The tall duke, now, has just the look of your garden spider; not the large-bellied kind, they are less dangerous; but your long-footed, meagre-bodied gentleman, that does not fatten on his diet, and whose threads are slender indeed, but not the less tenacious.

JETTER. Egmont is knight of the Golden Fleece, who dare

lay hands on him? He can be tried only by his peers, by the assembled knights of his order. Your own foul tongue and evil conscience betray you into this nonsense.

VANSEN. Think you that I wish him ill? I would you were in the right. He is an excellent gentleman. He once let off, with a sound drubbing, some good friends of mine, who would else have been hanged. Now take yourselves off! begone, I advise you! Yonder I see the patrol again commencing their round. They do not look as if they would be willing to fraternize with us over a glass. We must wait, and bide our time. I have a couple of nieces and a gossip of a tapster; if after enjoying themselves in their company, they are not tamed, they are regular wolves.

SCENE II.—*The Palace of Eulenberg, Residence of the* DUKE OF ALVA

SILVA *and* GOMEZ (*meeting*)

SILVA. Have you executed the duke's commands.?

GOMEZ. Punctually. All the day-patrols have received orders to assemble at the appointed time, at the various points that I have indicated. Meanwhile, they march as usual through the town to maintain order. Each is ignorant respecting the movements of the rest, and imagines the command to have reference to himself alone; thus in a moment the cordon can be formed, and all the avenues to the palace occupied. Know you the reason of this command?

SILVA. I am accustomed blindly to obey; and to whom can one more easily render obedience than to the duke, since the event always proves the wisdom of his commands?

GOMEZ. Well! Well! I am not surprised that you are become as reserved and monosyllabic as the duke, since you are obliged to be always about his person; to me, however, who am accustomed to the lighter service of Italy, it seems strange enough. In loyalty and obedience, I am the same old soldier as ever; but I am wont to indulge in gossip and discussion; here, you are all silent, and seem as though you knew not how to enjoy yourselves. The duke, methinks, is like a brazen tower without gates, the garrison of which must be furnished with wings. Not long ago I heard him say at the table of a gay, jovial fellow that he was like a bad spirit-shop, with a brandy sign displayed, to allure idlers, vagabonds, and thieves.

SILVA. And has he not brought us hither in silence?

GOMEZ. Nothing can be said against that. Of a truth, we, who witnessed the address with which he led the troops hither out of Italy, have seen something. How he advanced warily through friends and foes; through the French, both royalists and heretics; through the Swiss and their confederates; maintained the strictest discipline, and accomplished with ease, and without the slightest hindrance, a march that was esteemed so perilous!—We have seen and learned something.

SILVA. Here too! Is not everything as still and quiet as though there had been no disturbance?

GOMEZ. Why, as for that, it was tolerably quiet when we arrived.

SILVA. The provinces have become much more tranquil; if there is any movement now, it is only among those who wish to escape; and to them, methinks, the duke will speedily close every outlet.

GOMEZ. This service cannot fail to win for him the favour of the king.

SILVA. And nothing is more expedient for us than to retain his. Should the king come hither, the duke doubtless and all whom he recommends will not go without their reward.

GOMEZ. Do you really believe then that the king will come?

SILVA. So many preparations are being made, that the report appears highly probable.

GOMEZ. I am not convinced, however.

SILVA. Keep your thoughts to yourself then. For if it should not be the king's intention to come, it is at least certain that he wishes the rumour to be believed.

Enter FERDINAND

FERDINAND. Is my father not yet abroad?

SILVA. We are waiting to receive his commands.

FERDINAND. The princes will soon be here.

GOMEZ. Are they expected to-day?

FERDINAND. Orange and Egmont.

GOMEZ (*aside to* SILVA). A light breaks in upon me.

SILVA. Well, then, say nothing about it.

Enter the DUKE OF ALVA (*as he advances the rest draw back*)

ALVA. Gomez.

GOMEZ (*steps forward*). My lord.

ALVA. You have distributed the guards and given them their instructions?

GOMEZ. Most accurately. The day-patrols—

ALVA. Enough. Attend in the gallery. Silva will announce to you the moment when you are to draw them together, and to occupy the avenues leading to the palace. The rest you know.

GOMEZ. I do, my lord. [*Exit.*

ALVA. Silva.

SILVA. Here my lord.

ALVA. I shall require you to manifest to-day all the qualities which I have hitherto prized in you: courage, resolve, unswerving execution.

SILVA. I thank you for affording me an opportunity of showing that your old servant is unchanged.

ALVA. The moment the princes enter my cabinet, hasten to arrest Egmont's private secretary. You have made all needful preparations for securing the others who are specified?

SILVA. Rely upon us. Their doom, like a well-calculated eclipse, will overtake them with terrible certainty.

ALVA. Have you had them all narrowly watched?

SILVA. All. Egmont especially. He is the only one whose demeanour, since your arrival, remains unchanged. The live-long day he is now on one horse and now on another; he invites guests as usual, is merry and entertaining at table, plays at dice, shoots, and at night steals to his mistress. The others, on the contrary, have made a manifest pause in their mode of life; they remain at home, and, from the outward aspect of their houses, you would imagine that there was a sick man within.

ALVA. To work then, ere they recover in spite of us.

SILVA. I shall bring them without fail. In obedience to your commands we load them with officious honours; they are alarmed; cautiously, yet anxiously, they tender us their thanks, feel that flight would be the most prudent course, yet none venture to adopt it; they hesitate, are unable to work together, while the bond which unites them prevents their acting boldly as individuals. They are anxious to withdraw themselves from suspicion, and thus only render themselves more obnoxious to it. I already contemplate with joy the successful realization of your scheme.

ALVA. I rejoice only over what is accomplished, and not lightly over that; for there ever remains ground for serious and anxious thought. Fortune is capricious; the common, the worthless, she oft-times ennobles, while she dishonours with a contemptible issue the most maturely considered schemes. Await the arrival of the princes, then order Gomez to occupy the streets, and hasten yourself to arrest Egmont's secretary, and the others who are specified. This done, return, and announce to my son that he may bring me the tidings in the council.

SILVA. I trust this evening I shall dare to appear in your presence. (ALVA *approaches his son who has hitherto been standing in the gallery.*) I dare not whisper it even to myself; but my mind misgives me. The event will, I fear, be different from what he anticipates. I see before me spirits, who, still and thoughtful, weigh in ebon scales the doom of princes and of many thousands. Slowly the beam moves up and down; deeply the judges appear to ponder; at length one scale sinks, the other rises, breathed on by the caprice of destiny, and all is decided. [*Exit.*

ALVA (*advancing with his son*). How did you find the town?

FERDINAND. All is again quiet. I rode as for pastime, from street to street. Your well-distributed patrols hold Fear so tightly yoked, that she does not venture even to whisper. The town resembles a plain when the lightning's glare announces the impending storm: no bird, no beast is to be seen, that is not stealing to a place of shelter.

ALVA. Has nothing further occurred?

FERDINAND. Egmont, with a few companions, rode into the market-place; we exchanged greetings; he was mounted on an unbroken charger, which excited my admiration, " Let us hasten to break in our steeds," he exclaimed; " we shall need them ere long! " He said that he should see me again to-day; he is coming here, at your desire, to deliberate with you.

ALVA. He will see you again.

FERDINAND. Among all the knights whom I know here, he pleases me the best. I think we shall be friends.

ALVA. You are always rash and inconsiderate. I recognize in you the levity of your mother, which threw her unconditionally into my arms. Appearances have already allured you precipitately into many dangerous connections.

FERDINAND. You will find me ever submissive.

ALVA. I pardon this inconsiderate kindness, this heedless gaiety, in consideration of your youthful blood. Only forget not on what mission I am sent, and what part in it I would assign to you.

FERDINAND. Admonish me, and spare me not, when you deem it needful.

ALVA (*after a pause*). My son!

FERDINAND. My father!

ALVA. The princes will be here anon; Orange and Egmont. It is not mistrust that has withheld me till now from disclosing to you what is about to take place. They will not depart hence.

FERDINAND. What do you purpose?

ALVA. It has been resolved to arrest them.—You are astonished! Learn what you have to do; the reasons you shall know when all is accomplished. Time fails now to unfold them. With you alone I wish to deliberate on the weightiest, the most secret matters; a powerful bond holds us linked together; you are dear and precious to me; on you I would bestow everything. Not the habit of obedience alone would I impress upon you; I desire also to implant within your mind the power to realize, to command, to execute; to you I would bequeath a vast inheritance, to the king a most useful servant; I would endow you with the noblest of my possessions, that you may not be ashamed to appear among your brethren.

FERDINAND. How deeply am I indebted to you for this love, which you manifest for me alone, while a whole kingdom trembles before you!

ALVA. Now hear what is to be done. As soon as the princes have entered, every avenue to the palace will be guarded. This duty is confided to Gomez. Silva will hasten to arrest Egmont's secretary, together with those whom we hold most in suspicion. You, meanwhile, will take the command of the guards stationed at the gates and in the courts. Before all, take care to occupy the adjoining apartment with the trustiest soldiers. Wait in the gallery till Silva returns, then bring me any unimportant paper, as a signal that his commission is executed. Remain in the ante-chamber till Orange retires, follow him; I will detain Egmont here as though I had some further communication to make to him. At the end of the gallery demand Orange's sword, summon the guards, secure promptly the most dangerous man; I meanwhile will seize Egmont here.

FERDINAND. I obey, my father—for the first time with a heavy and an anxious heart.

ALVA. I pardon you; this is the first great day of your life.

Enter SILVA

SILVA. A courier from Antwerp. Here is Orange's letter. He does not come.

ALVA. Says the messenger so?

SILVA. No, my own heart tells me.

ALVA. In thee speaks my evil genius. (*After reading the letter, he makes a sign to the two, and they retire to the gallery.* ALVA *remains alone in front of the stage.*) He comes not! Till the last moment he delays declaring himself. He ventures not to come! So then, the cautious man, contrary to all expectations, is for once cautious enough to lay aside his wonted caution. The hour moves on! Let the finger travel but a short space over the dial, and a great work is done or lost—irrevocably lost; for the opportunity can never be retrieved, nor can our intention remain concealed. Long had I maturely weighed everything, foreseen even this contingency, and firmly resolved in my own mind what, in that case, was to be done; and now, when I am called upon to act, I can with difficulty guard my mind from being again distracted by conflicting doubts. Is it expedient to seize the others if he escape me? Shall I delay, and suffer Egmont to elude my grasp, together with his friends, and so many others who now, and perhaps for to-day only, are in my hands? How! Does destiny control even thee—the uncontrollable? How long matured! How well prepared! How great, how admirable the plan! How nearly had hope attained the goal! And now, at the decisive moment, thou art placed between two evils; as in a lottery, thou dost grasp in the dark future; what thou hast drawn remains still unrolled, to thee unknown whether it is a prize or a blank! (*He becomes attentive, like one who hears a noise, and steps to the window.*) 'Tis he! Egmont! Did thy steed bear thee hither so lightly, and started not at the scent of blood, at the spirit with the naked sword who received thee at the gate? Dismount! Lo, now thou hast one foot in the grave! And now both! Ay, caress him, and for the last time stroke his neck for the gallant service he has rendered thee. And for me no choice is left. The delusion, in which Egmont ventures here to-day, cannot a second time deliver him into my hands! Hark! (FERDI- NAND *and* SILVA *enter hastily.*) Obey my orders! I swerve not from my purpose. I shall detain Egmont here as best I may, till you bring me tidings from Silva. Then remain at hand. Thee, too, fate has robbed of the proud honour of arresting with thine own hand the king's greatest enemy. (*To* SILVA.) Be prompt! (*To* FERDINAND.) Advance to meet him.

> (ALVA *remains some moments alone, pacing the chamber in silence.*)

Enter EGMONT

EGMONT. I come to learn the king's commands; to hear what service he demands from our loyalty, which remains eternally devoted to him.

ALVA. He desires, before all, to hear your counsel.

EGMONT. Upon what subject? Does Orange come also? I thought to find him here.

ALVA. I regret that he fails us at this important crisis. The king desires your counsel, your opinion as to the best means of tranquillizing these states. He trusts indeed that you will zealously co-operate with him in quelling these disturbances, and in securing to these provinces the benefit of complete and permanent order.

EGMONT. You, my lord, should know better than I, that tranquillity is already sufficiently restored, and was still more so, till the appearance of fresh troops again agitated the public mind, and filled it anew with anxiety and alarm.

ALVA. You seem to intimate that it would have been more advisable if the king had not placed me in a position to interrogate you.

EGMONT. Pardon me! It is not for me to determine whether the king acted advisedly in sending the army hither, whether the might of his royal presence alone would not have operated more powerfully. The army is here, the king is not. But we should be most ungrateful were we to forget what we owe to the Regent. Let it be acknowledged! By her prudence and valour, by her judicious use of authority and force, of persuasion and finesse, she pacified the insurgents, and, to the astonishment of the world, succeeded, in the course of a few months, in bringing a rebellious people back to their duty.

ALVA. I deny it not. The insurrection is quelled; and the people appear to be already forced back within the bounds of obedience. But does it not depend upon their caprice alone to overstep these bounds? Who shall prevent them from again breaking loose? Where is the power capable of restraining them? Who will be answerable to us for their future loyalty and submission? Their own good-will is the sole pledge we have.

EGMONT. And is not the good-will of a people the surest, the noblest pledge? By heaven! when can a monarch hold himself more secure, ay, both against foreign and domestic foes, than when all can stand for one, and one for all?

ALVA. You would not have us believe, however, that such is the case here at present?

EGMONT. Let the king proclaim a general pardon; he will thus tranquillize the public mind; and it will be seen how speedily loyalty and affection will return, when confidence is restored.

ALVA. How! And suffer those who have insulted the majesty of the king, who have violated the sanctuaries of our religion, to go abroad unchallenged! living witnesses that enormous crimes may be perpetrated with impunity!

EGMONT. And ought not a crime of frenzy, of intoxication, to be excused, rather than horribly chastised? Especially when there is the sure hope, nay, more, where there is positive certainty that the evil will never again recur? Would not sovereigns thus be more secure? Are not those monarchs most extolled by the world and by posterity, who can pardon, pity, despise an offence against their dignity? Are they not on that account likened to God himself, who is far too exalted to be assailed by every idle blasphemy?

ALVA. And therefore, should the king contend for the honour of God and of religion, we for the authority of the king. What the supreme power disdains to avert, it is our duty to avenge. Were I to counsel, no guilty person should live to rejoice in his impunity.

EGMONT. Think you that you will be able to reach them all? Do we not daily hear that fear is driving them to and fro, and forcing them out of the land? The more wealthy will escape to other countries with their property, their children, and their friends; while the poor will carry their industrious hands to our neighbours.

ALVA. They will, if they cannot be prevented. It is on this account that the king desires counsel and aid from every prince, zealous co-operation from every stadtholder; not merely a description of the present posture of affairs, or conjectures as to what might take place were events suffered to hold on their course without interruption. To contemplate a mighty evil, to flatter oneself with hope, to trust to time, to strike a blow, like the clown in a play, so as to make a noise and appear to do something, when in fact one would fain do nothing; is not such conduct calculated to awaken a suspicion that those who act thus contemplate with satisfaction a rebellion, which they would not indeed excite, but which they are by no means unwilling to encourage?

EGMONT (*about to break forth, restrains himself, and after a brief pause, speaks with composure*). Not every design is obvious, and many a man's design is misconstrued. It is widely rumoured, however, that the object which the king has in view is not so much to govern the provinces according to uniform and clearly defined laws, to maintain the majesty of religion, and to give his people universal peace, as unconditionally to subjugate them, to rob them of their ancient rights, to appropriate their possessions, to curtail the fair privileges of the nobles, for whose sake alone they are ready to serve him with life and limb. Religion, it is said, is merely a splendid device, behind which every dangerous design may be contrived with the greater ease; the prostrate crowds adore the sacred symbols pictured there while behind lurks the fowler ready to ensnare them.

ALVA. This must I hear from you?

EGMONT. I speak not my own sentiments! I but repeat what is loudly rumoured, and uttered now here and now there by great and by humble, by wise men and fools. The Netherlanders fear a double yoke, and who will be surety to them for their liberty?

ALVA. Liberty! A fair word when rightly understood. What liberty would they have? What is the freedom of the most free? To do right! And in that the monarch will not hinder them. No! No! They imagine themselves enslaved, when they have not the power to injure themselves and others. Would it not be better to abdicate at once, rather than rule such a people? When the country is threatened by foreign invaders, the burghers, occupied only with their immediate interests, bestow no thought upon the advancing foe, and when the king requires their aid, they quarrel among themselves, and thus, as it were, conspire with the enemy. Far better is it to circumscribe their power, to control and guide them for their good, as children are controlled and guided. Trust me, a people grows neither old nor wise, a people remains always in its infancy.

EGMONT. How rarely does a king attain wisdom! And is

it not fit that the many should confide their interests to the many rather than to the one? And not even to the one, but to the few servants of the one, men who have grown old under the eyes of their master. To grow wise, it seems, is the exclusive privilege of these favoured individuals.

ALVA. Perhaps for the very reason that they are not left to themselves.

EGMONT. And therefore they would fain leave no one else to his own guidance. Let them do what they like, however; I have replied to your questions, and I repeat, the measures you propose will never succeed! They cannot succeed! I know my countrymen. They are men worthy to tread God's earth; each complete in himself, a little king, steadfast, active, capable, loyal, attached to ancient customs. It may be difficult to win their confidence, but it is easy to retain it. Firm and unbending! They may be crushed, but not subdued.

ALVA (*who during this speech has looked round several times*). Would you venture to repeat what you have uttered, in the king's presence?

EGMONT. It were the worse, if in his presence I were restrained by fear! The better for him and for his people, if he inspired me with confidence, if he encouraged me to give yet freer utterance to my thoughts.

ALVA. What is profitable, I can listen to as well as he.

EGMONT. I would say to him—'Tis easy for the shepherd to drive before him a flock of sheep; the ox draws the plough without opposition; but if you would ride the noble steed, you must study his thoughts, you must require nothing unreasonable, nor unreasonably, from him. The burgher desires to retain his ancient constitution; to be governed by his own countrymen; and why? Because he knows in that case how he shall be ruled, because he can rely upon their disinterestedness, upon their sympathy with his fate.

ALVA. And ought not the Regent to be empowered to alter these ancient usages? Should not this constitute his fairest privilege? What is permanent in this world? And shall the constitution of a state alone remain unchanged? Must not every relation alter in the course of time, and on that very account, an ancient constitution become the source of a thousand evils, because not adapted to the present condition of the people? These ancient rights afford, doubtless, convenient loopholes, through which the crafty and the powerful may creep, and wherein they may lie concealed, to the injury of the people and of the entire community; and it is on this account, I fear, that they are held in such high esteem.

EGMONT. And these arbitrary changes, these unlimited encroachments of the supreme power, are they not indications that one will permit himself to do what is forbidden to thousands? The monarch would alone be free, that he may have it in his power to gratify his every wish, to realize his every thought. And though we should confide in him as a good and virtuous sovereign, will he be answerable to us for his successor? That none who come after him shall rule without consideration, without forbearance! And who would deliver us from absolute caprice, should he send hither his servants, his minions, who, without knowledge of the country and its requirements, should govern according to their own good pleasure, meet with no opposition, and know themselves exempt from all responsibility?

ALVA (*who has meanwhile again looked round*). There is nothing more natural than that a king should choose to retain the power in his own hands, and that he should select as the instruments of his authority, those who best understand him, who desire to understand him, and who will unconditionally execute his will.

EGMONT. And just as natural is it, that the burgher should prefer being governed by one born and reared in the same land, whose notions of right and wrong are in harmony with his own, and whom he can regard as his brother.

ALVA. And yet the noble, methinks, has shared rather unequally with these brethren of his.

EGMONT. That took place centuries ago, and is now submitted to without envy. But should new men, whose presence is not needed in the country, be sent, to enrich themselves a second time, at the cost of the nation; should the people see themselves exposed to their bold, unscrupulous rapacity, it would excite a ferment that would not soon be quelled.

ALVA. You utter words to which I ought not to listen;—
I, too, am a foreigner.

EGMONT. That they are spoken in your presence is a sufficient proof that they have no reference to you.

ALVA. Be that as it may, I would rather not hear them
from you. The king sent me here in the hope that I should
obtain the support of the nobles. The king wills, and will
have his will obeyed. After profound deliberation, the king
at length discerns what course will best promote the welfare
of the people; matters cannot be permitted to go on as
heretofore; it is the king's intention to limit their power
for their own good; if necessary, to force upon them their
salvation: to sacrifice the more dangerous burghers in order
that the rest may find repose, and enjoy in peace the blessing of a wise government. This is his resolve; this I am
commissioned to announce to the nobles; and in his name
I require from them advice, not as to the course to be pursued—on that he is resolved—but as to the best means of
carrying his purpose into effect.

EGMONT. Your words, alas, justify the fears of the people,
the universal fear! The king has then resolved as no sovereign ought to resolve. In order to govern his subjects
more easily, he would crush, subvert, nay, ruthlessly destroy,
their strength, their spirit, and their self-respect! He would
violate the inmost core of their individuality, doubtless with
the view of promoting their happiness. He would annihilate them, that they may assume a new, a different form.
Oh! if his purpose be good, he is fatally misguided! It is
not the king whom we resist;—we but place ourselves in
the way of the monarch, who, unhappily, is about to take
the first rash step in a wrong direction.

ALVA. Such being your sentiments, it were a vain attempt
for us to endeavour to agree. You must indeed think poorly
of the king, and contemptibly of his counsellors, if you imagine that everything has not already been thought of and
maturely weighed. I have no commission a second time to
balance conflicting arguments. From the people I demand
submission;—and from you, their leaders and princes, I
demand counsel and support, as pledges of this unconditional duty.

EGMONT. Demand our heads, and your object is attained; to a noble soul it must be indifferent whether he stoop his neck to such a yoke, or lay it upon the block. I have spoken much to little purpose. I have agitated the air, but accomplished nothing.

Enter FERDINAND

FERDINAND. Pardon my intrusion. Here is a letter, the bearer of which urgently demands an answer.

ALVA. Allow me to peruse its contents. (*Steps aside.*)

FERDINAND (*to* EGMONT). 'Tis a noble steed that your people have brought, to carry you away.

EGMONT. I have seen worse. I have had him some time; I think of parting with him. If he pleases you we shall probably soon agree as to the price.

FERDINAND. We will think about it.

(ALVA *motions to his son, who retires to the back-ground.*)

EGMONT. Farewell! Allow me to retire; for, by heaven, I know not what more I can say.

ALVA. Fortunately for you, chance prevents you from making a fuller disclosure of your sentiments. You incautiously lay bare the recesses of your heart, and your own lips furnish evidence against you, more fatal than could be produced by your bitterest adversary.

EGMONT. This reproach disturbs me not. I know my own heart; I know with what honest zeal I am devoted to the king; I know that my allegiance is more true than that of many who, in his service, seek only to serve themselves. I regret that our discussion should terminate so unsatisfactorily, and trust that in spite of our opposing views, the service of the king, our master, and the welfare of our country, may speedily unite us; another conference, the presence of the princes who to-day are absent, may, perchance, in a more propitious moment, accomplish what at present appears impossible. In this hope I take my leave.

ALVA (*who at the same time makes a sign to* FERDINAND). Hold, Egmont!—Your sword!—(*The centre door opens and discloses the gallery, which is occupied with guards, who remain motionless.*)

EGMONT (*after a pause of astonishment*). This was the

intention? For this thou hast summoned me? (*Grasping his sword as if to defend himself.*) Am I then weaponless?

ALVA. The king commands. Thou art my prisoner. (*At the same time guards enter from both sides.*)

EGMONT (*after a pause*). The king?—Orange! Orange! (*after a pause, resigning his sword*). Take it! It has been employed far oftener in defending the cause of my king than in protecting this breast.

(*He retires by the centre door, followed by the guard and* ALVA'S *son.* ALVA *remains standing while the curtain falls.*)

ACT V

SCENE I.—*A Street. Twilight*

CLARA, BRACKENBURG, BURGHERS

BRACKENBURG. Dearest, for Heaven's sake, what wouldst thou do?

CLARA. Come with me, Brackenburg! Thou canst not know the people, we are certain to rescue him; for what can equal their love for him? Each feels, I could swear it, the burning desire to deliver him, to avert danger from a life so precious, and to restore freedom to the most free. Come! A voice only is wanting to call them together. In their souls the memory is still fresh of all they owe him, and well they know that his mighty arm alone shields them from destruction. For his sake, for their own sake, they must peril everything. And what do we peril? At most, our lives, which if he perish, are not worth preserving.

BLACKENBURG. Unhappy girl! Thou seest not the power that holds us fettered as with bands of iron.

CLARA. To me it does not appear invincible. Let us not lose time in idle words. Here comes some of our old, honest, valiant burghers! Hark ye, friends! Neighbours! Hark! —Say, how fares it with Egmont?

CARPÉNTER. What does the girl want? Tell her to hold her peace.

CLARA. Step nearer, that we may speak low, till we are united and more strong. Not a moment is to be lost!

Audacious tyranny, that dared to fetter him, already lifts
the dagger against his life. Oh, my friends! With the advancing twilight my anxiety grows more intense. I dread
this night. Come! Let us disperse; let us hasten from
quarter to quarter, and call out the burghers. Let every one
grasp his ancient weapons. In the market-place we meet
again, and every one will be carried onward by our gathering stream. The enemy will see themselves surrounded,
overwhelmed, and be compelled to yield. How can a handful
of slaves resist us? And he will return among us, he will
see himself rescued, and can for once thank us, us, who are
already so deeply in his debt. He will behold, perchance, ay
doubtless, he will again behold the morn's red dawn in the
free heavens.

CARPENTER. What ails thee, maiden?

CLARA. Can ye misunderstand me? I speak of the Count!
I speak of Egmont.

JETTER. Speak not the name! 'tis deadly.

CLARA. Not speak his name? How? Not Egmont's
name? Is it not on every tongue? Where stands it not in-
scribed? Often have I read it emblazoned with all its letters
among these stars. Not utter it? What mean ye? Friends!
good, kind neighbours, ye are dreaming; collect yourselves.
Gaze not upon me with those fixed and anxious looks! Cast
not such timid glances on every side! I but give utterance
to the wish of all. Is not my voice the voice of your own
hearts? Who, in this fearful night, ere he seeks his restless couch, but on bended knee will, in earnest prayer, seek
to wrest his life as a cherished boon from heaven? Ask
each other! Let each ask his own heart! And who but ex-
claims with me,—"Egmont's liberty, or death!"

JETTER. God help us! This is a sad business.

CLARA. Stay! Stay! Shrink not away at the sound of
his name, to meet whom ye were wont to press forward so
joyously!—When rumour announced his approach, when the
cry arose, "Egmont comes! He comes from Ghent!"—then
happy indeed were those citizens who dwelt in the streets
through which he was to pass. And when the neighing of
his steed was heard, did not every one throw aside his work,
while a ray of hope and joy, like a sunbeam from his counte-

nance, stole over the toil-worn faces that peered from every window. Then, as ye stood in the doorways, ye would lift up your children in your arms, and pointing to him, exclaim: "See, that is Egmont, he who towers above the rest! 'Tis from him that ye must look for better times than those your poor fathers have known." Let not your children inquire at some future day, "Where is he? Where are the better times ye promised us?"—Thus we waste the time in idle words! do nothing,—betray him.

SOEST. Shame on thee, Brackenburg! Let her not run on thus! Prevent the mischief!

BRACKENBURG. Dear Clara! Let us go! What will your mother say? Perchance—

CLARA. Thinkest thou I am a child, or frantic? What avails perchance?—With no vain hope canst thou hide from me this dreadful certainty . . . Ye shall hear me and ye will: for I see it, ye are overwhelmed, ye cannot hearken to the voice of your own hearts. Through the present peril cast but one glance into the past,—the recent past. Send your thoughts forward into the future. Could ye live, would ye live, were he to perish? With him expires the last breath of freedom. What was he not to you? For whose sake did he expose himself to the direst perils? His blood flowed, his wounds were healed for you alone. The mighty spirit, that upheld you all, a dungeon now confines, while the horrors of secret murder are hovering around. Perhaps he thinks of you—perhaps he hopes in you,—he who has been accustomed only to grant favours to others and to fulfil their prayers.

CARPENTER. Come, gossip.

CLARA. I have neither the arms, nor the vigour of a man; but I have that which ye all lack—courage and contempt of danger. O that my breath could kindle your souls! That, pressing you to this bosom, I could arouse and animate you! Come! I will march in your midst!—As a waving banner, though weaponless, leads on a gallant army of warriors, so shall my spirit hover, like a flame, over your ranks, while love and courage shall unite the dispersed and wavering multitude into a terrible host.

JETTER. Take her away; I pity her, poor thing!

[*Exeunt* BURGHERS.

BRACKENBURG. Clara! Seest thou not where we are?

CLARA. Where? Under the dome of heaven, which has so often seemed to arch itself more gloriously as the noble Egmont passed beneath it. From these windows I have seen them look forth, four or five heads one above the other; at these doors the cowards have stood, bowing and scraping, if he but chanced to look down upon them! Oh, how dear they were to me, when they honoured him. Had he been a tyrant they might have turned with indifference from his fall! But they loved him! O ye hands, so prompt to wave caps in his honour, can ye not grasp a sword? Brackenburg, and we? —do we chide them? These arms that have so often embraced him, what do they for him now? Stratagem has accomplished so much in the world. Thou knowest the ancient castle, every passage, every secret way.—Nothing is impossible,—suggest some plan—

BRACKENBURG. That we might go home!

CLARA. Well.

BRACKENBURG. There at the corner I see Alva's guard; let the voice of reason penetrate to thy heart! Dost thou deem me a coward? Dost thou doubt that for thy sake I would peril my life? Here we are both mad, I as well as thou. Dost thou not perceive that thy scheme is impracticable? Oh, be calm! Thou art beside thyself.

CLARA. Beside myself! Horrible. You, Brackenburg, are beside yourself. When you hailed the hero with loud acclaim, called him your friend, your hope, your refuge, shouted vivats as he passed;—then I stood in my corner, half opened the window, concealed myself while I listened, and my heart beat higher than yours who greeted him so loudly. Now it again beats higher! In the hour of peril you conceal yourselves, deny him, and feel not, that if he perish, you are lost.

BRACKENBURG. Come home.

CLARA. Home?

BRACKENBURG. Recollect thyself! Look around thee! These are the streets in which thou wert wont to appear only on the Sabbath-day, when thou didst walk modestly to church; where, over-decorous perhaps, thou wert displeased If I but joined thee with a kindly greeting. And now thou

dost stand, speak, and act before the eyes of the whole world.
Recollect thyself, love! How can this avail us?

CLARA. Home! Yes, I remember. Come, Brackenburg,
let us go home! Knowest thou where my home lies?

[*Exeunt.*

SCENE II.—*A Prison*
Lighted by a lamp, a couch in the back-ground

EGMONT (*alone*). Old friend! Ever faithful sleep, dost
thou too forsake me, like my other friends? How wert
thou wont of yore to descend unsought upon my free brow,
cooling my temples as with a myrtle wreath of love! Amidst
the din of battle, on the waves of life, I rested in thine
arms, breathing lightly as a growing boy. When tempests
whistled through the leaves and boughs, when the summits
of the lofty trees swung creaking in the blast, the inmost
core of my heart remained unmoved. What agitates thee
now? What shakes thy firm and steadfast mind? I feel it,
'tis the sound of the murderous axe, gnawing at thy root.
Yet I stand erect, but an inward shudder runs through my
frame. Yes, it prevails, this treacherous power; it under-
mines the firm, the lofty stem, and ere the bark withers,
thy verdant crown falls crashing to the earth.

Yet wherefore now, thou who hast so often chased the
weightiest cares like bubbles from thy brow, wherefore
canst thou not dissipate this dire foreboding which inces-
santly haunts thee in a thousand different shapes? Since
when hast thou trembled at the approach of death, amid
whose varying forms, thou wert wont calmly to dwell, as
with the other shapes of this familiar earth. But 'tis not
he, the sudden foe, to encounter whom the sound bosom
emulously pants;—'tis the dungeon, emblem of the grave,
revolting alike to the hero and the coward. How intolerable
I used to feel it, in the stately hall, girt round by gloomy
walls, when, seated on my cushioned chair, in the solemn
assembly of the princes, questions, which scarcely required
deliberation, were overlaid with endless discussions, while
the rafters of the ceiling seemed to stifle and oppress me.
Then I would hurry forth as soon as possible, fling myself

upon my horse with deep-drawn breath, and away to the wide champaign, man's natural element, where, exhaling from the earth, nature's richest treasures are poured forth around us, while, from the wide heavens, the stars shed down their blessings through the still air; where, like earth-born giants, we spring aloft, invigorated by our mother's touch; where our entire humanity and our human desires throb in every vein; where the desire to press forward, to vanquish, to snatch, to use his clenched fist, to possess, to conquer, glows through the soul of the young hunter; where the warrior, with rapid stride, assumes his inborn right to dominion over the world; and, with terrible liberty, sweeps like a desolating hailstorm over the field and grove, knowing no boundaries traced by the hand of man.

Thou art but a shadow, a dream of the happiness I so long possessed; where has treacherous fate conducted thee? Did she deny thee to meet the rapid stroke of never-shunned death, in the open face of day, only to prepare for thee a foretaste of the grave, in the midst of this loathsome corruption? How revolting its rank odour exhales from these damp stones! Life stagnates, and my foot shrinks from the couch as from the grave.

Oh care, care! Thou who dost begin prematurely the work of murder,—forbear;—Since when has Egmont been alone, so utterly alone in the world? 'Tis doubt renders thee insensible, not happiness. The justice of the king, in which through life thou hast confided, the friendship of the Regent, which, thou mayst confess it, was akin to love,— have these suddenly vanished, like a meteor of the night, and left thee alone upon thy gloomy path? Will not Orange, at the head of thy friends, contrive some daring scheme? Will not the people assemble, and with gathering might, attempt the rescue of their faithful friend?

Ye walls, which thus gird me round, separate me not from the well-intentioned zeal of so many kindly souls. And may the courage with which my glance was wont to inspire them, now return again from their hearts to mine. Yes! they assemble in thousands! they come! they stand beside me! their pious wish rises urgently to heaven, and implores a miracle; and if no angel stoops for my deliverance, I see them grasp eagerly their lance and sword. The gates are forced, the bolts are riven, the walls fall beneath their conquering hands, and Egmont advances joyously, to hail the freedom of the rising morn. How many well-known faces receive me with loud acclaim! O Clara! wert thou a man, I should see thee here the very first, and thank thee for that which it is galling to owe even to a king—liberty.

Scene III.—Clara's *House*

Clara (*enters from her chamber with a lamp and a glass of water; she places the glass upon the table and steps to the window*). Brackenburg, is it you? What noise was that? No one yet? No one! I will set the lamp in the window, that he may see that I am still awake, that I still watch for him. He promised me tidings. Tidings? horrible certainty!—Egmont condemned!—what tribunal has the right to summon him?—And they dare to condemn him!—Does the king condemn him, or the duke? And the Regent withdraws herself! Orange hesitates, and all his friends! —Is this the world, of whose fickleness and treachery I have heard so much, and as yet experienced nothing? Is this the world?—Who could be so base as to bear malice against one so dear? Could villainy itself be audacious enough to overwhelm with sudden destruction the object of a nation's homage? Yet so it is—it is—O Egmont, I held thee safe before God and man, safe as in my arms! What was I to thee. Thou hast called me thine, my whole being was devoted to thee. What am I now? In vain I stretch out my hand to the toils that environ thee. Thou helpless and I free!—Here is the key that unlocks my chamber door. My going out and my coming in, depend upon my own caprice; yet, alas; to aid thee I am powerless!—Oh, bind me that I may not despair; hurl me into the deepest dungeon, that I may dash my head against the damp walls, groan for freedom, and dream how I would rescue him if fetters did not hold me bound.—Now I am free, and in freedom lies the anguish of impotence.—Conscious of my own existence, yet unable to stir a limb in his behalf, alas! even this insignificant portion of thy being, thy Clara, is, like thee, a captive, and, separated from thee, consumes her expiring energies in the agonies of death.—I hear a stealthy step,—a cough—Brackenburg,—'tis he!—Kind, unhappy man, thy destiny remains ever the same; thy love opens to thee the door at night, alas! to what a doleful meeting. (*Enter* BRACKENBURG.) Thou com'st so pale, so terrified! Brackenburg! What is it?

BRACKENBURG. I have sought thee through perils and circuitous paths. The principal streets are occupied with troops;—through lanes and by-ways have I stolen to thee!

CLARA. Tell me, how is it?

BRACKENBURG (*seating himself*). O Clara, let me weep. I loved him not. He was the rich man who lured to better pasture the poor man's solitary lamb. I have never cursed him, God has created me with a true and tender heart. My life was consumed in anguish, and each day I hoped would end my misery.

CLARA. Let that be forgotten, Brackenburg! Forget thyself. Speak to me of him! Is it true? Is he condemned?

BRACKENBURG. He is! I know it.

CLARA. And still lives?

BRACKENBURG. Yes, he still lives.

CLARA. How canst thou be sure of that? Tyranny murders the hero in the night! His blood flows concealed from every eye. The people stunned and bewildered, lie buried in sleep, dream of deliverance, dream of the fulfilment of their impotent wishes, while, indignant at our supineness, his spirit abandons the world. He is no more! Deceive me not; deceive not thyself!

BRACKENBURG. No,—he lives! and the Spaniards, alas, are preparing for the people, on whom they are about to trample, a terrible spectacle, in order to crush for ever, by a violent blow, each heart that yet pants for freedom.

CLARA. Proceed! Calmly pronounce my death-warrant also! Near and more near I approach that blessed land, and already from those realms of peace, I feel the breath of consolation. Say on.

BRACKENBURG. From casual words, dropped here and there by the guards, I learned that secretly in the market-place they were preparing some terrible spectacle. Through

by-ways and familiar lanes I stole to my cousin's house,
and from a back window, looked out upon the market-place.
Torches waved to and fro, in the hands of a wide circle of
Spanish soldiers. I sharpened my unaccustomed sight, and
out of the darkness there arose before me a scaffold, black,
spacious, and lofty! The sight filled me with horror. Several persons were employed in covering with black cloth
such portions of the wood-work as yet remained white and
visible. The steps were covered last, also with black;—I
saw it all. They seemed preparing for the celebration of
some horrible sacrifice. A white crucifix, that shone like
silver through the night, was raised on one side. As I gazed
the terrible conviction strengthened in my mind. Scattered
torches still gleamed here and there; gradually they flickered
and went out. Suddenly the hideous birth of night returned
into its mother's womb.

CLARA. Hush, Brackenburg! Be still! Let this veil rest
upon my soul. The spectres are vanished; and thou, gentle
night, lend thy mantle to the inwardly fermenting earth,
she will no longer endure the loathsome burden, shuddering,
she rends open her yawning chasms, and with a crash swal-
lows the murderous scaffold. And that God, whom in their
rage they have insulted, sends down His angel from on
high; at the hallowed touch of the messenger bolts and bars
fly back; he pours around our friend a mild radiance, and
leads him gently through the night to liberty. My path leads
also through the darkness to meet him.

BRACKENBURG (*detaining her*). My child, whither wouldst
thou go? What wouldst thou do?

CLARA. Softly, my friend, lest some one should awake!
Lest we should awake ourselves! Know'st thou this phial,
Brackenburg? I took it from thee once in jest, when thou,
as was thy wont, didst threaten, in thy impatience, to end
thy days.—And now my friend—

BRACKENBURG. In the name of all the saints!

CLARA. Thou canst not hinder me. Death is my portion!
Grudge me not the quiet and easy death which thou hadst
prepared for thyself. Give me thine hand!—At the moment
when I unclose that dismal portal through which there is
no return, I may tell thee, with this pressure of the hand,

how sincerely I have loved, how deeply I have pitied thee.
My brother died young; I chose thee to fill his place; thy
heart rebelled, thou didst torment thyself and me, demanding
with ever increasing fervour that which fate had not destined for thee. Forgive me and farewell! Let me call thee
brother! 'Tis a name that embraces many names. Receive,
with a true heart, the last fair token of the departing spirit
—take this kiss. Death unites all, Brackenburg—us too it
will unite!

BRACKENBURG. Let me then die with thee! Share it! oh,
share it! There is enough to extinguish two lives.

CLARA. Hold! Thou must live, thou canst live.—Support
my mother, who, without thee, would be a prey to want.
Be to her what I can no longer be, live together, and weep
for me. Weep for our fatherland, and for him who could
alone have upheld it. The present generation must still
endure this bitter woe; vengeance itself could not obliterate
it. Poor souls, live on, through this gap in time, which is
time no longer. To-day the world suddenly stands still, its
course is arrested, and my pulse will beat but for a few
minutes longer. Farewell.

BRACKENBURG. Oh, live with us, as we live only for thy
sake! In taking thine own life, thou wilt take ours also;
still live and suffer. We will stand by thee, nothing shall
sever us from thy side, and love, with ever-watchful solicitude, shall prepare for thee the sweetest consolation in its
loving arms. Be ours! Ours! I dare not say, mine.

CLARA. Hush, Brackenburg! Thou feelest not what chord
thou touchest. Where hope appears to thee, I see only
despair.

BRACKENBURG. Share hope with the living! Pause on the
brink of the precipice, cast one glance into the gulf below,
and then look back on us.

CLARA. I have conquered; call me not back to the struggle.

BRACKENBURG. Thou art stunned; enveloped in night, thou
seekest the abyss. Every light is not yet extinguished, yet
many days!—

CLARA. Alas! Alas! Cruelly thou dost rend the veil
from before mine eyes. Yes, the day will dawn! Despite
its misty shroud it needs must dawn. Timidly the burgher

gazes from his window, night leaves behind an ebon speck; he looks, and the scaffold looms fearfully in the morning light. With re-awakened anguish the desecrated image of the Saviour lifts to the Father its imploring eyes. The sun veils his beams, he will not mark the hero's death-hour. Slowly the fingers go their round—one hour strikes after another—hold! Now is the time. The thought of the morning scares me into the grave.

(*She goes to the window as if to look out, and drinks secretly.*)

BRACKENBURG. Clara! Clara!

CLARA (*goes to the table, and drinks water*). Here is the remainder. I invite thee not to follow me. Do as thou wilt; farewell. Extinguish this lamp silently and without delay; I am going to rest. Steal quietly away, close the door after thee. Be still! Wake not my mother! Go, save thyself, if thou wouldst not be taken for my murderer. [*Exit.*

BRACKENBURG. She leaves me for the last time as she has ever done. What human soul could conceive how cruelly she lacerates the heart that loves her? She leaves me to myself, leaves me to choose between life and death, and both are alike hateful to me. To die alone! Weep, ye tender souls! Fate has no sadder doom than mine. She shares with me the death-potion, yet sends me from her side! She draws me after her, yet thrusts me back into life! Oh, Egmont, how enviable a lot falls to thee! She goes before thee! The crown of victory from her hand is thine, she brings all heaven to meet thee!—And shall I follow? Again to stand aloof? To carry this inextinguishable jealousy even to yon distant realms? Earth is no longer a tarrying place for me, and hell and heaven offer equal torture. Now welcome to the wretched the dread hand of annihilation!

[*Exit.*

(*The scene remains some time unchanged. Music sounds, indicating* CLARA'S *death; the lamp, which* BRACKENBURG *had forgotten to extinguish, flares up once or twice, and then suddenly expires. The scene changes to*

SCENE IV.—*A Prison*

EGMONT *is discovered sleeping on a couch. A rustling of keys is heard; the door opens; servants enter with torches;* FERDINAND *and* SILVA *follow, accompanied by soldiers.* EGMONT *starts from his sleep.*

EGMONT. Who are ye that thus rudely banish slumber from my eyes? What mean these vague and insolent glances? Why this fearful procession? With what dream of horror come ye to delude my half awakened soul?

SILVA. The duke sends us to announce your sentence.

EGMONT. Do ye also bring the headsman who is to execute it?

SILVA. Listen, and you will know the doom that awaits you.

EGMONT. It is in keeping with the rest of your infamous proceedings. Hatched in night and in night achieved, so would this audacious act of injustice shroud itself from observation!—Step boldly forth, thou who dost bear the sword concealed beneath thy mantle; here is my head, the freest ever severed by tyranny from the trunk.

SILVA. You err! The righteous judges who have condemned you will not conceal their sentence from the light of day.

EGMONT. Then does their audacity exceed all imagination and belief.

SILVA (*takes the sentence from an attendant, unfolds it, and reads*). " In the King's name, and invested by his Majesty with authority to judge all his subjects of whatever rank, not excepting the knights of the Golden Fleece, we declare—"

EGMONT. Can the king transfer that authority?

SILVA. " We declare, after a strict and legal investigation, thee, Henry, Count Egmont, Prince of Gaure, guilty of high treason, and pronounce thy sentence:—That at early dawn thou be led from this prison to the market-place, and that there, in sight of the people, and as a warning to all traitors, thou with the sword be brought from life to death. Given at Brussels." (*Date and year so indistinctly read as to be imperfectly heard by the audience.*) " Ferdinand, Duke of

Alva, President of the Tribunal of Twelve." Thou knowest now thy doom. Brief time remains for thee to prepare for the impending stroke, to arrange thy affairs, and to take leave of thy friends.

[*Exit* SILVA *with followers.* FERDINAND *remains with two torch-bearers. The stage is dimly lighted.*

EGMONT (*stands for a time as if buried in thought, and allows* SILVA *to retire without looking round. He imagines himself alone, and, on raising his eyes, beholds* ALVA's *son*). Thou tarriest here? Wouldst thou by thy presence augment my amazement, my horror? Wouldst thou carry to thy father the welcome tidings that in unmanly fashion I despair? Go. Tell him that he deceives neither the world nor me. At first it will be whispered cautiously behind his back, then spoken more and more loudly, and when at some future day the ambitious man descends from his proud eminence, a thousand voices will proclaim—that 'twas not the welfare of the state, not the honour of the king, not the tranquillity of the provinces, that brought him hither. For his own selfish ends he, the warrior, has counselled war, that in war the value of his services might be enhanced. He has excited this monstrous insurrection that his presence might be deemed necessary in order to quell it. And I fall a victim to his mean hatred, his contemptible envy. Yes, I know it, dying and mortally wounded I may utter it; long has the proud man envied me, long has he meditated and planned my ruin.

Even then, when still young, we played at dice together, and the heaps of gold, one after the other, passed rapidly from his side to mine; he would look on with affected composure, while inwardly consumed with rage, more at my success than at his own loss. Well do I remember the fiery glance, the treacherous pallor that overspread his features when, at a public festival, we shot for a wager before assembled thousands. He challenged me, and both nations stood by; Spaniards and Netherlanders wagered on either side; I was the victor; his ball missed, mine hit the mark, and the air was rent by acclamations from my friends. His shot now hits me. Tell him that I know this, that I know him, that the world despises every trophy that a paltry spirit erects for itself by base and surreptitious arts. And thou!

If it be possible for a son to swerve from the manners of his father, practise shame betimes, while thou art compelled to feel shame for him whom thou wouldst fain revere with thy whole heart.

FERDINAND. I listen without interrupting thee! Thy reproaches fall like blows upon a helmet. I feel the shock, but I am armed. They strike, they wound me not; I am sensible only to the anguish that lacerates my heart. Alas! Alas! Have I lived to witness such a scene? Am I sent hither to behold a spectacle like this?

EGMONT. Dost thou break out into lamentations? What moves, what agitates thee thus? Is it a late remorse at having lent thyself to this infamous conspiracy? Thou art so young, thy exterior is so prepossessing? Thy demeanour towards me was so friendly, so unreserved! So long as I beheld thee, I was reconciled with thy father; and crafty, ay, more crafty than he, thou hast lured me into the toils. Thou art the wretch! The monster! Whoso confides in him, does so at his own peril; but who could apprehend danger in trusting thee? Go! Go! rob me not of the few moments that are left me! Go, that I may collect my thoughts, the world forget, and first of all thyself!

FERDINAND. What can I say? I stand and gaze on thee, yet see thee not; I am scarcely conscious of my own existence. Shall I seek to excuse myself? Shall I assure thee that it was not till the last moment that I was made aware of my father's intentions? That I acted as a constrained, a passive instrument of his will? What signifies now the opinion thou mayst entertain of me? Thou art lost; and I, miserable wretch, stand here only to assure thee of it, only to lament thy doom.

EGMONT. What strange voice, what unexpected consolation comes thus to cheer my passage to the grave? Thou, the son of my first, of almost my only enemy, thou dost pity me, thou art not associated with my murderers? Speak! In what light must I regard thee?

FERDINAND. Cruel father! Yes, I recognize thy nature in this command. Thou didst know my heart, my disposition, which thou hast so often censured as the inheritance of a tender-hearted mother. To mould me into thine own likeness thou hast sent me hither. Thou dost compel me to behold this man on the verge of the yawning grave, in the grasp of an arbitrary doom, that I may experience the profoundest anguish; that thus, rendered callous to every fate, I may henceforth meet every event with a heart unmoved.

EGMONT. I am amazed! Be calm! Act, speak like a man.

FERDINAND. Oh, that I were a woman! That they might say—what moves, what agitates thee? Tell me of a greater, a more monstrous crime, make me the spectator of a more direful deed; I will thank thee, I will say: this was nothing.

EGMONT. Thou dost forget thyself. Consider where thou art!

FERDINAND. Let this passion rage, let me give vent to my anguish! I will not seem composed when my whole inner being is convulsed. Thee must I behold here? Thee? It is horrible! Thou understandest me not! How shouldst thou understand me? Egmont! Egmont!

(Falling on his neck.)

EGMONT. Explain this mystery.

FERDINAND. It is no mystery.

EGMONT. How can the fate of a mere stranger thus deeply move thee?

FERDINAND. Not a stranger! Thou art no stranger to me. Thy name it was that, even from my boyhood, shone before me like a star in heaven! How often have I made inquiries concerning thee, and listened to the story of thy deeds! The youth is the hope of the boy, the man of the youth. Thus didst thou walk before me, ever before me; I saw thee without envy, and followed after, step by step; at length I hoped to see thee—I saw thee, and my heart flew to thy embrace. I had destined thee for myself, and when I beheld thee, I made choice of thee anew. I hoped now to know thee, to live with thee, to be thy friend,—thy—'tis over now and I see thee here!

EGMONT. My friend, if it can be any comfort to thee, be assured that the very moment we met my heart was drawn towards thee. Now listen! Let us exchange a few quiet words. Tell me: is it the stern, the settled purpose of thy father to take my life?

FERDINAND. It is.

EGMONT. This sentence is not a mere empty scarecrow, designed to terrify me, to punish me through fear and intimidation, to humiliate me, that he may then raise me again by the royal favour?

FERDINAND. Alas, no! At first I flattered myself with this delusive hope; and even then my heart was filled with grief and anguish to behold thee thus. Thy doom is real! Is certain! No, I cannot command myself. Who will counsel, who will aid me, to meet the inevitable?

EGMONT. Hearken then to me! If thy heart is impelled so powerfully in my favour, if thou dost abhor the tyranny that holds me fettered, then deliver me! The moments are precious. Thou art the son of the all-powerful, and thou hast power thyself. Let us fly! I know the roads; the means of effecting our escape cannot be unknown to thee. These walls, a few short miles, alone separate me from my friends. Loose these fetters, conduct me to them; be ours. The king, on some future day, will doubtless thank my deliverer. Now he is taken by surprise, or perchance he is ignorant of the whole proceeding. Thy father ventures on this daring step, and majesty, though horror-struck at the deed, must needs sanction the irrevocable. Thou dost deliberate? Oh, contrive for me the way to freedom! Speak; nourish hope in a living soul.

FERDINAND. Cease! Oh, cease! Every word deepens my despair. There is here no outlet, no counsel, no escape.— 'Tis this thought that tortures me, that seizes my heart, and rends it as with talons. I have myself spread the net; I know its firm, inextricable knots; I know that every avenue is barred alike to courage and to stratagem. I feel that I too, like thyself, like all the rest, am fettered. Think'st thou that I should give way to lamentation if any means of safety remained untried? I have thrown myself at his feet, remonstrated, implored. He has sent me hither, in order to blast in this fatal moment, every remnant of joy and happiness that yet survived within my heart.

EGMONT. And is there no deliverance?

FERDINAND. None!

EGMONT (*stamping his foot*). No deliverance!—Sweet

life! Sweet, pleasant habitude of existence and of activity! from thee must I part! So calmly part! Not in the tumult of battle, amid the din of arms, the excitement of the fray, dost thou send me a hasty farewell; thine is no hurried leave; thou dost not abridge the moment of separation. Once more let me clasp thy hand, gaze once more into thine eyes, feel with keen emotion, thy beauty and thy worth, then resolutely tear myself away, and say;—depart!

FERDINAND. Must I stand by, and look passively on; unable to save thee, or to give thee aid! What voice avails for lamentation! What heart but must break under the pressure of such anguish?

EGMONT. Be calm!

FERDINAND. Thou canst be calm, thou canst renounce, led on by necessity, thou canst advance to the direful struggle, with the courage of a hero. What can I do? What ought I to do? Thou dost conquer thyself and us; thou art the victor; I survive both myself and thee. I have lost my light at the banquet, my banner on the field. The future lies before me, dark, desolate, perplexed.

EGMONT. Young friend, whom by a strange fatality, at the same moment, I both win and lose, who dost feel for me, who dost suffer for me the agonies of death,—look on me; —thou wilt not lose me. If my life was a mirror in which thou didst love to contemplate thyself, so be also my death. Men are not together only when in each other's presence;— the distant, the departed, also live for us. I shall live for thee, and for myself I have lived long enough. I have enjoyed each day; each day, I have performed, with prompt activity, the duties enjoined by my conscience. Now my life ends, as it might have ended, long, long, ago, on the sands of Gravelines. I shall cease to live; but I have lived. My friend, follow in my steps, lead a cheerful and a joyous life, and dread not the approach of death.

FERDINAND. Thou shouldst have saved thyself for us, thou couldst have saved thyself. Thou art the cause of thine own destruction. Often have I listened when able men discoursed concerning thee; foes and friends, they would dispute long as to thy worth; but on one point they were agreed, none ventured to deny, every one confessed, that thou wert treading a dangerous path. How often have I longed to warn thee! Hadst thou then no friends?

EGMONT. I was warned.

FERDINAND. And when I found all these allegations, point for point, in the indictment, together with thy answers, containing much that might serve to palliate thy conduct, but no evidence weighty enough fully to exculpate thee—

EGMONT. No more of this. Man imagines that he directs his life, that he governs his actions, when in fact his existence is irresistibly controlled by his destiny. Let us not dwell upon this subject; these reflections I can dismiss with ease—not so my apprehensions for these provinces; yet they too will be cared for. Could my blood flow for many, bring peace to my people, how freely should it flow! Alas! This may not be. Yet it ill becomes a man idly to speculate, when the power to act is no longer his. If thou canst restrain or guide the fatal power of thy father; do so. Alas, who can? —Farewell!

FERDINAND. I cannot leave thee.

EGMONT. Let me urgently recommend my followers to thy care! I have worthy men in my service; let them not be dispersed, let them not become destitute! How fares it with Richard, my secretary?

FERDINAND. He is gone before thee. They have beheaded him, as thy accomplice in high treason.

EGMONT. Poor soul!—Yet one word, and then farewell, I can no more. However powerfully the spirit may be stirred, nature at length irresistibly asserts her rights; and like a child, who, enveloped in a serpent's folds, enjoys refreshing slumber, so the weary one lays himself down to rest before the gates of death, and sleeps soundly, as though a toilsome journey yet lay before him.—One word more,—I know a maiden; thou wilt not despise her because she was mine. Since I can recommend her to thy care, I shall die in peace. Thy soul is noble; in such a man, a woman is sure to find a protector. Lives my old Adolphus? Is he free?

FERDINAND. The active old man, who always attended thee on horseback?

EGMONT. The same.

FERDINAND. He lives, he is free.

EGMONT. He knows her dwelling; let him guide thy steps thither, and reward him to his dying day, for having shown thee the way to this jewel.—Farewell!

FERDINAND. I cannot leave thee.

EGMONT (*urging him towards the door*). Farewell!

FERDINAND. Oh, let me linger yet a moment!

EGMONT. No leave-taking, my friend.

(*He accompanies* FERDINAND *to the door, and then tears himself away;* FERDINAND, *overwhelmed with grief, hastily retires.*)

EGMONT (*alone*)

EGMONT. Cruel man! Thou didst not think to render me this service through thy son. He has been the means of relieving my mind from the pressure of care and sorrow, from fear and every anxious feeling. Gently, yet urgently, nature claims her final tribute. 'Tis past!—'Tis resolved! And the reflections which, in the suspense of last night, kept me wakeful on my couch, now with resistless certainty lull my senses to repose.

(*He seats himself upon the couch; music*)

Sweet sleep! Like the purest happiness, thou comest most willingly, uninvited, unsought. Thou dost loosen the knots of earnest thoughts, dost mingle all images of joy and of sorrow, unimpeded the circle of inner harmony flows on, and wrapped in fond delusion, we sink into oblivion, and cease to be.

(*He sleeps; music accompanies his slumber. Behind his couch the wall appears to open and discovers a brilliant apparition. Freedom, in a celestial garb, surrounded by a glory, reposes on a cloud. Her features are those of* CLARA *and she inclines towards the sleeping hero. Her countenance betokens compassion, she seems to lament his fate. Quickly she recovers herself and with an encouraging gesture exhibits the symbols of freedom, the bundle of arrows, with the staff and cap. She encourages him to be of good cheer, and while she signifies to him that his death will secure the freedom of the provinces, she hails him as a conqueror, and extends to him a laurel crown. As the wreath*

approaches his head, EGMONT *moves like one asleep,
and reclines with his face towards her. She holds
the wreath suspended over his head;—martial music
is heard in the distance, at the first sound the vision
disappears. The music grows louder and louder.*
EGMONT *awakes. The prison is dimly illuminated
by the dawn.—His first impulse is to lift his hand
to his head, he stands up, and gazes round, his hand
still upraised.*)

The crown is vanished! Beautiful vision, the light of
day has frighted thee! Yes, they revealed themselves to
my sight uniting in one radiant form the two sweetest joys
of my heart. Divine Liberty borrowed the mien of my
beloved one; the lovely maiden arrayed herself in the celestial garb of my friend. In a solemn moment they appeared
united, with aspect more earnest than tender. With blood-
stained feet the vision approached, the waving folds of her
robe also were tinged with blood. It was my blood, and the
blood of many brave hearts. No! It shall not be shed in
vain! Forward! Brave people! The goddess of liberty
leads you on! And as the sea breaks through and destroys
the barriers that would oppose its fury, so do ye overwhelm
the bulwark of tyranny, and with your impetuous flood sweep
it away from the land which it usurps.   (*Drums.*)

Hark! Hark! How often has this sound summoned my
joyous steps to the field of battle and of victory! How
bravely did I tread, with my gallant comrades, the dangerous path of fame! And now, from this dungeon I shall
go forth, to meet a glorious death; I die for freedom, for
whose cause I have lived and fought, and for whom I now
offer myself up a sorrowing sacrifice.

(*The background is occupied by Spanish soldiers with
halberts.*)

Yes, lead them on! Close your ranks, ye terrify me not.
I am accustomed to stand amid the serried ranks of war,
and environed by the threatening forms of death, to feel,
with double zest, the energy of life.   (*Drums.*)

The foe closes round on every side! Swords are flashing;
courage, friends! Behind are your parents, your wives, your
children!   (*Pointing to the guard.*)

And these are impelled by the word of their leader, not by their own free will. Protect your homes! And to save those who are most dear to you, be ready to follow my example, and to fall with joy.

(*Drums. As he advances through the guards towards the door in the background, the curtain falls. The music joins in, and the scene closes with a symphony of victory.*

HERMANN AND DOROTHEA

BY
GOETHE

TRANSLATED BY
ELLEN FROTHINGHAM

INTRODUCTORY NOTE

THERE *are few modern poems of any country so perfect in their kind as the "Hermann and Dorothea" of Goethe. In clearness of characterization, in unity of tone, in the adjustment of background and foreground, in the conduct of the narrative, it conforms admirably to the strict canons of art; yet it preserves a freshness and spontaneity in its emotional appeal that are rare in works of so classical a perfection in form.*

The basis of the poem is a historical incident. In the year 1731 the Archbishop of Salzburg drove out of his diocese a thousand Protestants, who took refuge in South Germany, and among whom was a girl who became the bride of the son of a rich burgher. The occasion of the girl's exile was changed by Goethe to more recent times, and in the poem she is represented as a German from the west bank of the Rhine fleeing from the turmoil caused by the French Revolution. The political element is not a mere background, but is woven into the plot with consummate skill, being used, at one point, for example, in the characterization of Dorothea, who before the time of her appearance in the poem has been deprived of her first betrothed by the guillotine; and, at another, in furnishing a telling contrast between the revolutionary uproar in France and the settled peace of the German village.

The characters of the father and the minister Goethe took over from the original incident, the mother he invented, and the apothecary he made to stand for a group of friends. But all of these persons, as well as the two lovers, are recreated, and this so skilfully that while they are made notably familiar to us as individuals, they are no less significant as permanent types of human nature. The hexameter measure which he employed, and which is retained in the present translation, he handled with such charm that it has since seemed the natural verse for the domestic idyl— witness the obvious imitation of this, as of other features of the poem, in Longfellow's "Evangeline."

Taken as a whole, with its beauty of form, its sentiment, tender yet restrained, and the compelling pathos of its story, "Hermann and Dorothea" appeals to a wider public than perhaps any other product of its author.

HERMANN AND DOROTHEA

CALLIOPE

FATE AND SYMPATHY

"TRULY, I never have seen the market and street so
    deserted!
    How as if it were swept looks the town, or had
    perished! Not fifty
Are there, methinks, of all our inhabitants in it remaining.
What will not curiosity do! here is every one running,
Hurrying to gaze on the sad procession of pitiful exiles.
Fully a league it must be to the causeway they have to pass
    over,
Yet all are hurrying down in the dusty heat of the noonday.
I, in good sooth, would not stir from my place to witness the
    sorrows
Borne by good, fugitive people, who now, with their rescued
    possessions,
Driven, alas! from beyond the Rhine, their beautiful country,
Over to us are coming, and through the prosperous corner
Roam of this our luxuriant valley, and traverse its windings.
Well hast thou done, good wife, our son in thus kindly
    dispatching,
Laden with something to eat and to drink, and with store
    of old linen,
'Mongst the poor folk to distribute; for giving belongs to
    the wealthy.
How the youth drives, to be sure! What control he has
    over the horses!
Makes not our carriage a handsome appearance,—the new
    one? With comfort,

335

Four could be seated within, with a place on the box for the coachman.
This time, he drove by himself.   How lightly it rolled round the corner ! "
Thus, as he sat at his ease in the porch of his house on the market,
Unto his wife was speaking mine host of the Golden Lion.

Thereupon answered and said the prudent, intelligent housewife:
" Father, I am not inclined to be giving away my old linen:
Since it serves many a purpose; and cannot be purchased for money,
When we may want it.   To-day, however, I gave, and with pleasure,
Many a piece that was better, indeed, in shirts and in bed-clothes;
For I was told of the aged and children who had to go naked.
But wilt thou pardon me, father? thy wardrobe has also been plundered.
And, in especial, the wrapper that has the East-Indian flowers,
Made of the finest of chintz, and lined with delicate flannel,
Gave I away: it was thin and old, and quite out of the fashion."

Thereupon answered and said, with a smile, the excellent landlord:
" Faith! I am sorry to lose it, my good old calico wrapper,
Real East-Indian stuff: I never shall get such another.
Well, I had given up wearing it: nowadays, custom compels us
Always to go in surtout, and never appear but in jacket;
Always to have on our boots; forbidden are night-cap and slippers."

" See! " interrupted the wife; " even now some are yonder returning,

Who have beheld the procession: it must, then, already be
  over.
Look at the dust on their shoes! and see how their faces are
  glowing!
Every one carries his kerchief, and with it is wiping the
  sweat off.
Not for a sight like that would I run so far and so suffer,
Through such a heat; in sooth, enough shall I have in the
  telling."

  Thereupon answered and said, with emphasis, thus, the
    good father:
" Rarely does weather like this attend such a harvest as
  this is.
We shall be bringing our grain in dry, as the hay was before it.
Not the least cloud to be seen, so perfectly clear is the
  heaven;
And, with delicious coolness, the wind blows in from the
  eastward.
That is the weather to last! over-ripe are the cornfields
  already;
We shall begin on the morrow to gather our copious   ,
  harvest."

  Constantly, while he thus spoke, the crowds of men and
    of women
Grew, who their homeward way were over the market-place
  wending;
And, with the rest, there also returned, his daughters be-
  side him,
Back to his modernized house on the opposite side of the
  market,
Foremost merchant of all the town, their opulent neighbor,
Rapidly driving his open barouche,—it was builded in
  Landau.
Lively now grew the streets, for the city was handsomely
  peopled.
Many a trade was therein carried on, and large manu-
  factures.

Under their doorway thus the affectionate couple were
  sitting,
Pleasing themselves with many remarks on the wandering
  people.
Finally broke in, however, the worthy housewife, exclaiming:
"Yonder our pastor, see! is hitherward coming, and with
  him
Comes our neighbor the doctor, so they shall every thing
  tell us;
All they have witnessed abroad, and which 'tis a sorrow to
  look on."

  Cordially then the two men drew nigh, and saluted the
  couple;
Sat themselves down on the benches of wood that were
  placed in the doorway,
Shaking the dust from their feet, and fanning themselves
  with their kerchiefs.
Then was the doctor, as soon as exchanged were the mutual
  greetings,
First to begin, and said, almost in a tone of vexation:
"Such is mankind, forsooth! and one man is just like
  another,
Liking to gape and to stare when ill-luck has befallen his
  neighbor.
Every one hurries to look at the flames, as they soar in
  destruction;
Runs to behold the poor culprit, to execution conducted:
Now all are sallying forth to gaze on the need of these
  exiles,
Nor is there one who considers that he, by a similar fortune,
May, in the future, if not indeed next, be likewise o'ertaken.
Levity not to be pardoned, I deem; yet it lies in man's
  nature."

  Thereupon answered and said the noble, intelligent pastor;
Ornament he of the town, still young, in the prime of his
  manhood.

He was acquainted with life,—with the needs of his hearers
  acquainted;
Deeply imbued he was with the Holy Scriptures' importance,
As they reveal man's destiny to us, and man's disposition;
Thoroughly versed, besides, in best of secular writings.
"I should be loath," he replied, "to censure an innocent
  instinct,
Which to mankind by good mother Nature has always been
  given.
What understanding and reason may sometimes fail to ac-
  complish,
Oft will such fortunate impulse, that bears us resistlessly
  with it.
Did curiosity draw not man with its potent attraction,
Say, would he ever have learned how harmoniously fitted
  together
Worldly experiences are? For first what is novel he covets;
Then with unwearying industry follows he after the useful;
Finally longs for the good by which he is raised and
  ennobled.
While he is young, such lightness of mind is a joyous com-
  panion,
Traces of pain-giving evil effacing as soon as 'tis over.
He is indeed to be praised, who, out of this gladness of
  temper,
Has in his ripening years a sound understanding developed;
Who, in good fortune or ill, with zeal and activity labors:
Such an one bringeth to pass what is good, and repaireth
  the evil."

  Then broke familiarly in the housewife impatient, exclaiming:
"Tell us of what ye have seen; for that I am longing to
  hear of!"

  "Hardly," with emphasis then the village doctor made
  answer,
"Can I find spirits so soon after all the scenes I have
  witnessed.
Oh, the manifold miseries! who shall be able to tell them?

E'en before crossing the meadows, and while we were yet at
  a distance,
Saw we the dust; but still from hill to hill the procession
Passed away out of our sight, and we could distinguish but
  little.
But when at last we were come to the street that crosses the
  valley,
Great was the crowd and confusion of persons on foot and
  of wagons.
There, alas! saw we enough of these poor unfortunates
  passing,
And could from some of them learn how bitter the sorrow-
  ful flight was,
Yet how joyful the feeling of life thus hastily rescued.
Mournful it was to behold the most miscellaneous chattels,—
All those things which are housed in every well-furnished
  dwelling,
All by the house-keeper's care set up in their suitable places,
Always ready for use; for useful is each and important.—
Now these things to behold, piled up on all manner of
  wagons,
One on the top of another, as hurriedly they had been
  rescued.
Over the chest of drawers were the sieve and wool coverlet
  lying;
Thrown in the kneading-trough lay the bed, and the sheets
  on the mirror.
Danger, alas! as we learned ourselves in our great con-
  flagration
Twenty years since, will take from a man all power of
  reflection,
So that he grasps things worthless and leaves what is pre-
  cious behind him.
Here, too, with unconsidering care they were carrying with
  them
Pitiful trash, that only encumbered the horses and oxen;
Such as old barrels and boards, the pen for the goose, and
  the bird-cage.
Women and children, too, went toiling along with their
  bundles,

Panting 'neath baskets and tubs, full of things of no manner
of value:
So unwilling is man to relinquish his meanest possession.
Thus on the dusty road the crowded procession moved
forward,
All confused and disordered. The one whose beasts were
the weaker,
Wanted more slowly to drive, while faster would hurry
another.
Presently went up a scream from the closely squeezed women
and children,
And with the yelping of dogs was mingled the lowing of
cattle,
Cries of distress from the aged and sick, who aloft on the
wagon,
Heavy and thus overpacked, upon beds were sitting and
swaying.
Pressed at last from the rut and out to the edge of the
highway,
Slipped the creaking wheel; the cart lost its balance, and
over
Fell in the ditch. In the swing the people were flung to a
distance,
Far off into the field, with horrible screams; by good
fortune
Later the boxes were thrown and fell more near to the
wagon.
Verily all who had witnessed the fall, expected to see them
Crushed into pieces beneath the weight of trunks and of
presses.
So lay the cart all broken to fragments, and helpless the
people.
Keeping their onward way, the others drove hastily by them,
Each thinking only of self, and carried away by the current.
Then we ran to the spot, and found the sick and the
aged,—
Those who at home and in bed could before their lingering
ailments
Scarcely endure,—lying bruised on the ground, complaining
and groaning,

Choked by the billowing dust and scorched by the heat of
the noonday."

Thereupon answered and said the kind-hearted landlord,
with feeling:
" Would that our Hermann might meet them and give them
refreshment and clothing!
Loath should I be to behold them: the looking on suffering
pains me.
Touched by the earliest tidings of their so cruel afflictions,
Hastily sent we a mite from out of our super-abundance,
Only that some might be strengthened, and we might our-
selves be made easy.
But let us now no longer renew these sorrowful pictures
Knowing how readily fear steals into the heart of us mortals
And anxiety, worse to me than the actual evil.
Come with me into the room behind, our cool little parlor,
Where no sunbeam e'er shines, and no sultry breath ever
enters
Through its thickness of wall. There mother will bring us
a flagon
Of our old eighty-three, with which we may banish our
fancies.
Here 'tis not cosey to drink: the flies so buzz round the
glasses."
Thither adjourned they then, and all rejoiced in the coolness.

Carefully brought forth the mother the clear and glorious
vintage,
Cased in a well-polished flask, on a waiter of glittering
pewter,
Set round with large green glasses, the drinking cups meet
for the Rhine wine.
So sat the three together about the highly waxed table,
Gleaming and round and brown, that on mighty feet was
supported.
Joyously rang at once the glasses of landlord and pastor,
But his motionless held the third, and sat lost in reflection,
Until with words of good-humor the landlord challenged
him, saying,—

"Come, sir neighbor, empty your glass, for God in his
  mercy
Thus far has kept us from evil, and so in the future will
  keep us.
For who acknowledges not, that since our dread confla-
  gration,
When he so hardly chastised us, he now is continually
  blessing,
Constantly shielding, as man the apple of his eye watches
  over,
Holding it precious and dear above all the rest of his
  members?
Shall he in time to come not defend us and furnish us
  succor?
Only when danger is nigh do we see how great is his power.
Shall he this blooming town which he once by industrious
  burghers
Built up afresh from its ashes, and afterwards blessed with
  abundance,
Now demolish again, and bring all the labor to nothing?"

  Cheerfully said in reply the excellent pastor, and kindly:
"Keep thyself firm in the faith, and firm abide in this
  temper;
For it makes steadfast and wise when fortune is fair, and
  when evil,
Furnishes sweet consolation and animates hopes the sub-
  limest."

  Then made answer the landlord, with thoughts judicious
  and manly:
"Often the Rhine's broad stream have I with astonishment
  greeted,
As I have neared it again, after travelling abroad upon
  business.
Always majestic it seemed, and my mind and spirit exalted.
But I could never imagine its beautiful banks would so
  shortly
Be to a rampart transformed, to keep from our borders the
  Frenchman,

And its wide-spreading bed be a moat all passage to hinder.
See! thus nature protects, the stout-hearted Germans protect us,
And thus protects us the Lord, who then will be weakly despondent?
Weary already the combatants, all indications are peaceful.
Would it might be that when that festival, ardently longed for,
Shall in our church be observed, when the sacred *Te Deum* is rising,
Swelled by the pealing of organ and bells, and the blaring of trumpets,—
Would it might be that that day should behold my Hermann, sir pastor,
Standing, his choice now made, with his bride before thee at the altar,
Making that festal day, that through every land shall be honored,
My anniversary, too, henceforth of domestic rejoicing!
But I observe with regret, that the youth so efficient and active
Ever in household affairs, when abroad is timid and backward.
Little enjoyment he finds in going about among others;
Nay, he will even avoid young ladies' society wholly;
Shuns the enlivening dance which all young persons delight in."

Thus he spoke and listened; for now was heard in the distance
Clattering of horses' hoofs drawing near, and the roll of the wagon,
Which, with furious haste, came thundering under the gateway.

TERPSICHORE

HERMANN

NOW when of comely mien the son came into the chamber,
Turned with a searching look the eyes of the preacher upon him,
And, with the gaze of the student, who easily fathoms expression,
Scrutinized well his face and form and his general bearing.
Then with a smile he spoke, and said in words of affection:
"Truly a different being thou comest! I never have seen thee
Cheerful as now, nor ever beheld I thy glances so beaming.
Joyous thou comest, and happy: 'tis plain that among the poor people
Thou hast been sharing thy gifts, and receiving their blessings upon thee."

Quietly then, and with serious words, the son made him answer:
"If I have acted as ye will commend, I know not; but I followed
That which my heart bade me do, as I shall exactly relate you.
Thou wert, mother, so long in rummaging 'mong thy old pieces,
Picking and choosing, that not until late was thy bundle together;
Then too the wine and the beer took care and time in the packing.
When I came forth through the gateway at last, and out on the high-road,

Backward the crowd of citizens streamed with women and children,
Coming to meet me; for far was already the band of the exiles.
Quicker I kept on my way, and drove with speed to the village,
Where they were meaning to rest, as I heard, and tarry till morning.
Thitherward up the new street as I hasted, a stout-timbered wagon,
Drawn by two oxen, I saw, of that region the largest and strongest;
While, with vigorous steps, a maiden was walking beside them,
And, a long staff in her hand, the two powerful creatures was guiding,
Urging them now, now holding them back; with skill did she drive them.
Soon as the maiden perceived me, she calmly drew near to the horses,
And in these words she addressed me: ' Not thus deplorable always
Has our condition been, as to-day on this journey thou seest.
I am not yet grown used to asking gifts of a stranger,
Which he will often unwillingly give, to be rid of the beggar.
But necessity drives me to speak; for here, on the straw, lies
Newly delivered of child, a rich land-owner's wife, whom I scarcely
Have in her pregnancy, safe brought off with the oxen and wagon.
Naked, now in her arms the new-born infant is lying,
And but little the help our friends will be able to furnish,
If in the neighboring village, indeed, where to-day we would rest us,
Still we shall find them; though much do I fear they already have passed it.
Shouldst thou have linen to spare of any description, provided
Thou of this neighborhood art, to the poor in charity give it.'

"Thus she spoke, and the pale-faced mother raised herself feebly

Up from the straw, and towards me looked. Then said I in answer:

'Surely unto the good, a spirit from heaven oft speaketh,

Making them feel the distress that threatens a suffering brother.

For thou must know that my mother, already presaging thy sorrows,

Gave me a bundle to use it straightway for the need of the naked.'

Then I untied the knots of the string, and the wrapper of father's

Unto her gave, and gave her as well the shirts and the linen.

And she thanked me with joy, and cried: 'The happy believe not

Miracles yet can be wrought: for only in need we acknowledge

God's own hand and finger, that leads the good to show goodness.

What unto us he has done through thee, may he do to thee also!'

And I beheld with what pleasure the sick woman handled the linens,

But with especial delight the dressing-gown's delicate flannel.

'Let us make haste,' the maid to her said, 'and come to the village,

Where our people will halt for the night and already are resting.

There these clothes for the children I, one and all, straightway will portion.'

Then she saluted again, her thanks most warmly expressing,

Started the oxen; the wagon went on; but there I still lingered,

Still held the horses in check; for now my heart was divided

Whether to drive with speed to the village, and there the provisions

Share 'mong the rest of the people, or whether I here to the maiden
All should deliver at once, for her discreetly to portion.
And in an instant my heart had decided, and quietly driving
After the maiden, I soon overtook her, and said to her quickly:
'Hearken, good maiden;—my mother packed up not linen-stuffs only
Into the carriage, that I should have clothes to furnish the naked;
Wine and beer she added besides, and supply of provisions:
Plenty of all these things I have in the box of the carriage.
But now I feel myself moved to deliver these offerings also
Into thy hand; for so shall I best fulfil my commission.
Thou wilt divide them with judgment, while I must by chance be directed.'
Thereupon answered the maiden: 'I will with faithfulness portion
These thy gifts, that all shall bring comfort to those who are needy.'
Thus she spoke, and quickly the box of the carriage I opened,
Brought forth thence the substantial hams, and brought out the breadstuffs,
Bottles of wine and beer, and one and all gave to the maiden.
Willingly would I have given her more, but the carriage was empty.
All she packed at the sick woman's feet, and went on her journey.
I, with my horses and carriage, drove rapidly back to the city."

Instantly now, when Hermann had ceased, the talkative neighbor
Took up the word, and cried: "Oh happy, in days like the present,
Days of flight and confusion, who lives by himself in his dwelling,
Having no wife nor child to be clinging about him in terror!

Happy I feel myself now, and would not for much be called father;
Would not have wife and children to-day, for whom to be anxious.
Oft have I thought of this flight before; and have packed up together
All my best things already, the chains and old pieces of money
That were my sainted mother's, of which not one has been sold yet.
Much would be left behind, it is true, not easily gotten.
Even the roots and the herbs, that were with such industry gathered,
I should be sorry to lose, though the worth of the goods is but trifling.
If my purveyor remained, I could go from my dwelling contented.
When my cash I have brought away safe, and have rescued my person,
All is safe: none find it so easy to fly as the single."

"Neighbor," unto his words young Hermann with emphasis answered:
"I can in no wise agree with thee here, and censure thy language.
Is he indeed a man to be prized, who, in good and in evil,
Takes no thought but for self, and gladness and sorrow with others
Knows not how to divide, nor feels his heart so impel him?
Rather than ever to-day would I make up my mind to be married:
Many a worthy maiden is needing a husband's protection,
And the man needs an inspiriting wife when ill is impending."

Thereupon smiling the father replied: "Thus love I to hear thee!
That is a sensible word such as rarely I've known thee to utter."

Straightway, however, the mother broke in with quick-
    ness, exclaiming:
'Son, to be sure, thou art right! we parents have set the
    example;
Seeing that not in our season of joy did we choose one
    another;
Rather the saddest of hours it was that bound us together.
Monday morning—I mind it well; for the day that preceded
Came that terrible fire by which our city was ravaged—
Twenty years will have gone. The day was a Sunday as
    this is;
Hot and dry was the season; the water was almost ex-
    hausted.
All the people were strolling abroad in their holiday dresses,
'Mong the villages partly, and part in the mills and the
    taverns.
And at the end of the city the flames began, and went
    coursing
Quickly along the streets, creating a draught in their
    passage.
Burned were the barns where the copious harvest already
    was garnered;
Burned were the streets as far as the market: the house of
    my father,
Neighbor to this, was destroyed, and this one also fell
    with it.
Little we managed to save. I sat, that sorrowful night
    through,
Outside the town on the common, to guard the beds and the
    boxes.
Sleep overtook me at last, and when I again was awakened,
Feeling the chill of the morning that always descends before
    sunrise,
There were the smoke and the glare, and the walls and
    chimneys in ruins.
Then fell a weight on my heart; but more majestic than ever
Came up the sun again, inspiring my bosom with courage.
Then I rose hastily up, with a yearning the place to revisit
Whereon our dwelling had stood, and to see if the hens had
    been rescued,

Which I especially loved, for I still was a child in my
  feelings.
Thus as I over the still-smoking timbers of house and of
  court-yard
Picked my way, and beheld the dwelling so ruined and
  wasted,
Thou camest up to examine the place, from the other
  direction.
Under the ruins thy horse in his stall had been buried; the
  rubbish
Lay on the spot and the glimmering beams; of the horse
  we saw nothing.
Thoughtful and grieving we stood there thus, each facing
  the other,
Now that the wall was fallen that once had divided our
  court-yards.
Thereupon thou by the hand didst take me, and speak to me,
  saying,—
'Lisa, how camest thou hither?   Go back! thy soles must
  be burning;
Hot the rubbish is here: it scorches my boots, which are
  stronger.'
And thou didst lift me up, and carry me out through thy
  court-yard.
There was the door of the house left standing yet with its
  archway,
Just as 'tis standing now, the one thing only remaining.
Then thou didst set me down and kiss me; to that I ob-
  jected;
But thou didst answer and say with kindly significant
  language:
'See! my house lies in ruins: remain here and help me re-
  build it;
So shall my help in return be given to building thy
  father's.'
Yet did I not comprehend thee until thou sentest thy mother
Unto my father, and quick were the happy espousals ac-
  complished.
E'en to this day I remember with joy those half-consumed
  timbers,

And I can see once more the sun coming up in such
    splendor;
For 'twas the day that gave me my husband; and, ere the
    first season
Passed of that wild desolation, a son to my youth had been
    given.
Therefore I praise thee, Hermann, that thou, with an honest
    assurance,
Shouldst, in these sorrowful days, be thinking thyself of a
    maiden,
And amid ruins and war shouldst thus have the courage to
    woo her."

    Straightway, then, and with warmth, the father replied
    to her, saying:
"Worthy of praise is the feeling, and truthful also the
    story,
Mother, that thou hast related; for so indeed everything
    happened.
Better, however, is better. It is not the business of all men
Thus their life and estate to begin from the very foundation:
Every one needs not to worry himself as we and the rest
    did.
Oh, how happy is he whose father and mother shall give
    him,
Furnished and ready, a house which he can adorn with his
    increase.
Every beginning is hard; but most the beginning a house-
    hold.
Many are human wants, and every thing daily grows dearer,
So that a man must consider the means of increasing his
    earnings.
This I hope therefore of thee, my Hermann, that into our
    dwelling
Thou wilt be bringing ere long a bride who is handsomely
    dowered;
For it is meet that a gallant young man have an opulent
    maiden.
Great is the comfort of home whene'er, with the woman
    elected,

Enter the useful presents, besides, in box and in basket.

Not for this many a year in vain has the mother been busy

Making her daughter's linens of strong and delicate texture;

God-parents have not in vain been giving their vessels of silver,

And the father laid by in his desk the rare pieces of money;

For there a day will come when she, with her gifts and possessions,

Shall that youth rejoice who has chosen her out of all others.

Well do I know how good in a house is a woman's position,

Who her own furniture round her knows, in kitchen and chamber;

Who herself the bed and herself the table has covered.

Only a well-dowered bride should I like to receive to my dwelling.

She who is poor is sure, in the end, to be scorned by her husband;

And will as servant be held, who as servant came in with her bundle.

Men will remain unjust when the season of love is gone over.

Yes, my Hermann, thy father's old age thou greatly canst gladden,

If thou a daughter-in-law will speedily bring to my dwelling,

Out of the neighborhood here,—from the house over yonder, the green one.

Rich is the man, I can tell thee. His manufactures and traffic

Daily are making him richer; for whence draws the merchant not profit?

Three daughters only he has, to divide his fortune among them.

True that the eldest already is taken; but there is the second

Still to be had, as well as the third; and not long so, it may be.

I would never have lingered till now, had I been in thy place;

But had fetched one of the maidens, as once I bore off thy dear mother."

Modestly then did the son to the urgent father make
  answer:
" Truly 'twas my wish too, as well as thine own, to have
  chosen
One of our neighbor's daughters, for we had been brought
  up together;
Played, in the early days, about the market-place fountain;
And, from the other boys' rudeness, I often have been their
  defender.
That, though, is long since past: the girls, as they grew to
  be older,
Properly stayed in the house, and shunned the more bois-
  terous pastimes.
Well brought up are they, surely! I used sometimes to go
  over,
Partly to gratify thee, and because of our former ac-
  quaintance:
But no pleasure I ever could take in being among them;
For I was always obliged to endure their censures upon me.
Quite too long was my coat, the cloth too coarse, and the
  color
Quite too common; my hair was not cropped, as it should
  be, and frizzled.
I was resolved, at last, that I, also, would dress myself
  finely,
Just as those office-boys do who always are seen there on
  Sundays,
Wearing in summer their half-silken flaps, that dangle about
  them;
But I discovered, betimes, they made ever a laughing-stock
  of me.
And I was vexed when I saw it,—it wounded my pride; but
  more deeply
Felt I aggrieved that they the good-will should so far mis-
  interpret
That in my heart I bore them,—especially Minna the
  youngest.
It was on Easter-day that last I went over to see them;
Wearing my best new coat, that is now hanging up in the
  closet,

And having frizzled my hair, like that of the other young
fellows.
Soon as I entered, they tittered; but that not at me, as I
fancied.
Minna before the piano was seated; the father was present,
Hearing his daughters sing, and full of delight and good-
humor.
Much I could not understand of all that was said in the
singing;
But of Pamina I often heard, and oft of Tamino:
And I, besides, could not stay there dumb; so, as soon as
she ended,
Something about the words I asked, and about the two
persons.
Thereupon all were silent and smiled; but the father made
answer:
'Thou knowest no one, my friend, I believe, but Adam and
Eve?'
No one restrained himself longer, but loud laughed out then
the maidens,
Loud laughed out the boys, the old man held his sides for
his laughing.
I, in embarrassment, dropped my hat, and the giggling
continued,
On and on and on, for all they kept playing and singing.
Back to the house here I hurried, o'ercome with shame and
vexation,
Hung up my coat in the closet, and pulled out the curls with
my fingers,
Swearing that never again my foot should cross over that
threshold.
And I was perfectly right; for vain are the maidens, and
heartless.
E'en to this day, as I hear, I am called by them ever
'Tamino.'"

Thereupon answered the mother, and said: "Thou
shouldest not, Hermann,
Be so long vexed with the children: indeed, they are all of
them children.

Minna, believe me, is good, and was always disposed to
    thee kindly.
'Twas not long since she was asking about thee. Let her
    be thy chosen!"

Thoughtfully answered the son: "I know not. That mor-
    tification
Stamped itself in me so deeply, I never could bear to behold
    her
Seated before the piano or listen again to her singing."

Forth broke the father then, and in words of anger
    made answer:
"Little of joy will my life have in thee! I said it would
    be so
When I perceived that thy pleasure was solely in horses
    and farming:
Work which a servant, indeed, performs for an opulent
    master,
That thou doest; the father meanwhile must his son be de-
    prived of,
Who should appear as his pride, in the sight of the rest of
    the townsmen.
Early with empty hopes thy mother was wont to deceive me,
When in the school thy studies, thy reading and writing,
    would never
As with the others succeed, but thy seat would be always the
    lowest.
That comes about, forsooth, when a youth has no feeling
    of honor
Dwelling within his breast, nor the wish to raise himself
    higher.
Had but my father so cared for me as thou hast been
    cared for;
If he had sent me to school, and provided me thus with
    instructors,
I should be other, I trow, than host of the Golden Lion!"

Then the son rose from his seat and noiselessly moved
    to the doorway,

Slowly, and speaking no word. The father, however, in
    passion
After him called, " Yes, go, thou obstinate fellow! I know
    thee!
Go and look after the business henceforth, that I have not
    to chide thee;
But do thou nowise imagine that ever a peasant-born
    maiden
Thou for a daughter-in-law shalt bring into my dwelling, the
    hussy!
Long have I lived in the world, and know how mankind
    should be dealt with;
Know how to entertain ladies and gentlemen so that con-
    tented
They shall depart from my house, and strangers agreeably
    can flatter.
Yet I'm resolved that some day I one will have for a
    daughter,
Who shall requite me in kind and sweeten my manifold
    labors;
Who the piano shall play to me, too; so that there shall
    with pleasure
All the handsomest people in town and the finest assemble,
As they on Sundays do now in the house of our neighbor."
    Here Hermann
Softly pressed on the latch, and so went out from the
    chamber.

THALIA

THE CITIZENS

T HUS did the modest son slip away from the angry
upbraiding;
But in the tone he had taken at first, the father
continued:
"That comes not out of a man which he has not in him;
and hardly
Shall the joy ever be mine of seeing my dearest wish
granted:
That my son may not as his father be, but a better.
What would become of the house, and what of the city if
each one
Were not with pleasure and always intent on maintaining,
renewing,
Yea, and improving, too, as time and the foreigner teach us!
Man is not meant, forsooth, to grow from the ground like
a mushroom,
Quickly to perish away on the spot of ground that begot
him,
Leaving no trace behind of himself and his animate action!
As by the house we straightway can tell the mind of the
master,
So, when we walk through a city, we judge of the persons
who rule it.
For where the towers and walls are falling to ruin: where
offal
Lies in heaps in the gutters, and alleys with offal are littered;
Where from its place has started the stone, and no one
resets it;
Where the timbers are rotting away, and the house is
awaiting

Vainly its new supports,—that place we may know is ill
    governed.
Since if not from above work order and cleanliness down-
    ward,
Easily grows the citizen used to untidy postponement;
Just as the beggar grows likewise used to his ragged apparel.
Therefore I wished that our Hermann might early set out
    on some travels;
That he at least might behold the cities of Strasburg and
    Frankfort,
Friendly Mannheim, too, that is cheerful and evenly builded.
He that has once beheld cities so cleanly and large, never
    after
Ceases his own native city, though small it may be, to em-
    bellish.
Do not the strangers who come here commend the repairs
    in our gateway,
Notice our whitewashed tower, and the church we have
    newly rebuilded?
Are not all praising our pavement? the covered canals full
    of water,
Laid with a wise distribution, which furnish us profit and
    safety,
So that no sooner does fire break out than 'tis promptly
    arrested?
Has not all this come to pass since the time of our great
    conflagration?
Builder I six times was named by the council, and won the
    approval,
Won moreover the heartfelt thanks of all the good burghers,
Actively carrying out what I planned, and also fulfilling
What had by upright men been designed, and left uncom-
    pleted.
Finally grew the same zeal in every one of the council;
All now labor together, and firmly decided already
Stands it to build the new causeway that shall with the
    highroad connect us.
But I am sorely afraid that will not be the way with our
    children.
Some think only of pleasure and perishable apparel;

Others will cower at home, and behind the stove will sit
    brooding.
One of this kind, as I fear, we shall find to the last in our
    Hermann."

    Straightway answered and said the good and intelligent
        mother:
"Why wilt thou always, father, be doing our son such
    injustice?
That least of all is the way to bring thy wish to fulfilment.
We have no power to fashion our children as suiteth our
    fancy;
As they are given by God, we so must have them and love
    them;
Teach them as best we can, and let each of them follow
    his nature.
One will have talents of one sort, and different talents another.
Every one uses his own; in his own individual fashion,
Each must be happy and good. I will not have my Hermann
    found fault with;
For he is worthy, I know, of the goods he shall one day
    inherit;
Will be an excellent landlord, a pattern to burghers and
    builders;
Neither in council, as I can foresee, will he be the most
    backward.
But thou keepest shut up in his breast all the poor fellow's
    spirit,
Finding such fault with him daily, and censuring as thou
    but now hast."
And on the instant she quitted the room, and after him
    hurried,
Hoping she somewhere might find him, and might with
    her words of affection
Cheer him again, her excellent son, for well he deserved it.

    Thereupon when she was gone, the father thus smiling
        continued:
"What a strange folk, to be sure, are these women; and
    just like the children;

Both of them bent upon living according as suiteth their
    pleasure,
While we others must never do aught but flatter and praise
    them.
Once for all time holds good the ancients' trustworthy
    proverb:
'Whoever goes not forward comes backward.' So must
    it be always."

    Thereupon answered and said, in a tone of reflection, the
    doctor:
"That, sir neighbor, I willingly grant; for myself I am
    always
Casting about for improvement,—things new, so they be
    not too costly.
But what profits a man, who has not abundance of money,
Being thus active and stirring, and bettering inside and
    outside?
Only too much is the citizen cramped: the good, though
    he know it,
Has he no means to acquire because too slender his purse is,
While his needs are too great; and thus is he constantly
    hampered.
Many the things I had done; but then the cost of such
    changes
Who does not fear, especially now in this season of
    danger?
Long since my house was smiling upon me in modish
    apparel!
Long since great panes of glass were gleaming in all of
    the windows!
But who can do as the merchant does, who, with his re-
    sources,
Knows the methods as well by which the best is arrived at?
Look at that house over yonder,—the new one; behold
    with what splendor
'Gainst the background of green stand out the white spirals
    of stucco!
Great are the panes in the windows; and how the glass
    sparkles and glitters,

Casting quite into the shade the rest of the market-place
  houses!
Yet just after the fire were our two houses the finest,
This of the Golden Lion, and mine of the sign of the
  Angel.
So was my garden, too, throughout the whole neighborhood
  famous:
Every traveller stopped and gazed through the red palisa-
  does,
Caught by the beggars there carved in stone and the dwarfs
  of bright colors.
Then whosoever had coffee served in the beautiful grotto,—
Standing there now all covered with dust and partly in
  ruins,—
Used to be mightily pleased with the glimmering light of
  the mussels
Spread out in beautiful order; and even the eye of the critic
Used by the sight of my corals and potter's ore to be
  dazzled.
So in my parlor, too, they would always admire the painting,
Where in a garden are gaily dressed ladies and gentlemen
  walking,
And with their taper fingers are plucking and holding the
  flowers.
But who would look at it now! In sooth, so great my
  vexation
Scarcely I venture abroad. All now must be other and
  tasteful,
So they call it; and white are the laths and benches of
  wood-work;
Everything simple and smooth; no carving longer or gilding
Can be endured, and the woods from abroad are of all the
  most costly.
Well, I too should be glad could I get for myself something
  novel;
Glad to keep up with the times, and be changing my furni-
  ture often;
Yet must we all be afraid of touching the veriest trifle.
For who among us has means for paying the work-people's
  wages?

Lately I had an idea of giving the Archangel Michael,
Making the sign of my shop, another fresh coating of gilding,
And to the terrible dragon about his feet that is winding;
But I e'en let him stay browned as he is: I dreaded the
    charges."

EUTERPE

MOTHER AND SON

THUS entertaining themselves, the men sat talking. The mother
    Went meanwhile to look for her son in front of the dwelling,
First on the settle of stone, whereon 'twas his wont to be seated.
When she perceived him not there, she went farther to look in the stable,
If he were caring perhaps for his noble horses, the stallions,
Which he as colts had bought, and whose care he intrusted to no one.
And by the servant she there was told: He is gone to the garden.
Then with a nimble step she traversed the long, double court-yards,
Leaving the stables behind, and the well-builded barns, too, behind her;
Entered the garden, that far as the walls of the city extended;
Walked through its length, rejoiced as she went in every thing growing;
Set upright the supports on which were resting the branches
Heavily laden with apples, and burdening boughs of the pear-tree.
Next some caterpillars removed from a stout, swelling cabbage;
For an industrious woman allows no step to be wasted.
Thus was she come at last to the end of the far-reaching garden,
Where stood the arbor embowered in woodbine; nor there did she find him,

More than she had hitherto in all her search through the garden.

But the wicket was standing ajar, which out of the arbor,

Once by particular favor, had been through the walls of the city

Cut by a grandsire of hers, the worshipful burgomaster.

So the now dried-up moat she next crossed over with comfort,

Where, by the side of the road, direct the well-fencèd vine-yard,

Rose with a steep ascent, its slope exposed to the sun-shine.

Up this also she went, and with pleasure as she was ascend-ing

Marked the wealth of the clusters, that scarce by their leafage were hidden.

Shady and covered the way through the lofty middlemost alley,

Which upon steps that were made of unhewn blocks you ascended.

There were the Muscatel, and there were the Chasselas hanging

Side by side, of unusual size and colored with purple,

All set out with the purpose of decking the visitor's table;

While with single vine-stocks the rest of the hillside was covered,

Bearing inferior clusters, from which the delicate wine comes.

Thus up the slope she went, enjoying already the vintage,

And that festive day on which the whole country, rejoicing,

Picks and tramples the grapes, and gathers the must into vessels:

Fireworks, when it is evening, from every direction and corner

Crackle and blaze, and so the fairest of harvests is honored.

But more uneasy she went, her son after twice or thrice calling,

And no answer receiving, except from the talkative echo,

That with many repeats rang back from the towers of the city.

Strange it was for her to seek him; he never had gone to
a distance
That he told her not first, to spare his affectionate mother
Every anxious thought, and fear that aught ill had befallen.
Still did she constantly hope that, if further she went, she
should find him;
For the two doors of the vineyard, the lower as well as
the upper,
Both were alike standing open. So now she entered the
cornfield,
That with its broad expanse the ridge of the hill covered
over.
Still was the ground that she walked on her own; and the
crops she rejoiced in,—
All of them still were hers, and hers was the proud-waving
grain, too,
Over the whole broad field in golden strength that was
stirring.
Keeping the ridgeway, the footpath, between the fields she
went onward,
Having the lofty pear-tree in view, which stood on the
summit,
And was the boundary-mark of the fields that belonged to
her dwelling.
Who might have planted it, none could know, but visible
was it
Far and wide through the country; the fruit of the pear-
tree was famous.
'Neath it the reapers were wont to enjoy their meal at the
noon-day,
And the shepherds were used to tend their flocks in its
shadow.
Benches of unhewn stones and of turf they found set
about it.
And she had not been mistaken, for there sat her Hermann,
and rested,—
Sat with his head on his hand, and seemed to be viewing
the landscape
That to the mountains lay: his back was turned to his
mother.

Towards him softly she crept, and lightly touched on the
    shoulder;
Quick he turned himself round: there were tears in his
    eyes as he met her.

"Mother, how hast thou surprised me!" he said in con-
    fusion; and quickly
Wiped the high-spirited youth his tears away. But the
    mother,
"What! do I find thee weeping, my son?" exclaimed in
    amazement.
"Nay, that is not like thyself: I never before have so seen
    thee!
Tell me, what burdens thy heart? what drives thee here,
    to be sitting
Under the pear-tree alone? These tears in thine eyes, what
    has brought them?"

Then, collecting himself, the excellent youth made her
    answer:
"Truly no heart can that man have in his bosom of iron,
Who is insensible now to the needs of this emigrant people;
He has no brains in his head, who not for his personal
    safety,
Not for his fatherland's weal, in days like the present is
    anxious.
Deeply my heart had been touched by the sights and sounds
    of the morning;
Then I went forth and beheld the broad and glorious land-
    scape
Spreading its fertile slopes in every direction about us,
Saw the golden grain inclining itself to the reapers,
And the promise of well-filled barns from the plentiful har-
    vest.
But, alas, how near is the foe! The Rhine with its waters
Guards us, indeed; but, ah, what now are rivers and moun-
    tains
'Gainst that terrible people that onward bears like a tempest!
For they summon their youths from every quarter together,
Call up their old men too, and press with violence forward.

Death cannot frighten the crowd: one multitude follows
another.
And shall a German dare to linger behind in his homestead?
Hopes he perhaps to escape the everywhere threatening evil?
Nay, dear mother, I tell thee, to-day has made me regretful
That I was lately exempt, when out of our townsmen were
chosen
Those who should serve in the army. An only son I am
truly,
Also our business is great, and the charge of our household
is weighty.
Yet were it better, I deem, in the front to offer resistance
There on the border, than here to await disaster and
bondage.
So has my spirit declared, and deep in my innermost bosom
Courage and longing have now been aroused to live for my
country,
Yea, and to die, presenting to others a worthy example.
If but the strength of Germany's youth were banded to-
gether
There on the frontier, resolved that it never would yield to
the stranger,
Ah, he should not on our glorious soil be setting his foot-
steps,
Neither consuming before our eyes the fruit of our labor,
Ruling our men, and making his prey of our wives and our
daughters.
Hark to me, mother: for I in the depths of my heart am
determined
Quickly to do, and at once, what appears to me right and
in reason;
For he chooses not always the best who longest considers.
Hearken, I shall not again return to the house; but directly
Go from this spot to the city, and there present to the
soldiers
This right arm and this heart, to be spent in the father-
land's service.
Then let my father say if there be no feeling of honor
Dwelling within my breast, nor a wish to raise myself
higher."

Then with significant words spoke the good and intelligent
    mother,
While from her eyes the quick-starting tears were silently
    falling:
" Son, what change has come o'er thee to-day, and over thy
    temper,
That thou speakest no more, as thou yesterday didst, and
    hast always,
Open and free, to thy mother, and tellest exactly thy wishes?
Any one else, had he heard thee thus speak, would in sooth
    have commended,
And this decision of thine would have highly approved as
    most noble,
Being misled by thy tone and by thy significant language.
Yet have I nothing but censure to speak; for better I know
    thee.
Thou concealest thy heart, and thy thoughts are not such
    as thou tellest.
Well do I know that it is not the drum, not the trumpet
    that calls thee:
Neither in uniform wouldst thou figure in sight of the
    maidens;
Since, for all thou art honest and brave, it is thy vocation
Here in quiet to care for the farm and provide for the
    household.
Tell me honestly, therefore, what goads thee to such a
    decision? "

    Earnestly answered the son: "Nay, thou art mistaken,
    dear mother:
One day is not like another. The youth matures into man-
    hood:
Better in stillness oft ripening to deeds than when in the
    tumult
Wildering and wild of existence, that many a youth has
    corrupted.
And, for as still as I am and was always, there yet in my
    bosom
Has such a heart been shaped as abhors all wrong and
    injustice;

And I have learned aright between worldly things to dis-
　　tinguish.
Arm and foot, besides, have been mightily strengthened by
　　labor.
All this, I feel, is true: I dare with boldness maintain it.
Yet dost thou blame me with reason, O mother! for thou
　　hast surprised me
Using a language half truthful and half that of dissimu-
　　lation.
For, let me honestly own,—it is not the near danger that
　　calls me
Forth from my father's house; nor is it the lofty ambition
Helpful to be to my country, and terrible unto the
　　foeman.
They were but words that I spoke: they only were meant
　　for concealing
Those emotions from thee with which my heart is dis-
　　tracted;
And so leave me, O mother! for, since the wishes are
　　fruitless
Which in my bosom I cherish, my life must go fruitlessly
　　over.
For, as I know, he injures himself who is singly devoted,
When for the common cause the whole are not working
　　together."

　" Hesitate not," replied thereupon the intelligent mother,
" Every thing to relate me, the smallest as well as the
　　greatest.
Men will always be hasty, their thoughts to extremes ever
　　running:
Easily out of their course the hasty are turned by a hin-
　　drance.
Whereas a woman is clever in thinking of means, and will
　　venture
E'en on a roundabout way, adroitly to compass her object.
Let me know every thing, then; say wherefore so greatly
　　excited
As I ne'er saw thee before, why thy blood is coursing so
　　hotly,

Wherefore, against thy will, tears are filling thine eyes to
o'erflowing."

Then he abandoned himself, the poor boy, to his sorrow,
and weeping,
Weeping aloud on his kind mother's breast, he brokenly
answered:
"Truly my father's words to-day have wounded me sorely,—
Words which I have not deserved; not to-day, nor at any
time have I:
For it was early my greatest delight to honor my parents.
No one knew more, so I deemed, or was wiser than those
who begot me,
And had with strictness ruled throughout the dark season
of childhood.
Many the things, in truth, I with patience endured from
my playmates,
When the good-will that I bore them they often requited
with malice.
Often I suffered their flings and their blows to pass unre-
sented;
But if they ventured to ridicule father, when he of a
Sunday
Home from Church would come, with his solemn and
dignified bearing;
If they made fun of his cap-string, or laughed at the flowers
of the wrapper
He with such stateliness wore, which was given away but
this morning,—
Threateningly doubled my fist in an instant; with furious
passion
Fell I upon them, and struck out and hit, assailing them
blindly,
Seeing not where. They howled as the blood gushed out
from their noses:
Scarcely they made their escape from my passionate kicking
and beating.
Then, as I older grew, I had much to endure from my
father;
Violent words he oft vented on me, instead of on others,

When, at the board's last session, the council had roused
    his displeasure,
And I was made to atone for the quarrels and wiles of his
    colleagues.
Thou has pitied me often thyself; for much did I suffer,
Ever remembering with cordial respect the kindness of
    parents,
Solely intent on increasing for us their goods and posses-
    sions,
Much denying themselves in order to save for their children.
But, alas! saving alone, for the sake of a tardy enjoyment,—
That is not happiness: pile upon pile, and acre on acre,
Make us not happy, no matter how fair our estates may be
    rounded.
For the father grows old, and with him will grow old the
    children,
Losing the joy of the day, and bearing the care of to-
    morrow.
Look thou below, and see how before us in glory are lying,
Fair and abundant, the corn-fields; beneath them, the vine-
    yard and garden;
Yonder the stables and barns; our beautiful line of pos-
    sessions.
But when I look at the dwelling behind, where up in the
    gable
We can distinguish the window that marks my room in the
    attic;
When I look back, and remember how many a night from
    that window
I for the moon have watched; for the sun, how many a
    morning!
When the healthful sleep of a few short hours sufficed me,—
Ah, so lonely they seem to me then, the chamber and court-
    yard,
Garden and glorious field, away o'er the hill that is
    stretching;
All so desert before me lie: 'tis the wife that is wanting."

Thereupon spoke the good mother, and thus with intelligence answered:

"Son, not greater thy wish to bring thee a bride to thy
  chamber,
That thou mayst find thy nights a beautiful part of existence,
And that the work of the day may gain independence and
  freedom,
Than is thy father's wish too, and thy mother's. We always
  have counselled,—
Yea, we have even insisted,—that thou shouldst elect thee
  a maiden.
But I was ever aware, and now my heart gives me assurance,
That till the hour appointed is come, and the maiden ap-
  pointed
Shall with the hour appear, the choice will be left for the
  future,
While more strong than all else will be fear of grasping the
  wrong one.
If I may say it, my son, I believe thou already hast chosen;
For thy heart has been touched, and been made more than
  wontedly tender.
Speak it out honestly, then; for my soul has told me before-
  hand:
That same maiden it is, the exile, whom thou hast elected."

  "Thou has said, mother!" the son thereupon with eager-
  ness answered.
"Yes, it is she; and if I to-day as my bride do not bring
  her
Home to our dwelling, she from me will go, perhaps vanish
  for ever,
Lost in the war's confusion and sad movings hither and
  thither.
Mother, for ever in vain would then our abundant pos-
  sessions
Prosper before me, and seasons to come be in vain to me
  fruitful.
Yea, I should hold in aversion the wonted house and the
  garden:
Even my mother's love, alas! would not comfort my sorrow.
Every tie, so I feel in my heart, by love is unloosened
Soon as she fastens her own; and not the maid is it only

Leaves behind father and mother, to follow the man she
    has chosen.
He too, the youth, no longer knows aught of mother and
    father,
When he the maiden, his only beloved, sees vanishing from
    him.
Suffer me, then, to go hence wherever despair shall impel me:
Since by my father himself the decisive words have been
    spoken;
Since his house can no longer be mine if he shut out the
    maiden,
Her whom alone as my bride I desire to bring to our
    dwelling."

    Thereupon quickly made answer the good and intelligent
    mother:
"How like to rocks, forsooth, two men will stand facing
    each other!
Proud and not to be moved, will neither draw near to his
    fellow;
Neither will stir his tongue to utter the first word of kind-
    ness.
Therefore I tell thee, my son, a hope yet lives in my bosom,
So she be honest and good, thy father will let thee espouse
    her,
Even though poor, and against a poor girl so decisive his
    sentence.
Many a thing he is wont to speak out in his violent fashion
Which he yet never performs; and so what he denies will
    consent to.
Yet he requires a kindly word, and is right to require it:
He is the father! Besides we know that his wrath after
    dinner,—
When he most hastily speaks, and questions all others'
    opinions,—
Signifies naught; the full force of his violent will is excited
Then by the wine, which lets him not heed the language
    of others;
None but himself does he see and feel. But now is come
    evening,

Talk upon various subjects has passed between him and his
  neighbors.
Gentle, he is; I am sure now his little excitement is over,
And he can feel how unjust his passion has made him to
  others.
Come, let us venture at once: success is alone to the valiant!
Further we need the friends, still sitting together there with
  him;
And in especial the worthy pastor will give us assistance."

Thus she hastily spoke, and up from the stone then arising,
Drew from his seat her son, who willingly followed.   In
  silence
Both descended the hill, their important purpose revolving.

POLYHYMNIA

THE CITIZEN OF THE WORLD

THERE the three men, however, still sat conversing
together,
    With mine host of the Lion, the village doctor, and
        pastor;
And their talk was still on the same unvarying subject,
Turning it this way and that, and viewing from every
    direction.
But with his sober judgment the excellent pastor made
    answer:
"Here will I not contradict you. I know that man should
    be always
Striving for that which is better; indeed, as we see, he is
    reaching
Always after the higher, at least some novelty craving.
But be careful ye go not too far, for with this disposition
Nature has given us pleasure in holding to what is familiar;
Taught us in that to delight to which we have long been
    accustomed.
Every condition is good that is founded on reason and
    nature.
Many are man's desires, yet little it is that he needeth;
Seeing the days are short and mortal destiny bounded.
Ne'er would I censure the man whom a restless activity
    urges,
Bold and industrious, over all pathways of land and of
    ocean,
Ever untiring to roam; who takes delight in the riches,
Heaping in generous abundance about himself and his
    children.
Yet not unprized by me is the quiet citizen also,

Making the noiseless round of his own inherited acres,
Tilling the ground as the ever-returning seasons command
    him.
Not with every year is the soil transfigured about him;
Not in haste does the tree stretch forth, as soon as 'tis
    planted,
Full-grown arms towards heaven and decked with plenteous
    blossoms.
No: man has need of patience, and needful to him are also
Calmness and clearness of mind, and a pure and right
    understanding.
Few are the seeds he intrusts to earth's all-nourishing
    bosom;
Few are the creatures he knows how to raise and bring to
    perfection.
Centred are all his thoughts alone on that which is useful.
Happy to whom by nature a mind of such temper is given,
For he supports us all! And hail, to the man whose
    abode is
Where in a town the country pursuits with the city are
    blended.
On him lies not the pressure that painfully hampers the
    farmer,
Nor is he carried away by the greedy ambition of cities;
Where they of scanty possessions too often are given to
    aping,
Wives and daughters especially, those who are higher and
    richer.
Blessed be therefore thy son in his life of quiet employment;
Blessed the wife, of like mind with himself, whom he one
    day shall choose him."

  Thus he spoke; and scarce had he ended when entered
    the mother,
Holding her son by the hand, and so led him up to her
    husband.
"Father," she said, "how oft when we two have been
    chatting together,
Have we rejoiced in the thought of Hermann's future es-
    pousal,

When he should bring his bride to be the light of our
   dwelling!
Over and over again the matter we pondered: this maiden
Fixing upon for him first, and then that, with the gossip
   of parents.
But that day is now come; and Heaven at last has the
   maiden
Brought to him hither, and shown him; and now his heart
   has decided.
Said we not always then he should have his own choice in
   the matter?
Was it not just now thy wish that he might with lively
   affection
Feel himself drawn to some maiden? The hour is come
   that we hoped for.
Yes; he has felt and has chosen and come to a manly
   decision.
That same maiden it is that met him this morning, the
   stranger:
Say he may have her, or else, as he swears, his life shall
   be single."

   " Give her me, father," so added the son: " my heart has
      elected
Clear and sure; she will be to you both the noblest of
   daughters."

   But the father was silent. Then hastily rose the good
      pastor,
Took up the word and said: " The moment alone is decisive;
Fixes the life of man, and his future destiny settles.
After long taking of counsel, yet only the work of a moment
Every decision must be; and the wise alone seizes the right
   one.
Dangerous always it is comparing the one with the other
When we are making our choice, and so confusing our
   feelings.
Hermann is pure. From childhood up I have known him,
   and never
E'en as a boy was he wont to be reaching for this and the
   other:

What he desired **was** best for him too, and he held to it
    firmly.
Be not surprised and alarmed that now has appeared of a
    sudden,
What thou hast wished for so long. It is true that the
    present appearance
Bears not the form of the wish, exactly as thou hadst con-
    ceived it:
For our wishes oft hide from ourselves the object we wish
    for;
Gifts come down from above in the shapes appointed by
    Heaven.
Therefore misjudge not the maiden who now of thy dearly
    beloved,
Good and intelligent son has been first to touch the affec-
    tions:
Happy to whom at once his first love's hand shall be given,
And in whose heart no tenderest wish must secretly languish.
Yes: his whole bearing assures me that now his fate is
    decided.
Genuine love matures in a moment the youth into man-
    hood;
He is not easily moved; and I fear that if this be refused
    him,
Sadly his years will go by, those years that should be the
    fairest."

  Straightway then in a thoughtful tone the doctor made
    answer,
On whose tongue for a long time past the words had been
    trembling:
" Pray let us here as before pursue the safe middle course
    only.
Make haste slowly: that was Augustus the emperor's motto.
Willingly I myself place at my well-beloved neighbor's
    disposal,
Ready to do him what service I can with my poor under-
    standing.
Youth most especially stands in need of some one to guide it.
Let me therefore go forth that I may examine the maiden,

And may question the people among whom she lives and
who know her.
Me 'tis not easy to cheat: I know how words should be
valued."

Straightway the son broke in, and with wingèd words
made he answer:
" Do so, neighbor, and go and make thine inquiries; but
with thee
l should be glad if our minister here were joined in the errand:
Two such excellent men would be irreproachable judges.
O my father! believe me, she's none of those wandering
maidens,
Not one of those who stroll through the land in search
of adventure,
And who seek to ensnare inexperienced youth in their
meshes.
No: the hard fortunes of war, that universal destroyer,
Which is convulsing the earth and has hurled from its deep
foundations
Many a structure already, have sent the poor girl into exile.
Are not now men of high birth, the most noble, in misery
roaming?
Princes fly in disguise and kings are in banishment living.
So alas! also is she, the best among all of her sisters,
Driven an exile from home; yet, her personal sorrows
forgetting,
She is devoted to others; herself without help, she is
helpful.
Great is the want and the suffering over the earth that are
spreading:
Shall not some happiness, too, be begotten of all this afflic-
tion,
And shall not I in the arms of my wife, my trusted com-
panion,
Look back with joy to the war, as do ye to the great con-
flagration?"

Outspoke the father then in a tone of decision, and
answered:

" Strangely thy tongue has been loosened, my son, which
    many a year past
Seemed to have stuck in thy mouth, and only to move on
    compulsion !
I must experience to-day, it would seem, what threatens all
    fathers,
That the son's headstrong will the mother with readiness
    favors,
Showing too easy indulgence; and every neighbor sides
    with them
When there is aught to be carried against the father and
    husband.
But I will not oppose you, thus banded together: how could
    I?
For I already perceive here tears and defiance beforehand.
Go ye therefore, inquire, in God's name, bring me the
    daughter.
But if not so, then the boy is to think no more of the
    maiden."

Thus the father. The son cried out with joyful demeanor,
" Ere it is evening the noblest of daughters shall hither be
    brought you,
Such as no man with sound sense in his breast can fail to be
    pleased with.
Happy, I venture to hope, will be also the excellent maiden.
Yes; she will ever be grateful for having had father and
    mother
Given once more in you, and such as a child most delights in.
Now I will tarry no longer, but straightway harness the
    horses,
Drive forth our friends at once on the footsteps of my
    beloved,
Leaving them then to act for themselves, as their wisdom
    shall dictate,
Guide myself wholly, I promise, according to what they
    determine,
And, until I may call her my own, ne'er look on the maiden."
Thus he went forth: the others meanwhile remained in dis-
    cussion,

Rapid and earnest, considering deeply their great under-
taking.

Hermann hasted straightway to the stable, where quietly
standing
Found he the spirited stallions, the clean oats quickly de-
vouring,
And the well-dried hay that was cut from the richest of
meadows.
On them without delay the shining bits he adjusted,
Hastily drew the straps through the buckles of beautiful
plating,
Firmly fastened then the long broad reins, and the horses
Led without to the court-yard, whither the willing assistant
Had with ease, by the pole, already drawn forward the
carriage.
Next to the whipple-tree they with care by the neatly kept
traces
Joined the impetuous strength of the freely travelling
horses.
Whip in hand took Hermann his seat and drove under the
doorway.
Soon as the friends straightway their commodious places
had taken,
Quickly the carriage rolled off, and left the pavement be-
hind it,
Left behind it the walls of the town and the fresh-whitened
towers.
Thus drove Hermann on till he came to the well-known
causeway.
Rapidly, loitering nowhere, but hastening up hill and down
hill.
But as he now before him perceived the spire of the village,
And no longer remote the garden-girt houses were lying,
Then in himself he thought that here he would rein up the
horses.

Under the solemn shade of lofty linden-trees lying,
Which for centuries past upon this spot had been rooted,

Spread in front of the village a broad and grass-covered common,
Favorite place of resort for the peasants and neighboring townsfolk.
Here, at the foot of the trees, sunk deep in the ground was a well-spring;
When you descended the steps, stone benches you found at the bottom,
Stationed about the spring, whose pure, living waters were bubbling
Ceaselessly forth, hemmed in by low walls for convenience of drawing.
Hermann resolved that here he would halt, with his horses and carriage,
Under the shade of the trees. He did so, and said to the others:
" Here alight, my friends, and go your ways to discover
Whether the maiden in truth be worthy the hand that I offer.
That she is so, I believe; naught new or strange will ye tell me.
Had I to act for myself, I should go with speed to the village,
Where a few words from the maiden's own lips should determine my fortune.
Ye will with readiness single her out from all of the others,
For there can scarcely be one that to her may be likened in bearing.
But I will give you, besides, her modest attire for a token:
Mark, then, the stomacher's scarlet, that sets off the arch of her bosom,
Prettily laced, and the bodice of black fitting close to her figure;
Neatly the edge of her kerchief is plaited into a ruffle,
Which with a simple grace her chin's rounded outline encircles;
Freely and lightly rises above it the head's dainty oval;
And her luxuriant hair over silver bodkins is braided;
Down from under her bodice, the full, blue petticoat falling,
Wraps itself, when she is walking, about her neatly shaped ankles.

Yet one thing will I say, and would make it my earnest
    petition,—
Speak not yourselves with the maiden, nor let your intent
    be discovered;
Rather inquire of others, and hearken to what they may tell
    you.
When ye have tidings enough to satisfy father and mother,
Then return to me here, and we will consider what further.
So did I plan it all out in my mind while driving you
    hither."

    Thus he spoke. The friends thereupon went their way
    to the village,
Where, in the houses and gardens and barns, the people
    were swarming;
Wagons on wagons stood crowded together along the broad
    highway.
Men for the harnessed horses and lowing cattle were caring,
While the women were busy in drying their clothes on the
    hedges,
And in the running brook the children were merrily splashing.
Making their way through the pressure of wagons, of people
    and cattle,
Went the commissioned spies, and to right and to left looked
    about them,
If they a figure might see that answered the maiden's
    description;
But not one of them all appeared the beautiful damsel.
Denser soon grew the press. A contest arose round the
    wagons
'Mongst the threatening men, wherein blended the cries of
    the women.
Rapidly then to the spot, and with dignified step, came an
    elder,
Joined the clamoring group, and straightway the uproar was
    silenced,
As he commanded peace, and rebuked with a fatherly
    sternness.
"Has, then, misfortune," he cried, "not yet so bound us
    together,

That we have finally learned to bear and forbear one
another,
Though each one, it may be, do not measure his share of the
labor?
He that is happy, forsooth, is contentious! Will sufferings
never
Teach you to cease from your brawls of old between brother
and brother?
Grudge not one to another a place on the soil of the stranger;
Rather divide what ye have, as yourselves ye would hope to
find mercy."

Thus spoke the man and all became silent: restored to
good humor,
Peaceably then the people arranged·their cattle and wagons.
But when the clergyman now had heard what was said by
the stranger,
And had the steadfast mind of the foreign justice dis-
covered,
He to the man drew near and with words of meaning ad-
dressed him:
"True it is, father, that when in prosperity people are
living,
Feeding themselves from the earth, which far and wide
opens her bosom,
And in the years and months renews the coveted blessings,—
All goes on of itself, and each himself deems the wisest,
Deems the best, and so they continue abiding together,
He of greatest intelligence ranking no higher than others;
All that occurs, as if of itself, going quietly forward.
But let disaster unsettle the usual course of existence,
Tear down the buildings about us, lay waste the crops and
the garden,
Banish the husband and wife from their old, familiar-grown
dwelling,
Drive them to wander abroad through nights and days of
privation,—
Then, ah then! we look round us to see what man is the
wisest,
And no longer in vain his glorious words will be spoken.

Tell me, art thou not judge among this fugitive people,
Father, who thus in an instant canst bid their passions be
     quiet?
Thou dost appear to-day as one of those earliest leaders,
Who through deserts and wanderings guided the emigrant
     nations.
Yea, I could even believe I were speaking with Joshua or
     Moses."

Then with serious look the magistrate answered him,
     saying:
"Truly our times might well be compared with all others
     in strangeness,
Which are in history mentioned, profane or sacred tradition;
For who has yesterday lived and to-day in times like the
     present,
He has already lived years, events are so crowded together.
If I look back but a little, it seems that my head must be
     hoary
Under the burden of years, and yet my strength is still active.
Well may we of this day compare ourselves unto that
     people
Who, from the burning bush, beheld in the hour of their
     danger
God the Lord: we also in cloud and in fire have beheld
     him."

Seeing the priest was inclined to speak yet more with the
     stranger,
And was desirous of learning his story and that of his
     people,
Privately into his ear his companion hastily whispered:
"Talk with the magistrate further, and lead him to speak of
     the maiden.
I, however, will wander in search, and as soon as I find her,
Come and report to thee here." The minister nodded, as-
     senting;
And through the gardens, hedges, and barns, went the spy
     on his errand.

CLIO

THE AGE

NOW when the foreign judge had been by the minister
    questioned
    As to his people's distress, and how long their exile
    had lasted,
Thus made answer the man: "Of no recent date are our
    sorrows;
Since of the gathering bitter of years our people have
    drunken,—
Bitterness all the more dreadful because such fair hope had
    been blighted.
Who will pretend to deny that his heart swelled high in
    his bosom,
And that his freer breast with purer pulses was beating,
When we beheld the new sun arise in his earliest splen-
    dor,
When of the rights of men we heard, which to all should
    be common,
Were of a righteous equality told, and inspiriting freedom?
Every one hoped that then he should live his own life, and
    the fetters,
Binding the various lands, appeared their hold to be loos-
    ing,—
Fetters that had in the hand of sloth been held and self-
    seeking.
Looked not the eyes of all nations, throughout that calami-
    tous season,
Towards the world's capital city, for so it had long been
    considered,
And of that glorious title was now, more than ever, de-
    serving?

Were not the names of those men who first delivered the
    message,
Names to compare with the highest that under the heavens
    are spoken?
Did not, in every man, grow courage and spirit and lan-
    guage?
And, as neighbors, we, first of all, were zealously kindled.
Thereupon followed the war, and armèd bodies of French-
    men
Pressed to us nearer; yet nothing but friendship they seemed
    to be bringing;
Ay, and they brought it too; for exalted the spirit within
    them:
They with rejoicing the festive trees of liberty planted,
Promising every man what was his own, and to each his own
    ruling.
High beat the heart of the youths, and even the aged were
    joyful;
Gaily the dance began about the newly raised standard.
Thus had they speedily won, these overmastering French-
    men,
First the spirits of men by the fire and dash of their bearing,
Then the hearts of the women with irresistible graces.
Even the pressure of hungry war seemed to weigh on us
    lightly,
So before our vision did hope hang over the future,
Luring our eyes abroad into newly opening pathways.
Oh, how joyful the time when with her belovèd the maiden
Whirls in the dance, the longed-for day of their union
    awaiting!
But more glorious that day on which to our vision the
    highest
Heart of man can conceive seemed near and attainable to us.
Loosened was every tongue, and men—the aged, the strip-
    ling—
Spoke aloud in words that were full of high feeling and
    wisdom.
Soon, however, the sky was o'ercast. A corrupt generation
Fought for the right of dominion, unworthy the good to
    establish;

So that they slew one another, their new-made neighbors
  and brothers
Held in subjection, and then sent the self-seeking masses
  against us.
Chiefs committed excesses and wholesale plunder upon us,
While those lower plundered and rioted down to the lowest:
Every one seemed but to care that something be left for
  the morrow.
Great past endurance the need, and daily grew the oppres-
  sion:
They were the lords of the day; there was none to hear our
  complaining.
Then fell trouble and rage upon even the quietest spirit.
One thought only had all, and swore for their wrongs to
  have vengeance,
And for the bitter loss of their hope thus doubly deluded.
Presently Fortune turned and declared on the side of the
  German,
And with hurried marches the French retreated before us.
Ah! then as never before did we feel the sad fortunes of
  warfare:
He that is victor is great and good,—or at least he appears
  so,—
And he, as one of his own, will spare the man he has con-
  quered,
Him whose service he daily needs, and whose property
  uses.
But no law the fugitive knows, save of self-preservation,
And, with a reckless greed, consumes all the possessions
  about him;
Then are his passions also inflamed: the despair that is in
  him
Out of his heart breaks forth, and takes shape in criminal
  action.
Nothing is further held sacred; but all is for plunder. His
  craving
Turns in fury on woman, and pleasure is changed into
  horror.
Death he sees everywhere round him, and madly enjoys his
  last moments,

Taking delight in blood, in the shriekings of anguish exulting.
Thereupon fiercely arose in our men the stern resolution
What had been lost to avenge, and defend whate'er was remaining.
Every man sprang to his arms, by the flight of the foeman encouraged,
And by his blanching cheeks, and his timorous, wavering glances.
Ceaselessly now rang out the clanging peal of the tocsin.
Thought of no danger to come restrained their furious anger.
Quick into weapons of war the husbandman's peaceful utensils
All were converted; dripped with blood the scythe and the ploughshare.
Quarter was shown to none: the enemy fell without mercy.
Fury everywhere raged and the cowardly cunning of weakness.
Ne'er may I men so carried away by injurious passion
See again! the sight of the raging wild beast would be better.
Let not man prattle of freedom, as if himself he could govern!
Soon as the barriers are torn away, then all of the evil
Seems let loose, that by law had been driven deep back into corners."

"Excellent man!" thereupon with emphasis answered the pastor:
"Though thou misjudgest mankind, yet can I not censure thee for it.
Evil enough, I confess, thou hast had to endure from man's passions.
Yet wouldst thou look behind over this calamitous season,
Thou wouldst acknowledge thyself how much good thou also hast witnessed.
How many excellent things that would in the heart have lain hidden,

Had not danger aroused them, and did not necessity's
    pressure
Bring forth the angel in man, and make him a god of
    deliv'rance."

  Thereupon answered and said the reverend magistrate,
    smiling:
"There thou remindest me aptly of how we console the
    poor fellow,
After his house has been burned, by recounting the gold
    and the silver
Melted and scattered abroad in the rubbish, that still is
    remaining.
Little enough, it is true; but even that little is precious.
Then will the poor wretch after it dig and rejoice if he
    find it.
Thus I likewise with happier thoughts will gratefully
    turn me
Towards the few beautiful deeds of which I preserve the
    remembrance.
Yes, I will not deny, I have seen old quarrels forgotten,
Ill to avert from the state; I also have witnessed how
    friendship,
Love of parent and child, can impossibilities venture;
Seen how the stripling at once matured into man; how
    the aged
Grew again young; and even the child into youth was
    developed,
Yea, and the weaker sex too, as we are accustomed to call it,
Showed itself brave and strong and ready for every emer-
    gence.
Foremost among them all, one beautiful deed let me mention,
Bravely performed by the hand of a girl, an excellent
    maiden;
Who, with those younger than she, had been left in charge
    of a farmhouse,
Since there, also, the men had marched against the invader.
Suddenly fell on the house a fugitive band of marauders,
Eager for booty, who crowded straightway to the room of
    the women.

There they beheld the beautiful form of the fully grown
 maiden,
Looked on the charming young girls, who rather might still
 be called children.
Savage desire possessed them; at once with merciless passion
They that trembling band assailed and the high-hearted
 maiden.
But she had snatched in an instant the sword of one from
 its scabbard,
Felled him with might to the ground, and stretched him
 bleeding before her.
Then with vigorous strokes she bravely delivered the
 maidens,
Smiting yet four of the robbers; who saved themselves only
 by flying.
Then she bolted the gates, and, armed, awaited assistance."

Now when this praise the minister heard bestowed on
 the maiden,
Rose straightway for his friend a feeling of hope in his
 bosom,
And he had opened his lips to inquire what further befell
 her,
If on this mournful flight she now with her people were
 present;
When with a hasty step the village doctor approached
 them,
Twitched the clergyman's coat, and said in his ear in a
 whisper:
"I have discovered the maiden at last among several hundreds;
By the description I knew her, so come, let thine own eyes
 behold her!
Bring too the magistrate with thee, that so we may hear
 him yet further."
But as they turned to go, the justice was summoned to leave
 them,
Sent for by some of his people by whom his counsel was
 needed.

Straightway the preacher, however, the lead of the doctor
    had followed
Up to a gap in the fence where his finger he meaningly
    pointed.
"Seest thou the maiden?" he said: "she has made some
    clothes for the baby
Out of the well-known chintz,—I distinguish it plainly; and
    further
There are the covers of blue that Hermann gave in his
    bundle.
Well and quickly, forsooth, she has turned to advantage the
    presents.
Evident tokens are these, and all else answers well the
    description.
Mark how the stomacher's scarlet sets off the arch of her
    bosom,
Prettily laced, and the bodice of black fits close to her
    figure;
Neatly the edge of her kerchief is plaited into a ruffle,
Which, with a simple grace, her chin's rounded outline
    encircles;
Freely and lightly rises above it the head's dainty oval,
And her luxuriant hair over silver bodkins is braided.
Now she is sitting, yet still we behold her majestical
    stature,
And the blue petticoat's ample plaits, that down from her
    bosom
Hangs in abundant folds about her neatly shaped ankles,
She without question it is; come, therefore, and let us
    discover
Whether she honest and virtuous be, a housewifely maiden."

  Then, as the seated figure he studied, the pastor made
    answer:
"Truly, I find it no wonder that she so enchanted the strip-
    ling,
Since, to a man's experienced eye, she seems lacking in
    nothing.
Happy to whom mother Nature a shape harmonious has
    given!

Such will always commend him, and he can be nowhere a
    stranger.
All approach with delight, and all are delighted to linger,
If to the outward shape correspond but a courteous spirit.
I can assure thee, in her the youth has found him a maiden,
Who, in the days to come, his life shall gloriously brighten,
Standing with womanly strength in every necessity by him.
Surely the soul must be pure that inhabits a body so perfect,
And of a happy old age such vigorous youth is the promise."

  Thereupon answered and said the doctor in language of
    caution:
"Often appearances cheat; I like not to trust to externals.
For I have oft seen put to the test the truth of the proverb:
Till thou a bushel of salt with a new acquaintance hast
    eaten,
Be not too ready to trust him; for time alone renders thee
    certain
How ye shall fare with each other, and how well your
    friendship shall prosper.
Let us then rather at first make inquiries among the good
    people
By whom the maiden is known, and who can inform us about
    her."

  "Much I approve of thy caution," the preacher replied as
    he followed.
"Not for ourselves is the suit, and 'tis delicate wooing for
    others."

  Towards the good magistrate, then, the men directed their
    footsteps,
Who was again ascending the street in discharge of his
    duties.

  Him the judicious pastor at once addressed and with
    caution.
"Look! we a maiden have here descried in the neighboring
    garden,
Under an apple-tree sitting, and making up garments for
    children

Out of second-hand stuff that somebody doubtless has given;
And we were pleased with her aspect: she seems like a girl
    to be trusted.
Tell us whatever thou knowest: we ask it with honest
    intentions."

  Soon as the magistrate nearer had come, and looked into
    the garden,
" Her thou knowest already," he said; " for when I was
    telling
Of the heroic deed performed by the hand of that maiden,
When she snatched the man's sword, and delivered herself
    and her charges,
This was the one! she is vigorous born, as thou seest by her
    stature;
Yet she is good as strong, for her aged kinsman she tended
Until the day of his death, which was finally hastened by
    sorrow
Over his city's distress, and his own endangered possessions.
Also, with quiet submission, she bore the death of her lover,
Who a high-spirited youth, in the earliest flush of excite-
    ment,
Kindled by lofty resolve to fight for a glorious freedom,
Hurried to Paris, where early a terrible death he encoun-
    tered.
For as at home, so there, his foes were deceit and oppression."

  Thus the magistrate spoke. The others saluted and
    thanked him,
And from his purse a gold-piece the pastor drew forth;—
    for the silver
He had some hours before already in charity given,
When he in mournful groups had seen the poor fugitives
    passing;—
And to the magistrate handed it, saying: "Apportion the
    money
'Mongst thy destitute people, and God vouchsafe it an in-
    crease."
Put the stranger declined it, and, answering, said: " We
    have rescued

Many a dollar among us, with clothing and other possessions,
And shall return, as I hope, ere yet our stock is exhausted."

Then the pastor replied, and pressed the money upon him:
" None should be backward in giving in days like the present,
and no one
Ought to refuse to accept those gifts which in kindness are
offered.
None can tell how long he may hold what in peace he possesses,
None how much longer yet he shall roam through the land
of the stranger,
And of his farm be deprived, and deprived of the garden that
feeds him."

"Ay, to be sure!" in his bustling way interrupted the
doctor:
" If I had only some money about me, ye surely should have
it,
Little and big; for certainly many among you must need it.
Yet I'll not go without giving thee something to show what
my will is,
Even though sadly behind my good-will must lag the per-
formance."
Thus, as he spoke, by its straps his embroidered pocket of
leather,
Where his tobacco was kept, he drew forth,—enough was
now in it
Several pipes to fill,—and daintily opened, and portioned.
" Small is the gift," he added. The justice, however, made
answer:
" Good tobacco can ne'er to the traveller fail to be welcome."
Then did the village doctor begin to praise his canaster.

But the clergyman drew him away, and they quitted the
justice.
" Let us make haste," said the thoughtful man: " the youth's
waiting in torture;
Come! let him hear, as soon as he may, the jubilant tidings."

So they hastened their steps, and came to where under
the lindens
Hermann against the carriage was leaning. The horses
were stamping
Wildly the turf; he held them in check, and, buried in
musing,
Stood, into vacancy gazing before him; nor saw the two
envoys,
Till, as they came, they called out and made to him signals
of triumph.
E'en as far off as they then were, the doctor began to address
him;
But they were presently nearer come and then the good
pastor
Grasped his hand and exclaimed, interrupting the word of
his comrade:
"Hail to thee, O young man! thy true eye and heart have
well chosen;
Joy be to thee and the wife of thy youth; for of thee she is
worthy.
Come then and turn us the wagon, and drive straightway to
the village,
There the good maid to woo, and soon bring her home to thy
dwelling."

Still, however, the young man stood, without sign of
rejoicing
Hearing his messenger's words, though heavenly they were
and consoling.
Deeply he sighed as he said: "With hurrying wheels we
came hither,
And shall be forced, perchance, to go mortified homeward
and slowly.
For disquiet has fallen upon me since here I've been
waiting,
Doubt and suspicion and all that can torture the heart of
a lover.
Think ye we have but to come, and that then the maiden
will follow
Merely because we are rich, while she is poor and an exile?

Poverty, too, makes proud, when it comes unmerited!
Active
Seems she to be, and contented, and so of the world is she
mistress.
Think ye a maiden like her, with the manners and beauty
that she has,
Can into woman have grown, and no worthy man's love
have attracted?
Think ye that love until now can have been shut out from
her bosom?
Drive not thither too rashly: we might to our mortification
Have to turn softly homewards our horses' heads. For my
fear is
That to some youth already this heart has been given;
already
This brave hand has been clasped, has pledged faith to some
fortunate lover.
Then with my offer, alas! I should stand in confusion before
her."

Straightway the pastor had opened his lips to speak con-
solation,
When his companion broke in, and said in his voluble
fashion:
" Years ago, forsooth, unknown had been such a dilemma.
All such affairs were then conducted in regular fashion.
Soon as a bride for their son had been by the parents
selected,
First some family friend they into their councils would
summon,
Whom they afterwards sent as a suitor to visit the par-
ents
Of the elected bride. Arrayed in his finest apparel,
Soon after dinner on Sunday he sought the respectable
burgher,
When some friendly words were exchanged upon general
subjects,
He knowing how to direct the discourse as suited his pur-
pose.
After much circumlocution he finally mentioned the daughter,

Praising her highly, and praising the man and the house
  that had sent him.
Persons of tact perceived his intent, and the politic envoy
Readily saw how their minds were disposed, and explained
  himself further.
Then were the offer declined, e'en the 'no' brought not
  mortification;
But did it meet with success, the suitor was ever thereafter
Made the chief guest in the house on every festive occasion.
For, through the rest of their lives, the couple ne'er failed
  to remember
That 'twas by his experienced hand the first knot had been
  gathered.
All that, however, is changed, and, with many another good
  custom,
Quite fallen out of the fashion; for every man woos for
  himself now.
Therefore let every man hear to his face pronounced the
  refusal,
If a refusal there be, and stand shamed in the sight of the
  maiden!"

  "Let that be as it may!" made answer the youth, who had
    scarcely
Unto the words paid heed; but in silence had made his
  decision.
"I will go thither myself, will myself hear my destiny
  spoken
Out of the lips of a maiden in whom I a confidence cherish
Greater than heart of man has e'er before cherished in
  woman.
Say what she will, 'twill be good and wise; of that I am
  certain.
Should I behold her never again, yet this once will I see
  her;
Yet this once the clear gaze of those dark eyes will en-
  counter.
If I must press her ne'er to my heart, yet that neck and that
  bosom
Will I behold once more, that my arm so longs to encircle;

Once more that mouth will see, whose kiss and whose 'yes'
would for ever
Render me happy, from which a 'no' will for ever destroy
me.
But ye must leave me alone. Do not wait for me here;
but return ye
Back to my father and mother again, and give them the
knowledge
That their son has not been deceived, that the maiden is
worthy.
So then leave me alone! I shall follow the footpath that
crosses
Over the hill by the pear-tree, and thence descends through
our vineyard,
Taking a shorter way home. And oh, may I bring to our
dwelling,
Joyful and quick my beloved! but perhaps I alone may
come creeping
Over that path to the house, and ne'er again tread it with
gladness."

Thus he spoke, and gave up the reins to the hand of the
pastor,
Who understandingly grasped them, the foaming horses
controlling,
Speedily mounted the carriage, and sat in the seat of the
driver.

But thou didst hesitate, provident neighbor, and say in
remonstrance:
"Heart and soul and spirit, my friend, I willingly trust thee;
But as for life and limb, they are not in the safest of keeping,
When the temporal reins are usurped by the hand of the
clergy."

But thou didst laugh at his words, intelligent pastor, and
answer:
"Sit thee down, and contentedly trust me both body and
spirit;
For, in holding the reins, my hand grew long ago skilful,

Long has my eye been trained in making the nicest of turn-
    ings;
For we were practised well in driving the carriage in Stras-
    burg,
When I the youthful baron accompanied thither; then daily
Rolled the carriage, guided by me, through the echoing
    gateway,
Out over dusty roads till we reached the meadows and
    lindens,
Steering through groups of the town's-folk beguiling the
    day there with walking."

  Thereupon, half-reassured, the neighbor ascended the
    wagon,
Sat like one who for a prudent leap is holding him ready,
And the stallions sped rapidly homeward, desiring their
    stable.
Clouds of dust whirled up from under their powerful hoof-
    beats.
Long the youth stood there yet, and saw the dust in its
    rising,
Saw the dust as it settled again: he stood there unheeding.

ERATO

DOROTHEA

LIKE as the traveller, who, when the sun is approach-
    ing its setting,
       Fixes his eyes on it once again ere quickly it vanish,
Then on the sides of the rocks, and on all the darkening
    bushes,
Sees its hovering image; whatever direction he look in
That hastes before, and flickers and gleams in radiant
    colors,—
So before Hermann's eyes moved the beautiful shape of the
    maiden
Softly, and seeming to follow the path that led into the
    cornfield.
But he aroused from his wildering dream and turned himself
    slowly
Towards where the village lay and was wildered again; for
    again came
Moving to meet him the lofty form of the glorious maiden.
Fixedly gazed he upon her; herself it was and no phantom.
Bearing in either hand a larger jar and a smaller,
Each by the handle, with busy step she came on to the
    fountain.
Joyfully then he hastened to meet her; the sight of her gave
    him
Courage and strength; and thus the astonished girl he
    accosted:
"Do I then find thee, brave-hearted maiden, so soon again
    busy,
Rendering aid unto others, and happy in bringing them
    comfort?
Say why thou comest alone to this well which lies at such a
    distance,

When all the rest are content with the water they find in
the village?
This has peculiar virtues, 'tis true; and the taste is delicious.
Thou to that mother wouldst bring it, I trow, whom thy
faithfulness rescued."

Straightway with cordial greeting the kindly maiden made
answer:
"Here has my walk to the spring already been amply
rewarded,
Since I have found the good friend who bestowed so abun-
dantly on us;
For a pleasure not less than the gifts is the sight of the
giver.
Come, I pray thee, and see for thyself who has tasted thy
bounty;
Come, and the quiet thanks receive of all it has solaced.
But that thou straightway the reason mayst know for which
I am hither
Come to draw, where pure and unfailing the water is
flowing,
This I must tell thee,—that all the water we have in the
village
Has by improvident people been troubled with horses and
oxen
Wading direct through the source which brings the inhabi-
tants water.
And furthermore they have also made foul with their wash-
ings and rinsings
All the troughs of the village, and all the fountains have
sullied;
For but one thought is in all, and that how to satisfy
quickest
Self and the need of the moment, regardless of what may
come after."

Thus she spoke, and the broad stone steps meanwhile had
descended
With her companion beside her, and on the low wall of the
fountain

Both sat them down. She bent herself over to draw, and he
    also
Took in his hand the jar that remained, and bent himself
    over;
And in the blue of the heavens, they, seeing their image
    reflected,
Friendly greetings and nods exchanged in the quivering
    mirror.

  " Give me to drink," the youth thereupon in his gladness
    petitioned,
And she handed the pitcher. Familiarly sat they and rested,
Both leaning over their jars, till she presently asked her
    companion:
" Tell me, why I find thee here, and without thy horses and
    wagon,
Far from the place where I met thee at first? how camest
    thou hither?"

  Thoughtful he bent his eyes on the ground, then quietly
    raised them
Up to her face, and, meeting with frankness the gaze of
    the maiden,
Felt himself solaced and stilled. But then impossible was it,
That he of love should speak; her eye told not of affection,
Only of clear understanding, requiring intelligent answer.
And he composed himself quickly, and cordially said to
    the maiden:
" Hearken to me, my child, and let me reply to thy question.
'Twas for thy sake that hither I came; why seek to con-
    ceal it?
Know I live happy at home with both my affectionate
    parents,
Faithfully giving my aid their house and estates in directing,
Being an only son, and because our affairs are extensive.
Mine is the charge of the farm; my father bears rule in
    the household;
While the presiding spirit of all is the diligent mother.
But thine experience doubtless has taught thee how griev-
    ously servants,

Now through deceit, and now through their carelessness,
   harass the mistress,
Forcing her ever to change and replace one fault with another.
Long for that reason my mother has wished for a maid in
   the household,
Who not with hand alone, but with heart, too, will lend
   her assistance,
Taking the daughter's place, whom, alas! she was early
   deprived of.
Now when to-day by the wagon I saw thee, so ready and
   cheerful,
Witnessed the strength of thine arms, and thy limbs of such
   healthful proportion,
When thy intelligent speech I heard, I was smitten with
   wonder.
Hastening homeward, I there to my parents and neighbors
   the stranger
Praised as she well deserved. But I now am come hither
   to tell thee
What is their wish as mine.—Forgive me my stammering
   language."

   "Hesitate not," she, answering, said, "to tell me what
   follows.
Thou dost not give me offence; I have listened with gratitude
   to thee:
Speak it out honestly therefore; the sound of it will not
   alarm me.
Thou wouldst engage me as servant to wait on thy father
   and mother,
And to look after the well-ordered house of which ye are the
   owners;
And thou thinkest in me to find them a capable servant,
One who is skilled in her work, and not of a rude disposition.
Short thy proposal has been, and short shall be also my
   answer.
Yes, I will go with thee home, and the call of fate I will
   follow.
Here my duty is done: I have brought the newly made mother
Back to her kindred again, who are all in her safety rejoicing.

Most of our people already are gathered; the others will
    follow.
All think a few days more will certainly see them returning
Unto their homes; for such is the exile's constant delusion.
But by no easy hope do I suffer myself to be cheated
During these sorrowful days which promise yet more days
    of sorrow.
All the bands of the world have been loosed, and what shall
    unite them,
Saving alone the need, the need supreme, that is on us?
If in a good man's house I can earn my living by service,
Under the eye of an excellent mistress, I gladly will do it;
Since of doubtful repute, must be always a wandering
    maiden.
Yes, I will go with thee, soon as I first shall have carried
    the pitchers
Back to my friends, and prayed the good people to give me
    their blessing.
Come thou must see them thyself, and from their hands
    must receive me."

Joyfully hearkened the youth to the willing maiden's
    decision,
Doubtful whether he ought not at once to make honest con-
    fession.
Yet it appeared to him best to leave her awhile in her
    error,
Nor for her love to sue, before leading her home to his
    dwelling.
Ah! and the golden ring he perceived on the hand of the
    maiden,
Wherefore he let her speak on, and gave diligent ear to
    her language.

"Come," she presently said, "Let us back to the village;
    for maidens
Always are sure to be blamed if they tarry too long at
    the fountain.
Yet how delightful it is to chat by the murmuring water!"

Then from their seats they rose, and both of them turned
to the fountain
One more look behind, and a tender longing possessed them.
Both of the water-jars then in silence she took by the
handle,
Carried them up the steps, while behind her followed her
lover.
One of the pitchers he begged her to give him to lighten
the burden.
"Nay, let it be!" she said: "I carry them better so
balanced.
Nor shall the master, who is to command, be doing me
service.
Look not so gravely upon me, as thinking my fortune a
hard one.
Early a woman should learn to serve, for that is her calling;
Since through service alone she finally comes to the head-
ship,
Comes to the due command that is hers of right in the
household.
Early the sister must wait on her brother, and wait on her
parents;
Life must be always with her a perpetual coming and
going,
Or be a fetching and carrying, making and doing for
others.
Happy for her be she wonted to think no way is too grievous,
And if the hours of the night be to her as the hours of the
daytime;
If she find never a needle too fine, nor a labor too trifling;
Wholly forgetful of self, and caring to live but in others!
For she will surely, as mother, have need of every virtue,
When, in the time of her illness, the cries of her infant
arouse her
Calling for food from her weakness, and cares are to suffer-
ing added.
Twenty men bound into one were not able to bear such
a burden;
Nor is it meant that they should, yet should they with grati-
tude view it."

Thus she spoke, and was come, meanwhile, with her
  silent companion,
Far as the floor of the barn, at the furthermost end of the
  garden,
Where was the sick woman lying, whom, glad, she had left
  with her daughters,
Those late rescued maidens: fair pictures of innocence
  were they.
Both of them entered the barn; and, e'en as they did so,
  the justice,
Leading a child in each hand, came in from the other
  direction.
These had been lost, hitherto, from the sight of their sor-
  rowing mother;
But in the midst of the crowd the old man now had
  descried them.
Joyfully sprang they forward to meet their dear mother's
  embraces,
And to salute with delight their brother, their unknown
  companion.
Next upon Dorothea they sprang with affectionate greeting,
Asking for bread and fruit, but more than all else for some
  water.
So then she handed the water about; and not only the
  children
Drank, but the sick woman too, and her daughters, and with
  them the justice.
All were refreshed, and highly commended the glorious
  water;
Acid it was to the taste, and reviving, and wholesome to
  drink of.

Then with a serious face the maiden replied to them,
  saying:
"Friends, for the last time now to your mouth have I lifted
  my pitcher;
And for the last time by me have your lips been moistened
  with water.
But henceforth in the heat of the day when the draught
  shall refresh you,

When in the shade ye enjoy your rest beside a clear
  fountain,
Think of me then sometimes and of all my affectionate
  service,
Prompted more by my love than the duty I owed you as
  kindred.
I shall acknowledge as long as I live the kindness ye've
  shown me.
'Tis with regret that I leave you; but every one now is a
  burden,
More than a help to his neighbor, and all must be finally
  scattered
Far through a foreign land, if return to our homes be
  denied us.
See, here stands the youth to whom we owe thanks for the
  presents.
He gave the cloak for the baby, and all these welcome
  provisions.
Now he is come, and has asked me if I will make one in his
  dwelling,
That I may serve therein his wealthy and excellent par-
  ents.
And I refuse not the offer; for maidens must always be
  serving;
Burdensome were it for them to rest and be served in the
  household.
Therefore I follow him gladly. A youth of intelligence
  seems he,
And so will also the parents be, as becometh the wealthy.
So then farewell, dear friend; and mayst thou rejoice in
  thy nursling,
Living, and into thy face already so healthfully looking!
When thou shalt press him against thy breast in these gay-
  colored wrappings,
Oh, then remember the kindly youth who bestowed them
  upon us,
And who me also henceforth, thy sister, will shelter and
  nourish.
Thou, too, excellent man!" she said as she turned to the
  justice;

" Take my thanks that in many a need I have found thee
a father."

Then she knelt down on the floor by the side of the newly
made mother,
Kissing the weeping woman, and taking her low-whispered
blessing.

Thou, meanwhile, worshipful justice, wast speaking to
Hermann and saying:
" Justly mayst thou, my friend, be counted among the good
masters,
Careful to manage their household affairs with capable
servants.
For I have often observed how in sheep, as in horses and
oxen,
Men conclude never a bargain without making closest in-
spection,
While with a servant who all things preserves, if honest
and able,
And who will every thing lose and destroy, if he set to
work falsely,
Him will a chance or an accident make us admit to our
dwelling,
And we are left, when too late, to repent an o'er hasty
decision.
Thou understandest the matter it seems; because thou hast
chosen,
Thee and thy parents to serve in the house, a maid who is
honest.
Hold her with care; for as long as thy household is under
her keeping,
Thou shalt not want for a sister, nor yet for a daughter
thy parents."

Many were come, meanwhile, near relatives all of the
mother,
Bringing her various gifts, and more suitable quarters
announcing.
All of them, hearing the maiden's decision, gave Hermann
their blessing,

Coupled with glances of meaning, while each made his
    special reflections.
Hastily one and another would say in the ear of his
    neighbor:
"If in the master a lover she find, right well were she
    cared for."
Hermann took her at last by the hand, and said as he did
    so:
"Let us be going; the day is declining, and distant the
    city."
Eager and voluble then the women embraced Dorothea.
Hermann drew her away; but other adieus must be spoken:
Lastly the children with cries fell upon her and terrible
    weeping,
Clung to her garments, and would not their dear second
    mother should leave them.
But in a tone of command the women said, one and another:
"Hush now, children, she's going to the town, and will
    presently bring you
Plenty of nice sweet cake that was by your brother be-
    spoken
When by the stork just now he was brought past the shop
    of the baker.
Soon you will see her come back with sugar-plums splen-
    didly gilded."
Then did the little ones loose their hold, and Hermann,
    though hardly,
Tore her from further embraces away, and far-waving
    kerchiefs.

MELPOMENE

HERMANN AND DOROTHEA

TOWARDS the setting sun the two thus went on their
journey:
Close he had wrapped himself round with clouds por-
tending a tempest.
Out from the veil, now here and now there, with fiery
flashes,
Gleaming over the field shot forth the ominous lightning.
"May not these threatening heavens," said Hermann, "be
presently sending
Hailstones upon us and violent rains; for fair is the harvest."
And in the waving luxuriant grain they delighted together:
Almost as high it reached as the lofty shapes that moved
through it.

Thereupon spoke the maiden, and said to her guide
and companion:
"Friend, unto whom I soon am to owe so kindly a fortune,
Shelter and home, while many an exile's exposed to the
tempest,
Tell me concerning thy parents, I pray thee, and teach
me to know them,
Them whom with all my heart I desire to serve in the
future.
Who understands his master, more easily gives satisfaction,
Having regard to the things which to him seem chief
in importance,
And on the doing of which his firm-set mind is determined.
Tell me therefore, I pray, how to win thy father and
mother."

And to her question made answer the good and intelligent Hermann:

"Ah, what wisdom thou showest, thou good, thou excellent
   maiden,
Asking thus first of all concerning the tastes of my parents!
Know that in vain hitherto I have labored in serving my
   father,
Taking upon me as were it my own, the charge of the
   household;
Early and late at work in the fields, and o'erseeing the
   vineyard.
But my mother I fully content, who can value my service;
And thou wilt also appear in her eyes the worthiest of
   maidens,
If for the house thou carest, as were it thine own thou wast
   keeping.
Otherwise is it with father, who cares for the outward
   appearance.
Do not regard me, good maiden, as one who is cold and
   unfeeling,
That unto thee a stranger I straightway discover my
   father.
Nay, I assure thee that never before have words such as
   these are
Freely dropped from my tongue, which is not accustomed
   to prattle;
But from out of my bosom thou lurest its every secret.
Some of the graces of life my good father covets about him,
Outward signs of affection he wishes, as well as of honor;
And an inferior servant might possibly give satisfaction,
Who could turn these to account, while he might be dis-
   pleased with a better."

Thereupon said she with joy, the while her hastening
   footsteps
Over the darkening pathway with easy motion she quickened:
"Truly I hope to them both I shall equally give satisfaction:
For in thy mother's nature I find such an one as mine
   own is,
And to the outward graces I've been from my childhood
   accustomed.

Greatly was courtesy valued among our neighbors the
    Frenchmen,
During their earlier days; it was common to noble and
    burgher,
As to the peasant, and every one made it the rule of his
    household.
So, on the side of us Germans, the children were likewise
    accustomed
Daily to bring to their parents, with kissing of hands and
    with curtseys,
Morning good-wishes, and all through the day to be prettily
    mannered.
Every thing thus that I learned, and to which I've been used
    from my childhood,
All that my heart shall suggest, shall be brought into play
    for thy father.
But who shall tell me of thee, and how thyself shouldst
    be treated,
Thou the only son of the house, and henceforth **my**
    master?"

    Thus she said, and e'en as she spoke they stood under the
    pear-tree.
Down from the heavens the moon at her full was shedding
    her splendor.
Night had come on, and wholly obscured was the last gleam
    of sunlight,
So that contrasting masses lay side by side with each other,
Clear and bright as the day, and black with the shadows of
    midnight;
Gratefully fell upon Hermann's ear the kindly asked
    question
Under the shade of the glorious tree, the spot he so
    treasured,
Which but this morning had witnessed the tears he had
    shed for the exile.
And while they sat themselves down to rest them here
    for a little,
Thus spoke the amorous youth, as he grasped the hand of
    the maiden:

"Suffer thy heart to make answer, and follow it freely in all things."
Yet naught further he ventured to say although so propitious
Seemed the hour: he feared he should only haste on a refusal.
Ah, and he felt besides the ring on her finger, sad token!
Therefore they sat there, silent and still, beside one another.

First was the maiden to speak: "How sweet is this glorious moonlight!"
Said she at length: "It is as the light of the day in its brightness.
There in the city I plainly can see the houses and court-yards,
And in the gable—methinks I can number its panes—is a window."

"What thou seest," the modest youth thereupon made her answer,—
"What thou seest is our dwelling, to which I am leading thee downward,
And that window yonder belongs to my room in the attic,
Which will be thine perhaps, for various changes are making.
All these fields, too, are ours; they are ripe for the harvest to-morrow.
Here in the shade we will rest, and partake of our noontide refreshment.
But it is time we began our descent through the vineyard and garden;
For dost thou mark how yon threatening storm-cloud comes nearer and nearer,
Charged with lightning, and ready our fair full moon to extinguish?"

So they arose from their seats, and over the cornfields descended,
Through the luxuriant grain, enjoying the brightness of evening,
Until they came to the vineyard, and so entered into its shadow.
Then he guided her down o'er the numerous blocks that were lying,

Rough and unhewn on the pathway, and served as the steps
of the alley.
Slowly the maiden descended, and leaning her hands on his
shoulder,
While with uncertain beams, the moon through the leaves
overlooked them,
Ere she was veiled by the cloud, and so left the couple in
darkness.
Carefully Hermann's strength supported the maid that hung
o'er him;
But, not knowing the path and the rough-hewn steps that led
down it,
Missed she her footing, her ankle turned, and she surely
had fallen,
Had not the dexterous youth his arm outstretched in an
instant,
And his beloved upheld. She gently sank on his shoulder;
Breast was pressed against breast, and cheek against cheek.
Thus he stood there
Fixed as a marble statue, the force of will keeping him
steadfast,
Drew her not to him more closely, but braced himself under
her pressure.
Thus he the glorious burden felt, the warmth of her bosom,
And the perfume of her breath, that over his lips was
exhaling;
Bore with the heart of a man the majestic form of the
woman.

But she with playfulness said, concealing the pain that she
suffered:
"That is a sign of misfortune, so timorous persons would
tell us,
When on approaching a house we stumble not far from the
threshold;
And for myself, I confess, I could wish for a happier omen.
Let us here linger awhile that thy parents may not have to
blame thee,
Seeing a limping maid, and thou seem an incompetent landlord."

URANIA

PROSPECT

MUSES, O ye who the course of true love so willingly
favor,
Ye who thus far on his way the excellent youth
have conducted,
Even before the betrothal have pressed to his bosom the
maiden;
Further your aid vouchsafe this charming pair in uniting,
Straightway dispersing the clouds which over their happi-
ness lower!
Yet first of all declare what is passing meanwhile at the
Lion.

Now for the third time again the mother impatient had
entered
Where were assembled the men, whom anxious but now she
had quitted;
Spoke of the gathering storm, and the moonlight's rapid
obscuring;
Then of her son's late tarrying abroad and the dangers of
nightfall;
Sharply upbraided her friends that without having speech of
the maiden,
And without urging his suit, they had parted from Hermann
so early.

"Make it not worse than it is," the father replied with
displeasure.
"For, as thou seest, we tarry ourselves and are waiting the
issue."

Calmly, however, from where he was sitting the neighbor
made answer:

" Never in hours of disquiet like this do I fail to be grateful
Unto my late, blessed father, who every root of impatience
Tore from my heart when a child, and left no fibre re-
    maining;
So that I learned on the instant to wait as do none of your
    sages."

  " Tell us," the pastor returned, " what legerdemain he
    made use of."
" That will I gladly relate, for all may draw from it a
    lesson ;"
So made the neighbor reply. " When a boy I once stood of
    a Sunday
Full of impatience, and looking with eagerness out for the
    carriage
Which was to carry us forth to the spring that lies under
    the lindens.
Still the coach came not. I ran, like a weasel, now hither,
    now thither,
Up stairs and down, and forward and back, 'twixt the door
    and the window;
Even my fingers itched to be moving; I scratched on the
    tables,
Went about pounding and stamping, and hardly could keep
    me from weeping.
All was observed by the calm-tempered man; but at last
    when my folly
Came to be carried too far, by the arm he quietly took me,
Led me away to the window, and spoke in this serious
    language:
' Seest thou yonder the carpenter's shop that is closed for
    the Sunday?
He will re-open to-morrow, when plane and saw will be
    started,
And will keep on through the hours of labor from morning
    till evening.
But consider you this,—a day will be presently coming
When that man shall himself be astir and all of his work-
    men,
Making a coffin for thee to be quickly and skilfully finished,

Then that house of boards they will busily bring over
    hither,
Which must at last receive alike the impatient and patient,
And which is destined soon with close-pressing roof to be
    covered.'
Straightway I saw the whole thing in my mind as if it were
    doing;
Saw the boards fitting together, and saw the black color
    preparing,
Sat me down patiently then, and in quiet awaited the
    carriage.
Now when others I see, in seasons of anxious expectance,
Running distracted about, I cannot but think of the coffin."

Smiling, the pastor replied: "The affecting picture of
    death stands
Not as a dread to the wise, and not as an end to the pious.
Those it presses again into life, and teaches to use it;
These by affliction it strengthens in hope to future salvation.
Death becomes life unto both. Thy father was greatly
    mistaken
When to a sensitive boy he death in death thus depicted.
Let us the value of nobly ripe age, point out to the young
    man,
And to the aged the youth, that in the eternal progression
Both may rejoice, and life may in life thus find its com-
    pletion."

But the door was now opened, and showed the majestical
    couple.
Filled with amaze were the friends, and amazed the affec-
    tionate parents,
Seeing the form of the maid so well matched with that of
    her lover.
Yea, the door seemed too low to allow the tall figures to
    enter,
As they together now appeared coming over the threshold.

Hermann, with hurried words, presented her thus to his
    parents:

"Here is a maiden," he said; "such a one as ye wish in the
    household.
Kindly receive her, dear father: she merits it well; and
    thou, mother,
Question her straightway on all that belongs to a house-
    keeper's duty,
That ye may see how well she deserves to ye both to be
    nearer."

Quickly he then drew aside the excellent clergyman,
    saying:
"Help me, O worthy sir, and speedily out of this trouble;
Loosen, I pray thee, this knot, at whose untying I tremble.
Know that 'tis not as a lover that I have brought hither the
    maiden;
But she believes that as servant she comes to the house, and
    I tremble
Lest in displeasure she fly as soon as there's mention of
    marriage.
But be it straightway decided; for she no longer in error
Thus shall be left, and I this suspense no longer can suffer.
Hasten and show us in this a proof of the wisdom we
    honor."

Towards the company then the clergyman instantly turned
    him;
But already, alas! had the soul of the maiden been troubled,
Hearing the father's speech: for he, in his sociable fashion,
Had in these playful words, with the kindest intention ad-
    dressed her:
"Ay, this is well, my child! with delight I perceive that my
    Hermann
Has the good taste of his father, who often showed his in
    his young days,
Leading out always the fairest to dance, and bringing the
    fairest
Finally home as his wife; our dear little mother here that
    was.
For by the bride that a man shall elect we can judge what
    himself is,

Tell what the spirit is in him, and whether he feel his own
value.
Nor didst thou need for thyself, I'll engage, much time for
decision;
For, in good sooth, methinks, he's no difficult person to
follow."

Hermann had heard but in part; his limbs were inwardly
trembling,
And of a sudden a stillness had fallen on all of the circle.

But by these words of derision, for such she could not
but deem them,
Wounded, and stung to the depths of her soul, the excellent
maiden,
Stood, while the fugitive blood o'er her cheeks and e'en to
her bosom
Poured its flush. But she governed herself, and her cour-
age collecting,
Answered the old man thus, her pain not wholly concealing:
"Truly for such a reception thy son had in no wise pre-
pared me,
When he the ways of his father described, the excellent
burgher.
Thou art a man of culture, I know, before whom I am
standing;
Dealest with every one wisely, according as suits his
position;
But thou hast scanty compassion, it seems, on one such as
I am,
Who, a poor girl, am now crossing thy threshold with pur-
pose to serve thee;
Else, with such bitter derision, thou wouldst not have made
me remember
How far removed my fortune from that of thyself and thy
son is.
True, I come poor to thy house, and bring with me naught
but my bundle
Here where is every abundance to gladden the prosperous
inmates.

Yet I know well myself; I feel the relations between us.
Say, is it noble, with so much of mockery straightway to
greet me,
That I am sent from the house while my foot is scarce yet
on the threshold?"

'Anxiously Hermann turned and signed to his ally the
pastor
That he should rush to the rescue and straightway dispel
the delusion.
Then stepped the wise man hastily forward and looked on
the maiden's
Tearful eyes, her silent pain and repressed indignation,
And in his heart was impelled not at once to clear up the
confusion,
Rather to put to the test the girl's disquieted spirit.
Therefore he unto her said in language intended to try her:
"Surely, thou foreign-born maiden, thou didst not maturely
consider,
When thou too rashly decidedst to enter the service of
strangers,
All that is meant by the placing thyself 'neath the rule of
a master;
For by our hand to a bargain the fate of the year is de-
termined,
And but a single 'yea' compels to much patient endurance.
Not the worst part of the service the wearisome steps to be
taken,
Neither the bitter sweat of a labor that presses unceasing;
Since the industrious freeman must toil as well as the
servant.
But 'tis to bear with the master's caprice when he censures
unjustly,
Or when, at variance with self, he orders now this, now the
other;
Bear with the petulance, too, of the mistress, easily angered,
And with the rude, overbearing ways of unmannerly
children.
All this is hard to endure, and yet to go on with thy duties
Quickly, without delay, nor thyself grow sullen and stubborn.

Yet thou appearest ill fitted for this, since already so deeply
Stung by the father's jests: whereas there is nothing more
  common
Than for a girl to be teased on account of a youth she may
  fancy."

  Thus he spoke. The maiden had felt the full force of
  his language,
And she restrained her no more; but with passionate out-
  burst her feelings
Made themselves way; a sob broke forth from her now
  heaving bosom,
And, while the scalding tears poured down, she straightway
  made answer:
"Ah, that rational man who thinks to advise us in sorrow,
Knows not how little of power his cold words have in
  relieving
Ever a heart from that woe which a sovereign fate has
  inflicted.
Ye are prosperous and glad; how then should a pleasantry
  wound you?
Yet but the lightest touch is a source of pain to the sick
  man.
Nay, concealment itself, if successful, had profited nothing.
Better show now what had later increased to a bitterer
  anguish,
And to an inward consuming despair might perhaps have
  reduced me.
Let me go back! for here in this house I can tarry no
  longer.
I will away, and wander in search of my hapless companions,
Whom I forsook in their need; for myself alone choosing
  the better.
This is my firm resolve, and I therefore may make a con-
  fession
Which might for years perhaps have else lain hid in my
  bosom.
Deeply indeed was I hurt by the father's words of derision;
Not that I'm sensitive, proud beyond what is fitting a
  servant;

But that my heart in truth had felt itself stirred with
affection
Towards the youth who to-day had appeared to my eyes as
a savior.
When he first left me there on the road, he still remained
present,
Haunting my every thought; I fancied the fortunate maiden
Whom as a bride, perhaps, his heart had already elected.
When at the fountain I met him again, the sight of him
wakened
Pleasure as great as if there had met me an angel from
heaven;
And with what gladness I followed, when asked to come as
his servant.
True, that I flattered myself in my heart,—I will not deny
it,—
While we were hitherward coming, I might peradventure
deserve him,
Should I become at last the important stay of the house-
hold.
Now I, alas! for the first time see what risk I was run-
ning,
When I would make my home so near to the secretly loved
one;
Now for the first time feel how far removed a poor maiden
Is from an opulent youth, no matter how great her
deserving.
All this I now confess, that my heart ye may not misin-
terpret,
In that 'twas hurt by a chance to which I owe my awaking.
Hiding my secret desires, this dread had been ever before
me,
That at some early day he would bring him a bride to his
dwelling;
And ah, how could I then my inward anguish have suf-
fered!
Happily I have been warned, and happily now has my
bosom
Been of its secret relieved, while yet there is cure for the
evil.

But no more; I have spoken; and now shall nothing detain me
Longer here in a house where I stay but in shame and confusion,
Freely confessing my love and that foolish hope that I cherished.
Not the night which abroad is covered with lowering storm clouds;
Not the roll of the thunder—I hear its peal—shall deter me;
Not the pelt of the rain which without is beating in fury;
Neither the blustering tempest; for all these things have I suffered
During our sorrowful flight, and while the near foe was pursuing.
Now I again go forth, as I have so long been accustomed,
Carried away by the whirl of the times, and from every thing parted.
Fare ye well! I tarry no longer; all now is over."

Thus she spoke and back to the door she hastily turned her,
Still bearing under her arm, as she with her had brought it, her bundle.
But with both of her arms the mother seized hold of the maiden,
Clasping her round the waist, and exclaiming, amazed and bewildered:
"Tell me, what means all this? and these idle tears, say, what mean they?
I will not let thee depart: thou art the betrothed of my Hermann."

But still the father stood, observing the scene with displeasure,
Looked on the weeping girl, and said in a tone of vexation:
"This then must be the return that I get for all my indulgence,
That at the close of the day this most irksome of all things should happen!

For there is naught I can tolerate less than womanish
  weeping,
Violent outcries, which only involve in disorder and passion,
What with a little of sense had been more smoothly adjusted.
Settle the thing for yourselves: I'm going to bed; I've no
  patience
Longer to be a spectator of these your marvellous doings."
Quickly he turned as he spoke, and hastened to go to the
  chamber
Where he was wonted to rest, and his marriage bed was
  kept standing,
But he was held by his son, who said in a tone of entreaty:
"Father, hasten not from us, and be thou not wroth with
  the maiden.
I, only I, am to blame as the cause of all this confusion,
Which by his dissimulation our friend unexpectedly height-
  ened.
Speak, O worthy sir; for to thee my cause I intrusted.
Heap not up sorrow and anger, but rather let all this be
  ended;
For I could hold thee never again in such high estimation,
If thou shouldst show but delight in pain, not superior
  wisdom."

Thereupon answered and said the excellent clergyman,
  smiling:
"Tell me, what other device could have drawn this charming confession
Out of the good maiden's lips, and thus have revealed her
  affection?
Has not thy trouble been straightway transformed into gladness and rapture?
Therefore speak up for thyself; what need of the tongue of
  another?"

Thereupon Hermann came forward, and spoke in these
  words of affection:
"Do not repent of thy tears, nor repent of these passing
  distresses;
For they complete my joy, and—may I not hope it—thine
  also?

Not to engage the stranger, the excellent maid, **as a ser-**
vant,
Unto the fountain I came; but to sue for thy love I **came**
thither.
Only, alas! my timorous look could thy heart's inclination
Nowise perceive; I read in thine eyes of nothing but kindness,
As from the fountain's tranquil mirror thou gavest me
greeting.
Might I but bring thee home, the half of my joy was accomplished.
But thou completest it unto me now; oh, blest be thou for
it!"
Then with a deep emotion the maiden gazed on the stripling;
Neither forbade she embrace and kiss, the summit of rapture,
When to a loving pair they come as the longed-for assurance,
Pledge of a lifetime of bliss, that appears to them **now**
never-ending.

Unto the others, meanwhile, the pastor had made **ex-**
planation.
But with feeling and grace the maid now advanced to **the**
father,
Bent her before him, and kissing the hand he would **fain**
have withholden,
Said: "Thou wilt surely be just and forgive one so **startled**
as I was,
First for my tears of distress, and now for the tears **of my**
gladness.
That emotion forgive me, and oh! forgive me this also.
For I can scarce comprehend the happiness newly vouch-
safed me.
Yes, let that first vexation of which I, bewildered, **was**
guilty
Be too the last. Whatever the maid of affectionate **service**
Faithfully promised, shall be to thee now **performed by the**
daughter."

Straightway then, concealing his tears, the father embraced her,
Cordially, too, the mother came forward and kissed her with
fervor,
Pressing her hands in her own: the weeping women were
silent.

Thereupon quickly he seized, the good and intelligent
pastor,
First the father's hand, and the wedding-ring drew from
his finger,—
Not so easily either: the finger was plump and detained
it,—
Next took the mother's ring also, and with them betrothed
he the children,
Saying: "These golden circlets once more their office per-
forming
Firmly a tie shall unite, which in all things shall equal the
old one,
Deeply is this young man imbued with love of the maiden,
And, as the maiden confesses, her heart is gone out to him
also.
Here do I therefore betroth you and bless for the years
that are coming,
With the consent of the parents, and having this friend as
a witness."

Then the neighbor saluted at once, and expressed his good
wishes;
But when the clergyman now the golden circlet was drawing
Over the maiden's hand, he observed with amazement the
other,
Which had already by Hermann been anxiously marked at
the fountain.
And with a kindly raillery thus thereupon he addressed
her:
"So, then thy second betrothal is this? let us hope the first
bridegroom
May not appear at the altar, and so prohibit the marriage."

But she, answering, said: " Oh, let me to this recollection
Yet one moment devote; for so much is due the good giver,
Him who bestowed it at parting, and never came back to
    his kindred.
All that should come he foresaw, when in haste the passion
    for freedom,
When a desire in the newly changed order of things to be
    working,
Urged him onward to Paris, where chains and death he
    encountered.
' Fare thee well,' were his words; ' I go, for all is in motion
Now for a time on the earth, and every thing seems to be
    parting.
E'en in the firmest states fundamental laws are dissolving;
Property falls away from the hand of the ancient possessor;
Friend is parted from friend; and so parts lover from lover.
Here I leave thee, and where I shall find thee again, or if
    ever,
Who can tell? Perhaps these words are our last ones to-
    gether.
Man's but a stranger here on the earth, we are told and
    with reason;
And we are each of us now become more of strangers than
    ever.
Ours no more is the soil, and our treasures are all of them
    changing:
Silver and gold are melting away from their time-honored
    patterns.
All is in motion as though the already-shaped world into
    chaos
Meant to resolve itself backward into night, and to shape
    itself over.
Mine thou wilt keep thine heart, and should we be ever
    united
Over the ruins of earth, it will be as newly made creatures,
Beings transformed and free, no longer dependent on for-
    tune;
For can aught fetter the man who has lived through days
    such as these are!
But if it is not to be, that, these dangers happily over,

Ever again we be granted the bliss of mutual embraces,
Oh, then before thy thoughts so keep my hovering image
That with unshaken mind thou be ready for good or for
evil!
Should new ties allure thee again, and a new habitation,
Enter with gratitude into the joys that fate shall prepare
thee;
Love those purely who love thee; be grateful to them who
show kindness.
But thine uncertain foot should yet be planted but lightly,
For there is lurking the twofold pain of a new separa-
tion.
Blessings attend thy life; but value existence no higher
Than thine other possessions, and all possessions are cheat-
ing!'.
Thus spoke the noble youth, and never again I beheld him.
Meanwhile I lost my all, and a thousand times thought of
his warning.
Here, too, I think of his words, when love is sweetly pre-
paring
Happiness for me anew, and glorious hopes are reviving.
Oh forgive me, excellent friend, that e'en while I hold thee
Close to my side I tremble! So unto the late-landed sailor
Seem the most solid foundations of firmest earth to be
rocking.'

Thus she spoke, and placed the two rings on her finger
together.
But her lover replied with a noble and manly emotion:
"So much the firmer then, amid these universal convul-
sions,
Be, Dorothea, our union! We two will hold fast and con-
tinue,
Firmly maintaining ourselves, and the right to our ample
possessions.
For that man, who, when times are uncertain, is faltering
in spirit,
Only increases the evil, and further and further transmits it;
While he refashions the world, who keeps himself stead-
fastly minded.

Poorly becomes it the German to give to these fearful excitements

Aught of continuance, or to be this way and that way inclining.

This is our own! let that be our word, and let us maintain it!

For to those resolute peoples respect will be ever accorded,

Who for God and the laws, for parents, women and children,

Fought and died, as together they stood with their front to the foeman.

Thou art mine own; and now what is mine, is mine more than ever.

Not with anxiety will I preserve it, and trembling enjoyment;

Rather with courage and strength. To-day should the enemy threaten,

Or in the future, equip me thyself and hand me my weapons.

Let me but know that under thy care are my house and dear parents,

Oh! I can then with assurance expose my breast to the foeman.

And were but every man minded like me, there would be an upspring

Might against might, and peace should revisit us all with its gladness."